face2face

Starter Teacher's Book

Chris Redston

CAMBRIDGE
UNIVERSITY PRESS

University Printing House, Cambridge CB2 8BS, United Kingdom

Cambridge University Press is part of the University of Cambridge.

It furthers the University's mission by disseminating knowledge in the pursuit of education, learning and research at the highest international levels of excellence.

www.cambridge.org
Information on this title: www.cambridge.org/9781107650411

© Cambridge University Press 2013

First published 2013

Printed in Poland by Opolgraf

A catalogue record for this publication is available from the British Library

Library of Congress Cataloguing in Publication data

ISBN 978-1-107-65041-1 Starter Teacher's Book with DVD
ISBN 978-1-107-65440-2 Starter Student's Book with DVD-ROM
ISBN 978-1-107-61476-5 Starter Workbook with Key
ISBN 978-1-107-61477-2 Starter Workbook without Key
ISBN 978-1-107-62168-8 Starter Class Audio CDs (3)
ISBN 978-1-107-61473-4 Starter Testmaker Audio CD-ROM with Audio CD
ISBN 978-1-107-61475-8 Starter Presentation Plus DVD-ROM
ISBN 978-1-107-62268-5 Starter Student's Book with DVD-ROM and Online Workbook Pack
ISBN 978-1-139-87007-8 Starter Online Workbook (e-commerce for Students)
ISBN 978-1-139-86357-5 Starter Online Workbook (Teacher Access)

Additional resources for this publication at www.cambridge.org/elt/face2face

Contents

Photocopiable Materials

Welcome to face2face Second edition!

face2face Second edition

face2face Second edition is a general English course for adults and young adults who want to learn to communicate quickly and effectively in today's world. Based on the communicative approach, it combines the best in current methodology with innovative new features designed to make learning and teaching easier. Each self-contained double-page lesson is easily teachable off the page with minimal preparation.

The **face2face** Second edition syllabus integrates the learning of new language with skills development and places equal emphasis on vocabulary and grammar. The course uses a guided discovery approach to learning, first allowing students to check what they know, then helping them to work out the rules for themselves through carefully structured examples and concept questions.

There is a strong focus on listening and speaking throughout **face2face** Second edition. Innovative *Help with Listening* sections help students to understand natural spoken English in context and there are numerous opportunities for communicative, personalised speaking practice. The *Real World* lessons in each unit focus on the functional and situational language students need for day-to-day life.

This language can now be presented using video material on the Teacher's DVD. For more on the **face2face** approach, see p20.

All new language is included in the interactive *Language Summaries* in the back of the Student's Book and is regularly recycled and reviewed. Students can also review new language in the *Extra Practice* section in the Student's Book, on the Self-study DVD-ROM and in the Workbook.

The Student's Book provides approximately 70 hours of core teaching material, which can be extended to 100 hours with the inclusion of the photocopiable materials and extra ideas in this Teacher's Book.

The vocabulary selection in **face2face** Second edition has been informed by the *English Vocabulary Profile* (see p15) as well as the *Cambridge International Corpus* and the *Cambridge Learner Corpus*.

face2face Second edition is fully compatible with the *Common European Framework of Reference for Languages* (CEFR) and gives students regular opportunities to evaluate their progress. The Starter Student's Book covers CEFR level A1 (see p14–p19).

face2face Second edition Starter Components

Student's Book with Self-study DVD-ROM

The **Student's Book** provides 10 thematically linked units, each with four lessons of two pages. Each lesson takes approximately 90 minutes (see p6–p9).

The **Self-study DVD-ROM** is an invaluable resource for students with over 300 exercises in all language areas, a Review Video for each unit, *My Test* and *My Progress* sections, where students evaluate their own progress, and an interactive Phonemic Symbols chart. In addition there is an e-Portfolio with *Grammar Reference*, *Word List*, *Word Cards*, plus a *My Work* section where students can build a digital portfolio of their work. (See the photocopiable user instructions on p11–p13.)

Teacher's Book with Teacher's DVD

This **Teacher's Book** includes *Teaching Tips*, *Classroom Activities and Games* and *Teaching Notes* for each lesson, as well as an extensive bank of photocopiable materials (see p3). The **Teacher's DVD** contains video presentation material for all the *Real World* lessons in the Student's Book, as well as printable PDFs of all the Teaching Notes and photocopiable materials (see p10).

Class Audio CDs

The three **Class Audio CDs** contain all the listening material for the Student's Book and the listening sections of the *Progress Tests* for units 5 and 10.

Workbook and Online Workbook

The **Workbook** provides further practice of all language presented in the Student's Book. It also includes a 20-page *Reading and Writing Portfolio* based on the CEFR.

The **Online Workbook** provides students with the same Workbook exercises in an easy-to-use online format, as well as additional audio and supporting activities. It also allows teachers to monitor students' work online.

Testmaker CD-ROM and Audio CD

The **Testmaker** enables teachers to create, edit, save and print their own tests, choosing exercises from the Progress Tests and a bank of extra questions. Testmaker also allows teachers to produce two versions of each test to prevent students from sharing answers.

Website

Visit www.cambridge.org/elt/face2face2 for bilingual Word Lists, sample materials, full details of how **face2face** covers the language areas specified by the CEFR – and much more!

New Features of face2face Second edition Starter

Rob / Sally

NEW optional **VIDEO** presentation material for all ▷ **REAL WORLD** lessons in the Student's Book.

Last weekend

8 **a** VIDEO ▷ 9.2 CD3 ▷ 46 It's Monday morning. Watch or listen to Rob and Sally talk about last weekend. Put photos A–D in the order they talk about them.

b Work in pairs. How much can you remember? Choose the correct words or phrases.

1 Sally went to see her *brother* / *sister* last weekend.
2 They went shopping on *Saturday* / *Sunday* afternoon.
3 They *enjoyed* / *didn't enjoy* their evening at the theatre.
4 *Sally* / *Her brother* doesn't like art galleries very much.
5 They had lunch with *some friends* / *their parents*.
6 Rob went to a *Turkish* / *Spanish* restaurant on Saturday.

c Watch or listen again. Check your answers.

NEW Teacher's DVD with all the Real World video presentation material, Teacher's Notes and photocopiable materials from this Teacher's Book.

NEW full-page **Extra Practice and Progress Portfolio** sections for each unit in the back of the Student's Book provide further controlled practice of all new language.

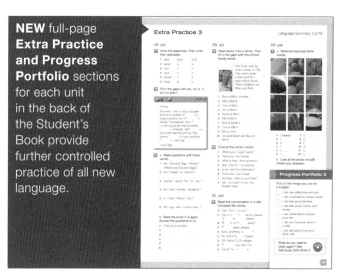

NEW Help with Pronunciation sections at the end of each unit in the Student's Book enable students to improve their pronunciation and help them to communicate more effectively.

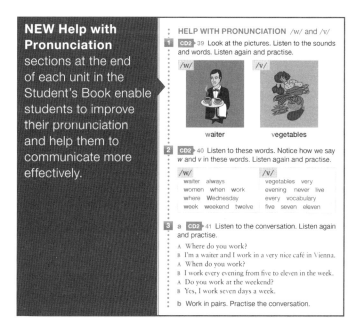

HELP WITH PRONUNCIATION /w/ and /v/

1 CD2 ▷ 39 Look at the pictures. Listen to the sounds and words. Listen again and practise.

/w/ — waiter
/v/ — vegetables

2 CD2 ▷ 40 Listen to these words. Notice how we say w and v in these words. Listen again and practise.

/w/	/v/
waiter always	vegetables very
women when work	evening never live
where Wednesday	every vocabulary
week weekend twelve	five seven eleven

3 **a** CD2 ▷ 41 Listen to the conversation. Listen again and practise.

A Where do you work?
B I'm a waiter and I work in a very nice café in Vienna.
A When do you work?
B I work every evening from five to eleven in the week.
A Do you work at the weekend?
B Yes, I work seven days a week.

b Work in pairs. Practise the conversation.

NEW Self-study DVD-ROM with over 300 practice exercises, review video, customisable tests, e-Portfolio and much more!

A Guide to the Student's Book

Lessons A and B in each unit introduce and practise new vocabulary and grammar in realistic contexts.

The menu lists the language taught in each lesson.

Help with Grammar sections ask students to focus on the rules of meaning and form themselves before checking with the teacher or in the *Language Summary*.

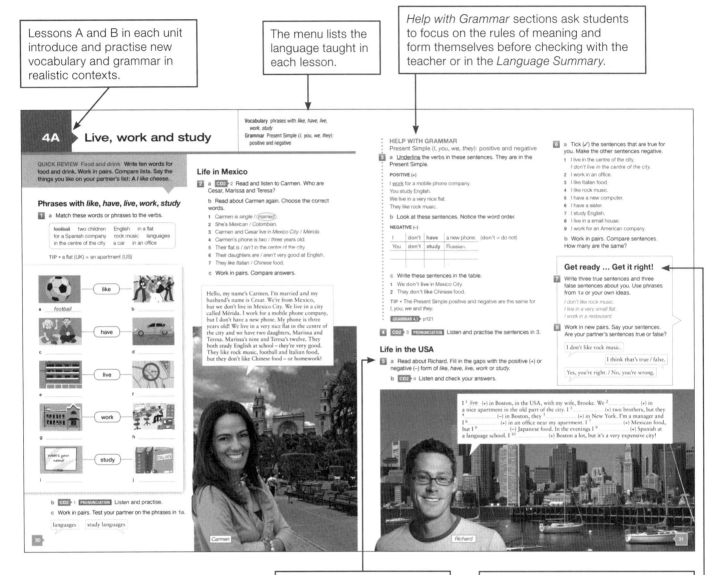

Controlled practice exercises check students have understood the meaning and form of new language.

Get ready … Get it right! sections are structured communicative speaking tasks that focus on both accuracy and fluency. The *Get ready …* stage provides the opportunity for students to plan the language and content of what they are going to say before *Getting it right!* when they do the communicative stage of the activity.

Reduced sample pages from the **face2face**
Second edition Starter Student's Book

Quick Reviews at the beginning of each lesson recycle previously learned language and get the class off to a lively, student-centred start.

New grammar structures are always presented in context in a listening or reading text.

Help with Listening sections focus on the areas that make spoken English so difficult to understand and teach students how to listen more effectively.

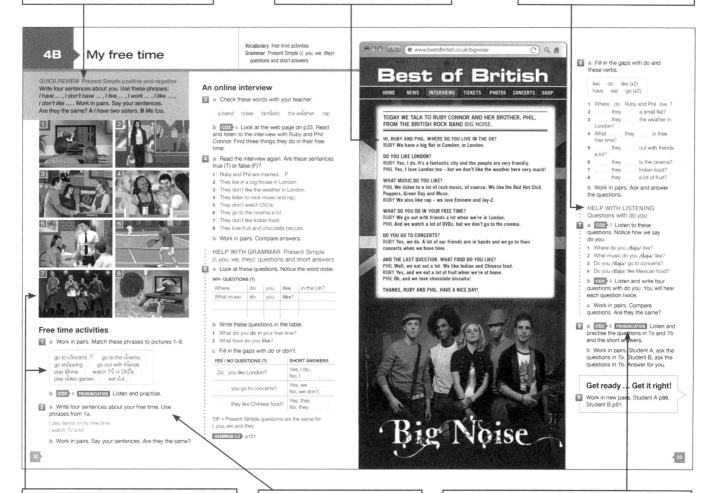

New vocabulary is usually presented visually. Students are often asked to match words to pictures before checking with their teacher or in the *Language Summary.*

There are practice activities immediately after the presentation of vocabulary to help consolidate the new language.

The PRONUNCIATION icon indicates a drill or a practice activity designed to improve students' pronunciation. The integrated pronunciation syllabus includes drills for all new vocabulary and grammar.

Reduced sample pages from the **face2face** Second edition Starter Student's Book

A Guide to the Student's Book

Lesson C REAL WORLD lessons focus on the functional and situational language that students need to communicate effectively in an English environment.

Add variety to your lessons by presenting *Real World* language visually, using the new video clips on the Teacher's DVD.

Real World sections focus on the language that students need in a particular situation or context, often using easy-to-follow flow charts.

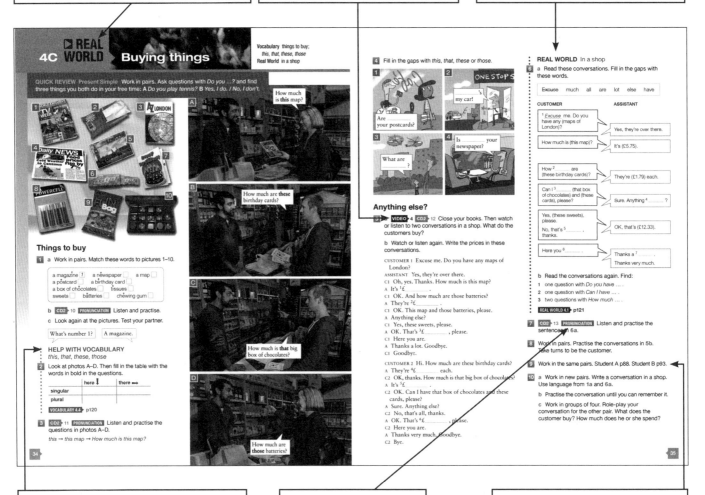

Help with Vocabulary sections ask students to focus on meaning and form of new vocabulary themselves before checking with the teacher or in the *Language Summary*.

The integrated pronunciation syllabus includes drills for all new *Real World* language.

The *Pair and Group Work* section at the back of the Student's Book provides a wide variety of communicative speaking practice activities.

Reduced sample pages from the **face2face**
Second edition Starter Student's Book

Lesson D VOCABULARY AND SKILLS lessons present and practise new vocabulary through visual contexts and reading texts.

Key vocabulary in listening and reading texts is pre-taught before students listen or read.

Help with Pronunciation sections help students with specific areas of pronunciation that they often find problematic.

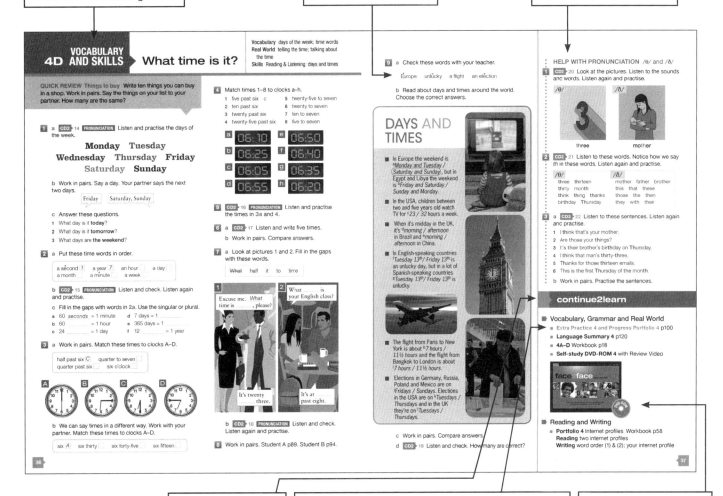

The *continue2learn* sections show students where they can continue practising and extending their knowledge of the language taught in the unit.

There is a full-page *Extra Practice* section in the back of the Student's Book, which provides revision of key language from the unit. Students can also monitor their progress by completing the *Progress Portfolio*, which is based on the requirements of the *Common European Framework of Reference for Languages*.

The Self-study DVD-ROM provides further practice activities, review video, drills, customisable tests and c-Portfolio section.

Reduced sample pages from the **face2face** Second edition Starter Student's Book

Teacher's DVD Instructions

The Teacher's DVD contains the *Real World* video presentation material as well as printable PDFs of all the Teaching Notes and photocopiable materials from this Teacher's Book.

- To play the *Real World* video presentation material you can use the DVD in a DVD player or in a computer. Insert the DVD and follow the instructions on the main menu.
- To access the PDFs on a computer with a Windows operating system, double click *My Computer*. Right click on the CD/DVD drive and choose *Explore*. Open the 'Teaching Notes and Photocopiable Materials' folder and double-click on the PDFs you want to view or print.
- To access the PDFs on a computer with a Mac operating system, double-click on the DVD icon on the desktop. Open the 'Teaching Notes and Photocopiable Materials' folder and double-click on the PDFs you want to view or print.

Choose a video.

Choose to have the subtitles on or off.

Get help to access the PDFs of the Teaching Notes and photocopiable materials.

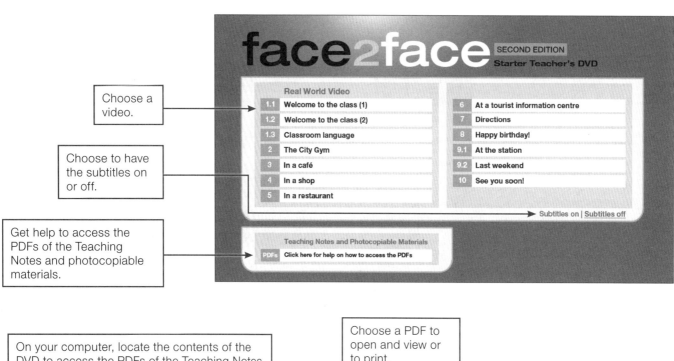

On your computer, locate the contents of the DVD to access the PDFs of the Teaching Notes and photocopiable materials.

Choose a PDF to open and view or to print.

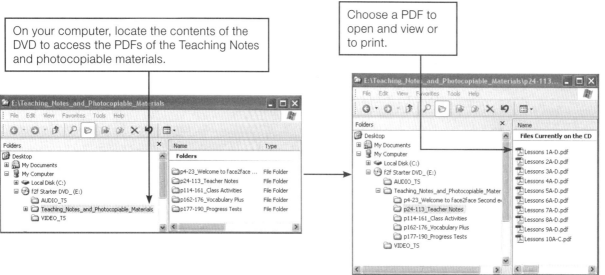

To view or print the Teaching Notes and photocopiable materials you will need a software program that can read PDFs such as Adobe® Reader®, which is free to download and install at www.adobe.com.

Self-study DVD-ROM Instructions

Installing the Self-study DVD-ROM to your hard disk

- Insert the **face2face** Second edition Starter Self-study DVD-ROM into your CD/DVD drive. The DVD-ROM will automatically start to install. Follow the installation instructions on your screen.

- On a Windows PC, if the DVD-ROM does not automatically start to install, open *My Computer*, locate your CD/DVD drive and open it to view the contents of the DVD-ROM. Double-click on the *CambridgeApplicationInstaller* file. Follow the installation instructions on your screen.

- On a Mac, if the DVD-ROM does not automatically start to install, double-click on the **face2face** DVD icon on your desktop. Double-click on the *CambridgeApplicationInstaller* file. Follow the installation instructions on your screen.

Support

If you need help with installing the DVD-ROM, please visit: www.cambridge.org/elt/support

System requirements

Windows
- Intel Pentium 4 2GHz or faster
- Microsoft® Windows® XP (SP3), Windows® Vista® (SP2), Windows® 7 and Windows® 8
- Minimum 1GB RAM
- Minimum 750MB of hard drive space
- Adobe® Flash® Player 10.3.183.7 or later

Mac OS
- Intel Core™ Duo 1.83GHz or faster
- Mac OSX 10.5 or later
- Minimum 1GB RAM
- Minimum 750MB of hard drive space
- Adobe® Flash® Player 10.3.183.7 or later

Unit menus

Choose a unit.

Practise the new language from each lesson.

Listen and practise new language. You can also record your own pronunciation.

Watch the Review Video and do the activities.

Use the navigation bar to go to different areas of the DVD-ROM.

Create vocabulary and grammar tests for language in the Student's Book.

Listen to the main recordings from the Student's Book and read the scripts.

Go to the home screen.

Look at the Phonemic Symbols chart and practise the pronunciation of vowels and consonant sounds.

Check *My Progress* to see your scores for completed activities.

Explore the e-Portfolio. See p12.

Get help on using the Self-study DVD-ROM.

Go to Cambridge Dictionaries Online.

Activities

Read the instructions.

Click play ▶ to listen to audio.

Record your own pronunciation of words and sentences. Send these recordings to the *My Work* section of the e-Portfolio. See p13.

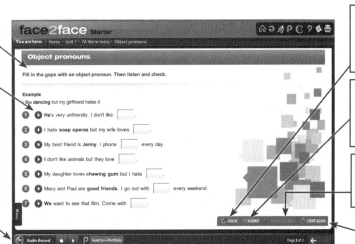

Check your answers. Sometimes activities then give you extra help or the Audio Script.

Submit your answers when you have finished the activity. Your score is recorded in *My Progress*.

After submitting your answers, see the correct answers.

Start the activity again.

Self-study DVD-ROM Instructions

e-Portfolio

Find all the Grammar Reference from the Student's Book.

Find words and phrases from the Student's Book.

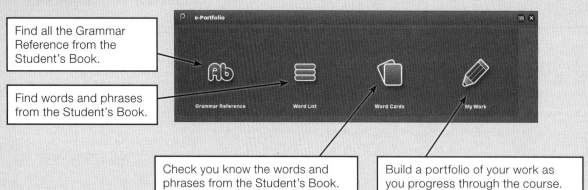

Check you know the words and phrases from the Student's Book.

Build a portfolio of your work as you progress through the course.

Grammar Reference

Choose a unit to see all the grammar in that Student's Book unit.

Choose a grammar point from the Student's Book.

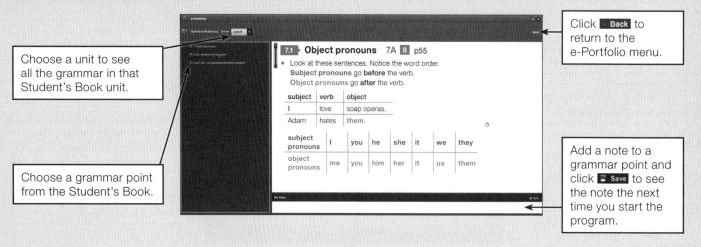

Click **Back** to return to the e-Portfolio menu.

Add a note to a grammar point and click **Save** to see the note the next time you start the program.

Word List

Choose a lesson to see the words in the Student's Book. Then choose a topic to see the main vocabulary sets in each lesson.

Choose a word to see its definition, an example sentence and the lesson in the Student's Book where it first appears. Listen to the word in British or American English.

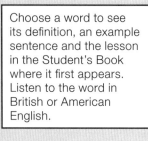

Click **Add** to add a new word to the Word List.

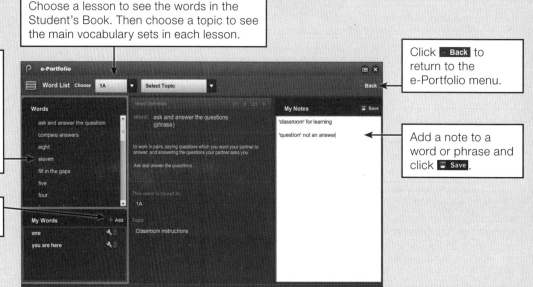

Click **Back** to return to the e-Portfolio menu.

Add a note to a word or phrase and click **Save**.

Word Cards

Choose the number of words.

Choose to have the Word Cards in alphabetical order or not.

Click **Start Again** to move all the cards back to the middle pile and start again.

Choose a unit.

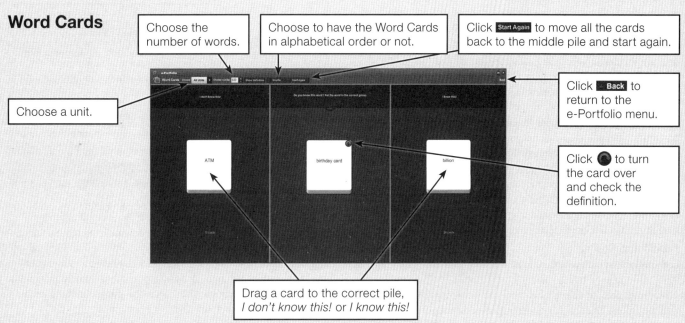

Click **Back** to return to the e-Portfolio menu.

Click ● to turn the card over and check the definition.

Drag a card to the correct pile, *I don't know this!* or *I know this!*

My Work

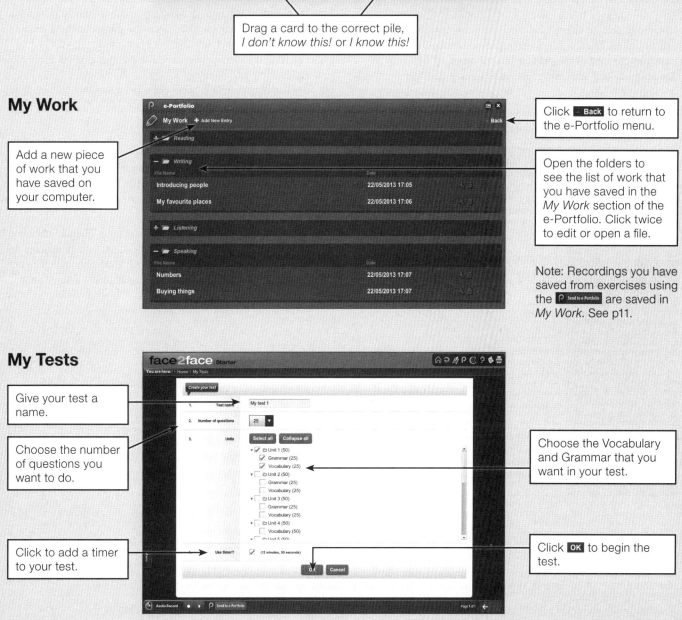

Add a new piece of work that you have saved on your computer.

Click **Back** to return to the e-Portfolio menu.

Open the folders to see the list of work that you have saved in the *My Work* section of the e-Portfolio. Click twice to edit or open a file.

Note: Recordings you have saved from exercises using the **Send to e-Portfolio** are saved in *My Work*. See p11.

My Tests

Give your test a name.

Choose the number of questions you want to do.

Click to add a timer to your test.

Choose the Vocabulary and Grammar that you want in your test.

Click **OK** to begin the test.

▶ The Common European Framework (CEFR)

What is the Common European Framework (CEFR)?

Since the early 1970s, a series of Council of Europe initiatives has developed a description of the language knowledge and skills that people need to live, work and survive in any European country. *Waystage 1990*[1], *Threshold 1990*[2] and *Vantage*[3] detail the knowledge and skills required at different levels of ability. In 2001, the contents of these documents were further developed into sets of 'can do' statements or 'competences' and officially launched as the *Common European Framework of Reference for Languages: Learning, teaching, assessment (CEFR)*[4]. A related document, *The European Language Portfolio*, encourages learners to assess their progress by matching their competence against the 'can do' statements.

face2face Second edition has been developed to include comprehensive coverage of the requirements of the CEFR. The table above right shows how **face2face** Second edition relates to the CEFR and the examinations which can be taken at each level through Cambridge English Language Assessment, which is a member of ALTE (The Association of Language Testers in Europe).

CEFR level:		Cambridge English exams:
	face2face	
C1	Advanced	Advanced (CAE)
B2	Upper Intermediate	First (FCE)
B1 +	Intermediate	Preliminary (PET)
B1	Pre-intermediate	
A2	Elementary	Key (KET)
A1	Starter	

In the spirit of *The European Language Portfolio* developed from the CEFR, **face2face** Second edition provides a Progress Portfolio for each unit in the Student's Book. Students are encouraged to assess their ability to use the language they have learned so far and to review any aspects they are unsure of by using the Self-study DVD-ROM. In the Workbook there is a 20-page *Reading and Writing Portfolio* section (2 pages for each unit) linked to the CEFR and a comprehensive list of 'can do' statements in the *Reading and Writing Progress Portfolio*, which allows students to track their own progress.

face2face Second edition Starter and CEFR level A1

		A1
UNDERSTANDING	Listening	I can understand familiar words and very basic phrases concerning myself, my family and immediate concrete surroundings when people speak slowly and clearly.
	Reading	I can understand familiar names, words and very simple sentences, for example on notices and posters or in catalogues.
SPEAKING	Spoken interaction	I can interact in a simple way provided the other person is prepared to repeat or rephrase things at a slower rate of speech and help me formulate what I'm trying to say. I can ask and answer simple questions in areas of immediate need or on very familiar topics.
	Spoken production	I can use simple phrases and sentences to describe where I live and people I know.
WRITING	Writing	I can write a short, simple postcard, for example sending holiday greetings. I can fill in forms with personal details, for example, entering my name, nationality and address on a hotel registration form.

The table on the left describes the general degree of skill required at level A1 of the CEFR. The 'can do' statements for A1 are listed in the *Common European Framework of Reference for Languages: Learning, teaching, assessment.*

The Listening, Reading, Speaking and Writing tables on p16–p19 show where the required competencies for level A1 are covered in **face2face** Second edition Starter. For more information about how **face2face** covers the areas specified by the CEFR, see our website: www.cambridge.org/elt/face2face

[1]*Waystage 1990* J A van Ek and J L M Trim, Council of Europe, Cambridge University Press ISBN 0 521 56707 6
[2]*Threshold 1990* J A van Ek and J L M Trim, Council of Europe, Cambridge University Press ISBN 0 521 56706 8
[3]*Vantage* J A van Ek and J L M Trim, Council of Europe, Cambridge University Press ISBN 0 521 56705 X
[4]*Common European Framework of Reference for Languages: Learning, teaching, assessment* (2001) Council of Europe Modern Languages Division, Strasbourg, Cambridge University Press ISBN 0 521 00531 0

English Vocabulary Profile

What is the English Vocabulary Profile?

The English Vocabulary Profile is part of English Profile, a ground-breaking and innovative programme which is shaping the future of English language learning, teaching and assessment worldwide. Endorsed by the Council of Europe, English Profile provides a unique benchmark for progress in English by clearly describing the language that learners need at each level of the Common European Framework (CEFR).

The CEFR is already widely used around the world to assess language ability. However, because it is 'language neutral' it needs to be interpreted appropriately for each language. English Profile makes the CEFR even more relevant to English language teachers by showing the specific vocabulary, grammar and functional language that students can be expected to master at each level in English. By making the CEFR more accessible in this way, it provides unparalleled support for the development of curricula and teaching materials, and in assessing students' language proficiency.

The English Vocabulary Profile shows, in both British and American English, which words and phrases learners around the world know at each level – A1 to C2 – of the CEFR. Rather than providing a syllabus of the vocabulary that learners *should* know, the English Vocabulary Profile verifies what they *do* know at each level. CEFR levels are assigned not just to the words themselves, but to each individual meaning of these words. So, for instance, the word *first* is assigned level A1 for the meaning *coming before the others*, A2 for *the most important*, B2 in the expression *at first sight* and C1 for the phrase *first and foremost*. The capitalised guidewords help the user to navigate longer entries, and phrases are listed separately within an entry.

face2face Second edition Starter and the English Vocabulary Profile

The vocabulary taught in **face2face** Second edition Starter has been informed by the English Vocabulary Profile to ensure that the majority of the new words and phrases taught in the Student's Book are A1 (or A2).

To find out more about the English Vocabulary Profile and the English Profile project or to get involved, visit www.englishprofile.org

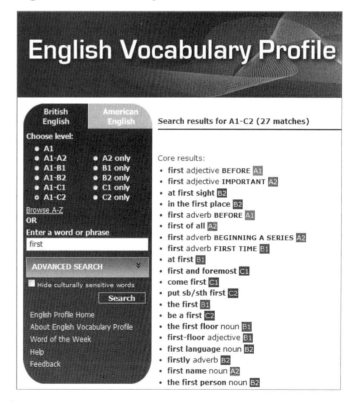

English Profile is a collaborative project between:

CEFR Tables: Listening and Reading

Listening

A language user at level A1 can:	1	2	3
understand basic greetings and phrases (*Hello, Excuse me*, etc.)	1A 1C	2A 2C 2D	3C
understand simple questions about themselves	1A 1B 1C	2B 2C 2D	3B
understand very short dialogues	1A 1B 1C	2B 2C 2D	3B 3C 3D
understand numbers, prices and times	1A	2D	3C
understand short simple directions			

Reading

A language user at level A1 can:	1	2	3
understand very short, simple texts, a single phrase at a time	WBP1		3A
pick out familiar names, words and phrases in very short, simple texts			3A
pick out information from catalogues, posters and calendars of public events about the time and place of films, concerts, etc.			
get an idea of the content of simpler informational material and short, simple descriptions (especially if there is visual support)			
understand information about people in newspapers, etc., (age, place of residence, etc.)			
understand simple forms well enough to give basic personal details		2C WBP2	
understand common commands	This competence is practised throughout the course in the rubrics.		
follow instructions that have clear pictures and few words	This competence is practised throughout the course in the rubrics.		
follow short, simple written directions			
understand short, simple messages on postcards			WBP3
understand simple messages written by friends or colleagues about everyday situations (text messages, invitations, etc.)			

1A = face2face Second edition Starter Student's Book Lesson 1A
WBP1 = face2face Second edition Starter Workbook Reading and Writing Portfolio 1

4	5	6	7	8	9	10
4B 4C	5C	6C	7B 7C 7D			10B 10C
4B	5A	6D	7A 7B	8B 8C	9B 9D	10B 10C
4B 4C 4D	5B 5C	6B 6C	7B 7C 7D	8B 8C	9C	10B
4C 4D	5A 5C	6C		8C 8D	9C	
			7C			

4	5	6	7	8	9	10
4A 4B WPB4	5B 5D WBP5	6A	7A WBP7	8A	9A 9B 9D	10A
4A 4B WPB4	5D WPB5		7A WBP7	8A	9A 9B 9D	10A
4D		6C		WBP8		
WPB4		6A WBP6		8A 8D	9A 9B WBP9	10A
4B	5D WBP5				9A	
			7C			
						WBP10

CEFR Tables: Speaking and Writing

Speaking

A language user at level A1 can:	1	2	3
introduce someone and use basic greeting and leave-taking expressions	1A	2C	
ask and answer simple questions and initiate and respond to simple statements in areas of immediate need or on very familiar topics	1A 1B 1C 1D	2A 2B 2C 2D	3A 3B 3C
ask and answer questions about themselves and other people, where they live, things they have, poeple they know	1B		3A 3D
give personal information (address, telephone number, etc.)	1A 1B 1C	2A 2B 2C 2D	3B
describe where he/she lives			
handle numbers, quantities, costs and times	1A	2C 2D	3C
make simple purchases			3C
ask people for things and give people things			3C
indicate time by such phrases as *next week, in November, on Monday*, etc.			
says when he/she doesn't understand	1C		
ask someone to repeat what they say	1C		

Writing

A language user at level A1 can:	1	2	3
copy familiar words and short phrases	This competence is practised throughout the Student's Book and Workbook.		
spell his/her address, nationality and other personal details	1B 1C WBP1	2A2C WBP2	
write sentences and simple phrases about themselves and others (where they live and what they do, etc.)	WBP1		3D
fill in a questionnaire or form with personal details		2C WBP2	
write a greetings card			
write a simple postcard			WBP3
link words or groups of words with very basic linear connectors (*and, but, so, because*, etc.)			WBP3

1A = **face2face** Second edition Starter Student's Book Lesson 1A
WBP1 = **face2face** Second edition Starter Workbook Reading and Writing Portfolio 1

4	5	6	7	8	9	10
						10C
4A 4B 4D	5A	6A 6B	7A 7C	8A 8B	9A 9B 9C 9D	10A 10B 10C
4B	5A 5B	6B 6D	7A 7B 7D	8B 8C	9B 9C 9D	10B 10C
4A	5A 5D			8A 8C	9A	10A
4B		6A 6B				
4C 4D	5C	6A 6B		8C 8D	9C 9D	
4C		6C			9C	
4C	5C	6C			9C	
	5A 5B 5D	6C		8A 8B 8C	9A 9B	10A 10B 10C

4	5	6	7	8	9	10
4A 4B WBP4	5A 5B 5D WBP5	6A 6D WBP6	7A 7B WBP7	8A WBP8	9A 9B 9C WBP9	10A 10B
						WBP10
	WBP5		WBP7		WBP9	

The face2face Approach

Listening

A typical listening practice activity checks students' understanding of gist and then asks questions about specific details. The innovative *Help with Listening* sections in **face2face** Second edition Starter take students a step further by focusing on the underlying reasons why listening to English can be so problematic. Activities in these sections:

- introduce the concept of stress on words and phrases.
- focus on sentence stress and its relationship to the important information in a text.
- explain why words are often linked together in natural spoken English.
- help students to identify and understand contractions.
- introduce some common weak forms.
- show students how these features of connected speech give spoken English its natural rhythm.

For *Teaching Tips* on Listening, see p21.

Speaking

All the lessons in Starter Student's Book and the *Class Activities* photocopiables provide students with numerous speaking opportunities. Many of these activities focus on accuracy, while the fluency activities help students to gain confidence and try out what they have learned. For fluency activities to be truly 'fluent', however, students often need time to formulate their ideas before they speak, and this preparation is incorporated into the *Get ready ... Get it right!* activities.

For *Teaching Tips* on Speaking, see p22.

Reading and Writing

In the **face2face** Starter Student's Book, reading texts from a variety of genres are used both to present new language and to provide reading practice. In addition, there are a number of writing activities which consolidate the language input of the lesson.

For classes that require more practice of reading and writing skills, there is the 20-page Reading and Writing Portfolio in the Starter Workbook. This section contains 10 double-page stand-alone lessons, one for each unit of the Student's Book, which students can do at home or in class. The topics and content of these lessons are based on the CEFR reading and writing competencies for level A1. At the end of this section there is a list of 'can do' statements that allows students to track their progress.

Vocabulary

face2face recognises the importance of vocabulary in successful communication. There is lexical input in every lesson, which is consolidated for student reference in the *Language Summaries* in the back of the Student's Book.

In addition, each unit in the Student's Book includes at least one *Help with Vocabulary* section. These sections are designed to guide students towards a better understanding of the lexical systems of English.

For longer courses and/or more able students, this Teacher's Book also contains one *Vocabulary Plus* worksheet for each unit (p167–p176). These stand-alone worksheets introduce and practise new vocabulary that is not included in the Student's Book.

For *Teaching Tips* on Vocabulary, see p22.

Grammar

Grammar is a central strand in the **face2face** Second edition Starter syllabus and new grammar structures are always introduced in context in a listening or a reading text. We believe students are more likely to understand and remember new language if they have actively tried to work out the rules for themselves. Therefore in the *Help with Grammar* sections students are often asked to focus on the meaning and form of the structure for themselves before checking with the teacher or in the appropriate *Language Summary*. All new grammar forms are practised in regular recorded pronunciation drills and communicative speaking activities, and consolidated through written practice.

For *Teaching Tips* on Grammar, see p12.

Functional and Situational Language

face2face places great emphasis on the functional and situational language students need to communicate effectively in an English-speaking environment. Each unit has a double-page *Real World* lesson that introduces and practises this language in a variety of situations. This language can now be presented either by using video clips on the Teacher's DVD or by using the recordings on the Class Audio CDs.

Pronunciation

Pronunciation is integrated throughout the Student's Book. Drills for all new vocabulary, grammar structures and *Real World* language are included on the Class Audio CDs. These drills focus on sentence stress, weak forms, intonation, etc. Students also practise individual sounds that are often problematic for learners of English in the *Help with Pronunciation* sections at the end of each unit. These drills are also included on the Self-study DVD-ROM.

For *Teaching Tips* on Pronunciation, see p23.

Reviewing and Recycling

We believe that regular revision and recycling of language are essential to students' language development, so language is recycled in every lesson of the **face2face** Starter Student's Book. Opportunities for review are also provided in the Quick Review sections at the beginning of every lesson, the full-page *Extra Practice* section and the 10 photocopiable *Progress Tests* in this Teacher's Book (p180–p191).

For *Teaching Tips* on Revision and Recycling, see p23.

Teaching Tips

Teaching Starter Classes

Teaching Starter classes can often be challenging as well as rewarding. Starter students can lack confidence and might not have studied a language formally before. Here are some tips to help you teach Starter classes.

- Each lesson in the Student's Book is carefully staged and takes students step-by-step from presentation to practice. Go slowly and methodically through the material exercise by exercise, making sure students understand each point before moving on.
- Keep your instructions in class short, clear and to the point. Students can often get lost if the teacher talks too much in English. It is perfectly acceptable to use imperatives to give instructions (*Look at exercise 3. Work in pairs.*, etc.). Teach the words and phrases in Classroom Instructions, SB p135, early in the course.
- Most exercises in the Student's Book have an example already filled in. Use these examples to check that the class knows what to do before asking them to work on their own or in pairs.
- Take time to demonstrate communicative activities with the class. At Starter level, demonstration is often a more effective way to give instructions than telling students what to do. You can demonstrate activities yourself or use a confident student as your partner.
- Do a lot of drilling. This helps to build students' confidence and allows them time to practise new language in a controlled way. All new vocabulary, grammar and *Real World* language is included on the Class Audio CDs to provide clear models of new language. See the tips on drilling on p23.
- Using the board is particularly important with Starter students. In the Teaching Notes (p24–p113) this icon ✍ indicates a point in the lesson where it may be useful for you to use the board.
- When using the board, try to involve students in what you are writing by asking questions (*What's the next word? Where's the stress?*, etc.). Give students time to copy what you have written and leave useful language on the board so that students can refer to it during the lesson.
- Show students the Language Summaries on SB p114–p133 early on in the course and encourage them to refer to this in class and when doing homework.
- Starter students need a lot of revision and recycling throughout the course. See the tips on reviewing and recycling on p23.
- It is, of course, very useful to know the students' first language. If you have a monolingual class, you may want to use the students' language to give or check instructions for speaking activities, or to deal with students' queries. However, try to speak to the class in English as much as possible, as this will help establish the classroom as an English-speaking environment.
- Remember that at Starter level, encouragement and praise are very important, particularly for weaker students.

Teaching Mixed Levels

In Starter classes, teachers often have a mixture of real beginners and 'false' beginners. Here are some tips to help you deal with teaching low-level mixed-ability classes.

- Work at the pace of the average student. Try not to let the fastest or slowest students dictate the pace.
- To avoid stronger students dominating, nominate the quieter ones to answer easier questions.
- Ask stronger and more confident students to demonstrate activities for the whole class.
- Allow time for students to check answers in pairs or groups before checking with the whole class.
- Encourage stronger students to help weaker ones, for example, if a student has finished an activity, ask him/her to work with a slower student.
- Give students time to think by asking them to write down answers rather than calling them out. This helps avoid the more able students dominating the class.
- When monitoring during pair and group work, go to the weaker students first to check that they have understood the instructions and are doing the activity correctly.
- Plan which students are going to work together in pair and group work. Vary the interaction so stronger students sometimes work with weaker students, and at other times (e.g. during freer speaking activities) they work with other students of the same level.
- Don't feel that you have to wait for everyone in the class to finish an exercise. It is usually best to stop an activity when most of the class have finished.
- Vary the amount and type of correction you give according to the level of the student, in order to push stronger students and to avoid overwhelming those who are less confident. Remember to praise successful communication as well as correct language.
- Focus on the effort made by each student and measure his/her progress against his/her personal standard. Remember that at this level, encouragement and praise are very important, particularly for weaker students.
- Give weaker students extra homework from the Workbook or the Self-study DVD-ROM.

Listening

- For most Starter students, listening to spoken English is usually very challenging. Be sensitive to the difficulties that students might be having and play a recording several times if necessary.
- At this level, activities where students listen and read at the same time are very useful, as they allow students to 'tune in' to spoken English and make the connection between what they hear and the written word. Make full use of these 'listen and read' activities in class.
- For other listening activities, you can ask students to read the Audio and Video Scripts (SB p107–p113) when they listen for a second or third time.

Teaching Tips

- Before asking students to listen to a recording, establish the context, the characters and what information you want them to listen for. If the recording is a 'listen and read' activity, check students are looking at the correct text on the page before you begin.
- Give students time to read the comprehension questions in the Student's Book and deal with any problems in these questions before playing a recording.
- Make full use of the *Help with Listening* sections in the Student's Book, which help students to understand natural spoken English.
- Encourage students to listen again to the classroom recordings on their Self-study DVD-ROM at home. These are in the *Class Audio* section of the home page for each unit.

Speaking

Pair and Group Work

- Make full use of all the communicative speaking activities in the Student's Book, particularly the *Get ready … Get it right!* sections. These allow students to work out what language they are going to use before they do the communicative stage of the activity, which will help them to retain the accuracy that has been built up during the lesson.
- Help students with the language they need to do speaking tasks by drawing their attention to the 'transactional language' in the speech bubbles.
- Try to ensure that students work with a number of different partners during a class. If it is difficult for students to swap places, you can ask them to work with students behind or in front of them as well as on either side of them.
- It is often useful to provide a model of the tasks you expect students to do. For example, before asking students to talk about their family in pairs, you can talk about your family with the whole class.
- Go around the class and monitor students while they are speaking in pairs or groups. You can provide extra language or ideas and correct any language or pronunciation which is impeding communication.
- When giving feedback on speaking, remember to praise good communication as well as good English, and focus on the result of the task as well as the language.
- Use the photocopiable *Class Activities* (p127–p161) to provide extra communicative speaking practice in class.

Correction

- When you hear a mistake, it is often useful to correct it immediately and ask the student to say the word or phrase again in the correct form, particularly if the mistake relates to the language from the lesson.
- Alternatively, when you point out a mistake to a student you can encourage him/her to correct it himself/herself before giving him/her the correct version.

- Another approach to correction during a freer speaking activity is to note down any mistakes you hear, but not correct them immediately. At the end of the activity write the mistakes on the board. Students can then work in pairs and correct the mistakes. Alternatively, you can discuss the mistakes with the whole class.

Vocabulary

- Most of the new vocabulary in **face2face** Second edition Starter is presented pictorially, and students are usually asked to match words with pictures themselves. If all your class are real beginners, consider introducing new vocabulary yourself first by bringing in pictures, flashcards, objects, etc. and teaching the words one by one. You can then use the first exercise in the Student's Book as practice.
- Make full use of the *Help with Vocabulary* sections in the Student's Book. These focus on lexical grammar and help students to understand the underlying patterns of how vocabulary is used in sentences. Go through each point with the whole class or ask students to do the exercises themselves before you check answers with the class, as shown in the Teaching Notes.
- Make students aware of collocations in English (e.g. *start work, go to the beach*, etc.) by pointing them out when they occur and encouraging students to record them in their notebooks.
- Review and recycle vocabulary at every opportunity in class, using the *Extra Practice* sections, the *Language Summaries* and the photocopiable *Class Activities*.
- Use the photocopiable *Vocabulary Plus* worksheets (p167–p176). These worksheets introduce and practise extra vocabulary which is not included in the Student's Book. They can be used for self-study in class or as homework, or as the basis of a classroom lesson.

Grammar

- Make full use of the *Help with Grammar* sections in the Student's Book. These highlight the rules for form and use of each grammar point. Go through each point with the whole class, or ask students to do the exercises themselves before you check answers with the class, as shown in the Teaching Notes.
- Sentences in the grammar tables in the Student's Book are often colour-coded. When using these tables, use the pink and blue words to highlight the underlying grammatical patterns of new language.
- Teach your students useful grammatical terms (e.g. *noun, verb, Present Simple*, etc.) when the opportunity arises. However, try not to overload students with terminology at this level.
- If you know the students' first language, highlight grammatical differences between their language and English. This raises their awareness of potential problems if they try to translate. It is also useful to show students when a grammatical structure in English is the same as in their own language.

Pronunciation

Drilling

- Make full use of the pronunciation drills on the Class Audio CDs. These drills give standard British native-speaker models of the language taught.
- Note that there are already sufficient pauses built into these recorded drills for students to repeat chorally without you having to pause the recording. If students are finding a particular word or sentences difficult to pronounce, you can pause the recording and ask each student to repeat individually before continuing.
- Point out to the class that all the recorded drills are also on the *Self-study DVD-ROM*. Encourage students to use these for pronunciation practice on their computer at home.
- For variety, model and drill the sentences yourself instead of using the recordings. When you model a phrase or sentence, make sure that you speak at normal speed with natural stress and contractions. Repeat the target language two or three times before asking the whole class to repeat after you in a 'choral drill'.
- After choral drilling it is usually helpful to do some individual drilling. Start with the strongest students and drill around the class in random order.
- As the aim of drilling is accuracy, you should correct students when they make a mistake. However, avoid making the students feel uncomfortable and don't spend too long with one student.
- After drilling new language, you can ask two students to practise alternate lines of a conversation from where they are sitting, with the rest of the class listening. This 'open pairs' technique is very useful to check students' pronunciation before they go on to practise in 'closed pairs'. It can also be used after students have worked in closed pairs to check their performance of the task.
- Praise students for good/comprehensible pronunciation and acknowledge weak students' improvement, even if their pronunciation is not perfect.

Helping students with stress and intonation

- Point out the stress marks (*) on all new vocabulary in the vocabulary boxes in the lessons and the *Language Summaries*. Note that only the main stress in each new word or phrase is shown. For example, in the phrase *finish work*, the main stress on *work* is shown, but the secondary stress on *finish* is not. We feel this simplified system is the most effective way of encouraging students to stress words and phrases correctly.
- When drilling new vocabulary, pay particular attention to words that sound different from how they are spelt. Words that students often find difficult to pronounce are highlighted in the Teaching Notes for each lesson.
- When you write words or sentences on the board, mark the stress in the correct place or ask the students to tell you which syllables or words are stressed.
- When you model sentences yourself, it may be helpful

to over-emphasise the stress pattern to help students hear the stress. You can also 'beat' the stress with your hand or fist.

- Emphasise that intonation is an important part of meaning in English and often shows how we feel. For example, a falling intonation on the word *please* can sound very impolite to a native English speaker.
- Encourage students to copy the intonation pattern of model sentences on the recorded drills, particularly in the *Real World* sections in lesson C of each unit.

Helping students with sounds

- Make full use of the *Help with Pronunciation* sections at the end of each unit in the Student's Book. These focus on sounds in English that that learners from most countries find difficult to reproduce.
- If students are having problems making a particular sound, you can demonstrate the shape of the mouth and the position of the tongue in front of the class (or draw this on the board). Often students can't say these sounds simply because they don't know the mouth position required. The mouth positions for all sounds in the *Help with Pronunciation* sections can be found in the Teaching Notes for each unit.
- Draw students' attention to the English sounds which are the same in their own language(s) as well as highlighting the ones that are different.
- Encourage students to use the pronunciation activities in each unit of the *Self-study DVD-ROM* at home. Students can also use the phonemes section of the *Self-study DVD-ROM* to practise individual sounds.

Reviewing and Recycling

- Use the *Quick Reviews* at the beginning of each lesson. They are easy to set up and should take no more than five to ten minutes. They are a good way of getting the class to speak immediately as well as reviewing what students have learned in previous lessons.
- Exploit the *Extra Practice* sections for each unit (SB p97–p106). They can be done in class when students have finished the unit, or set for homework. Note that the exercises in the *Extra Practice* sections are organised in lesson order, so individual exercises can be used as fillers at the beginning or end of a lesson.
- Encourage students to use the *Self-study DVD-ROM* to review each lesson at home. Also encourage students to review new language by reading the *Language Summary* for the lesson.
- Set homework after every class. The **face2face** Second edition Starter Workbook has a section for each lesson in the Student's Book, which reviews all the key language taught in that lesson.
- Give students a *Progress Test* (p180–p191) after each unit of the Student's Book. These can be done in class or given for homework.

1A ▶ What's your name?
Student's Book p6–p7

Vocabulary numbers 0–12
Grammar *I, my, you, your*
Real World saying hello; introducing people;
phone numbers; saying goodbye

Hello!

1 **a** **CD1▶1** Focus students on conversation 1 in the photo. Play the recording. Students listen and read the conversation. Play the recording again if necessary.

Check that students understand the sentences in the conversation. Point out that when giving our name, we can say *I'm …* or *My name's …* . You can also teach *And you.* as an alternative to *You too.*

b **PRONUNCIATION** Play the recording again, pausing after each sentence for students to repeat. Alternatively, model each sentence yourself and ask students to repeat chorally and individually. For **Teaching Tips** on drilling, see p23 of this book.

c Demonstrate the activity yourself by role-playing the conversation with a confident student. Then ask students to practise the conversation with four other students, either by moving around the room or by talking to students sitting near them. Students should use their own first names.

EXTRA IDEA

• Before asking students to practise the conversation in pairs, choose two confident students and ask them to practise the conversation for the class. Students don't need to leave their seats. Correct students' pronunciation as necessary, then ask them to practise the conversation again. Repeat this 'open pairs' procedure with other students. If this technique works well with your class, use it when appropriate in future lessons.

---

d Focus students on the speech bubbles. Use the third speech bubble to teach students *Hi = Hello.* Then ask students to take turns to introduce themselves to the class.

EXTRA IDEA

• ✍ Draw a plan of the class seating arrangements on the board and write in the students' names as they introduce themselves to the class. Leave the plan on the board for students to refer to during the lesson.

---

2 **a** **CD1▶2** Focus students on conversation 2 in the photo. Play the recording. Students listen and read. Check students understand all the sentences in the conversation. Remind students that *Hi = Hello* and point out that *I'm fine. = I'm OK.* You can also point out that *Hi* is more informal than *Hello.*

b **PRONUNCIATION** Play the recording again, pausing after each sentence for students to repeat. Alternatively, model each sentence yourself and ask students to repeat chorally and individually.

c Demonstrate the activity yourself by role-playing the conversation with a confident student. Then ask students to practise the conversation with four other students, either by moving around the room or by talking to students sitting near them. Students should use their own first names.

HELP WITH GRAMMAR *I, my, you, your*

Help with Grammar sections help students to examine examples of new language and discover the rules of meaning, form and use for themselves. Students should usually do the exercises on their own or in pairs before you check the answers with the class.

For more information on the **face2face** approach to Grammar, see p20.

For **Teaching Tips** on Grammar, see p22.

3 **a–b** Focus students on the example in **3a** and use this to teach the phrase *Fill in the gaps.* Students do the exercises on their own or in pairs. Check answers with the class. ✍ Alternatively, do the exercise on the board with the whole class.

• **a Answers** 2 I 3 My
• **b Answers** 2 you 3 You 4 your
• Highlight the difference between *I/my* and *you/your*.
• Point out that we use *I/you* + **verb** (*I read*, *you listen*, etc.) and *my/your* + **noun** (*my name*, *your book*, etc.).
• Also point out that we always use a capital *I* when we refer to ourselves.
• You can also tell students that there is no polite form of *you* in English.
• Students may ask you about the meaning of *'m, are* and *'s*. Tell the class they are part of the verb *be*, and that *I'm = I am* and *name's = name is*. We suggest that you don't go into detail about the verb *be* at this stage of the course and encourage students to treat the new language as fixed phrases. Note that the verb *be* is taught systematically in units 2 and 3.

EXTRA IDEA

• Highlight the Language Summary reference **GRAMMAR 1.1▶** at the end of the exercise and ask students to turn to Language Summary 1, SB (Student's Book) p114–p115. Ask students to find **GRAMMAR 1.1▶** and give them time to read the information. Point out that all the new language in each unit is included in the Language Summaries, and that this language is organised into three sections: Vocabulary, Grammar and Real World.

---

4 `CD1` **3** `PRONUNCIATION` Focus students on the sentences in **3**. Play the recording. Students listen and practise.

Note that in most of the recorded drills there are already sufficient pauses for students to repeat chorally without you pausing the recording yourself.

5 **a** Students do the exercise on their own, then compare answers in pairs.

b `CD1` **4** Play the recording (SB p107). Students listen and check their answers. Check answers with the class.

A
SUE	Hello, **my** name's Sue. What's **your** name?
MARIO	Hello, **I'm** Mario.
SUE	Nice to meet **you**.
MARIO	**You** too.

B
ADAM	Hi, Meg.
MEG	Hi, Adam. How are **you**?
ADAM	**I'm** fine, thanks. And **you**?
MEG	**I'm** OK, thanks.

c Students practise the conversations in pairs. Ask a few pairs to role-play the conversations for the class.

Introducing people

6 **a** `CD1` **5** Focus students on conversation 3 in the photo. Play the recording. Students listen and read the conversation. Check students understand that we use *this is …* to introduce people.

b `PRONUNCIATION` Play the recording again, pausing after each sentence for students to repeat. Alternatively, model each sentence yourself and ask students to repeat chorally and individually.

c Put students into groups of three. Students practise conversation 3 in their groups, using their own names.
Ask a few groups to role-play their conversations for the class. Alternatively, ask students to move around the room and introduce people to each other.

Numbers 0–12

7 **a** `CD1` **6** `PRONUNCIATION` Teach the word *number*. Play the recording. Students listen and repeat the numbers. Alternatively, model the words yourself and ask students to repeat chorally and individually.
Highlight the pronunciation of *zero* /ˈzɪərəʊ/ and *eight* /eɪt/. Repeat the drill if necessary.

b Demonstrate the activity by saying four numbers and asking students to write them down. Check they have the correct answers. Students then do the exercise in pairs.

> **EXTRA IDEA**
>
> • Students work in pairs and count alternately from 0 to 12. They can then count backwards alternately from 12 to 0.

Phone numbers

8 **a** `CD1` **7** Pre-teach *phone number*. Play the recording. Students listen and read the questions and answers.
Check students understand *mobile number* and *home number* by referring to the photos.
Point out the **TIP** on how to say *0* and double digits (*44*, etc.) in phone numbers. Note that we can also say *zero* in phone numbers instead of 'oh'.
`PRONUNCIATION` Play the recording again, pausing after each sentence for students to repeat chorally and individually. Highlight the pronunciation of *mobile* /ˈməʊbaɪl/ and *double* /ˈdʌbəl/.

b Students do the exercise in pairs.

9 **a** `CD1` **8** Play the recording (SB p107). Students listen and write the numbers. Play the recording again if necessary.

b Students compare answers in pairs.
Check answers with the class by eliciting the phone numbers and writing them on the board.
You can also use the recording to teach *Yes, that's right. Thanks.* and *Thank you.*

A 020 7599 6320   **B** 07655 421769
C 0034 91 532 67 53

Get ready … Get it right!

There is a *Get ready … Get it right!* activity at the end of every A and B lesson. The *Get ready …* stage helps students to collect their ideas and prepare the language that they need to complete the task. The *Get it right!* stage gives students the opportunity to use the language they have learned in the lesson in a communicative (and often personalised) context. These two-stage activities help students to become more fluent without losing the accuracy they have built up during the controlled practice stages of the lesson.
For more information on the **face2face** approach to Speaking, see p20. For **Teaching Tips** on Speaking and correction, see p22.

10 Put students into pairs, student A and student B. Student As turn to SB p86 and student Bs turn to SB p91. Check they are all looking at the correct exercise.

a Focus students on the *you* column in the table. Students practise saying the numbers on their own.

b Students do the exercise with their partner. They are not allowed to look at each other's books.

c Students compare tables and check their partner has written the phone numbers correctly.

Goodbye!

11 **a** **CD1** 9 Focus students on conversation 4 in the photo. Play the recording. Students listen and read the conversation.

Check students understand the words and sentences in the conversation. Point out that *Bye = Goodbye*. You can teach *See you tomorrow.* and *See you next class.* as alternatives to *See you soon.*

PRONUNCIATION Play the recording again, pausing after each sentence for students to repeat chorally and individually. Alternatively, model and drill the sentences yourself.

b Students move around the room and say goodbye to other students, or say goodbye to students sitting near the m.

1B Where's she from?

Student's Book p8–p9

Vocabulary countries
Grammar he, his, she, her
Real World *Where are you from?*

QUICK REVIEW *Quick Reviews* begin each lesson in a fun, student-centred way. They are short activities which review previously taught language and are designed to last about five or ten minutes. For **Teaching Tips** on Reviewing and Recycling, see p23.

This activity reviews phone numbers. Students work on their own and write two phone numbers. These can be real or invented numbers. Students do the rest of the activity in pairs. Students then check that their partner's numbers are correct.

Countries

1 Check students remember numbers 1–12. Focus students on the map of the world. Pre-teach *map* and *country*.

Use the example (*Italy*) to show that students should write the correct numbers of the countries in the boxes next to each vocabulary item.

Students do the exercise on their own or in pairs. Check answers with the class.

Point out that we use capital letters for countries (*Italy*, *Brazil*, etc.). Also point out *the* in *the USA* and *the UK*.

Note that *the USA* is also called *the US*, *the States*, *the United States* or *America*. Also note that *the UK* refers to England, Scotland, Wales and Northern Ireland, and we can say *the UK* or *Britain* /ˈbrɪtən/. The term *Great Britain* refers to the island that contains England, Scotland and Wales, not the country.

Brazil **3**; Russia **10**; the USA **1**; Germany **5**; Egypt **9**; Australia **12**; Mexico **2**; Turkey **8**; the UK **4**; China **11**; Spain **6**

HELP WITH LISTENING Word stress

Help with Listening sections are designed to help students understand natural spoken English. They focus on phonological aspects of spoken English which make listening problematic for students.

For more information on the **face2face** approach to Listening, see p20. For **Teaching Tips** on Listening, see p21.

This *Help with Listening* section introduces students to the concept of word stress.

2 **CD1** 10 Focus students on the vocabulary box in **1** and point out how stress is marked in the Student's Book (•). Play the recording. Students listen and notice the word stress.

Use the countries to teach *syllable* and point out the number of syllables in each country (*Italy* = three syllables, *Brazil* = two syllables, etc.).

Also highlight that *Spain* doesn't have a stress mark because it is a one-syllable word.

3 **CD1** 10 **PRONUNCIATION** Play the recording again. Students listen and practise. Check students copy the word stress correctly.

Highlight the pronunciation of *Egypt* /ˈiːdʒɪpt/, *Australia* /ɒsˈtreɪliə/ and *Turkey* /ˈtɜːki/.

4 Focus students on the speech bubbles and check students understand *What's number ... ?*.

Students do the activity in pairs. While they are working, monitor and correct any pronunciation mistakes that you hear.

Where are you from?

5 **a** Focus students on the photo of Stefan and Emel on SB p9. Check students remember these people from lesson 1A.

CD1 11 Play the recording. Students listen to the conversation and fill in the gaps. Check answers with the class.

EMEL	Where are you from, Stefan?
STEFAN	I'm from **Russia**. And you?
EMEL	I'm from **Turkey**.

b **CD1** 12 **PRONUNCIATION** Play the recording (SB p107). Students listen and practise.

c Focus students on the speech bubbles. Check that students know where the countries *Peru*, *Libya* and *Indonesia* are. Pre-teach *city* and ask students which country *Prague* /prɑːg/ is in (the Czech /tʃek/ Republic). Also highlight that we say *I'm from + city*: *I'm from Prague.*, etc.

Model and drill *Perú*, *Líbya* and *Indonésia*, highlighting the stress on each country.

Students take turns to tell the class which country they are from.

┌─ **EXTRA IDEAS** ─────────────────────────┐

• If you have a multilingual class, write all the students' countries on the board. Mark the stress on each country. Model and drill any new countries with the class.

• If your students are all from the same country or city, ask them to say which city, town or district they are from instead.

└───┘

d Students practise the conversation in groups. Alternatively, students move around the room and practise the conversation with other students.

What's his name?

6 **a** Students do the exercise on their own. Check answers with the class.

2a 3d 4c

b **CD1** 13 **PRONUNCIATION** Play the recording. Students listen and practise. Check that students pronounce the contractions (*What's*, *He's*, etc.) correctly. Repeat the drill if necessary.

HELP WITH GRAMMAR *he, his, she, her*

7 **a–b** Focus students on the example in **7a**. Students do the exercises on their own or in pairs. Check answers with the class. Alternatively, do the exercise on the board with the whole class.

• **a Answers** 2 His 3 he 4 He
• **b Answers** 2 Her 3 she 4 She
• Highlight the difference between *he/his* (male) and *she/her* (female).
• Point out that we use *he/she* + verb (*he's*, etc.) and *his/her* + noun (*his name*, etc.).
• Also highlight the difference in pronunciation between *he's* /hiːz/ and *his* /hɪz/.
• Students may ask you about the meaning of *'s* in the example sentences. Tell the class that *'s* = *is* and is part of the verb *be*. However, we suggest that you encourage students to treat the new language as fixed phrases at this stage of the course. Note that the verb *be* is taught systematically in units 2 and 3.

8 **a** Focus students on the six countries in the box and the people and countries 1–6 on SB p9. Ask students the name of the person in 1 (Marcel) and which country he's from (France). Highlight the example sentence under the vocabulary box.

Students do the exercise in pairs.

b **CD1** 14 Play the recording (SB p107). Students listen and check their answers.

Check answers with the class by eliciting the sentences and writing them on the board.

2 Her name's Ayumi and she's from Japan.
3 His name's Leon and he's from Poland.
4 Her name's Mai and she's from Thailand.
5 His name's Ricardo and he's from Colombia.
6 Her name's Gita and she's from India.

┌─ **EXTRA IDEA** ──────────────────────────┐

• To give your students extra pronunciation practice, play the recording again and ask students to repeat the sentences. Check they are pronouncing the contractions (*name's*, *he's*, etc.) correctly.

└───┘

Get ready ... Get it right!

9 Put students into pairs, student A and student B. Student As turn to SB p87 and student Bs turn to SB p92. Check they are all looking at the correct exercise.

a Focus students on the photo. Give students a few moments to read the names and countries of the people.

Students work with their partner. Student A in each pair asks about people 1, 3 and 5, as shown in the speech bubbles, and writes the answers in the correct places in his/her book. While students are working, monitor and check their questions for accuracy.

Note that the names have been chosen as they are easy for most nationalities to spell. However, if the English script is new to your students, you may choose to do this *Get ready ... Get it right!* activity after you have done lesson 1C, where the alphabet and the question *How do you spell that?* are taught and practised.

b Student B in each pair asks about people 2, 4 and 6, as shown in the speech bubbles, and writes the answers in the correct places in his/her book. When they have finished, students can compare books with their partners and check their answers.

c Give students one minute to memorise the people's names and countries.

d Ask students to close their books. Students work with their partners and take turns to ask where the people are from, as shown in the speech bubbles.

Finally, ask students to tell the class where each person is from.

> **EXTRA IDEA**
>
> • Use the photocopiable **Class Activity** 1B Where's he from? p127 (Instructions p114), which provides further speaking practice of the language from the lesson.

> **FURTHER PRACTICE**
>
> **Ph** **Class Activity** 1B Where's he from? p127 (Instructions p114)
> • Note that **Ph** refers to activities, worksheets and tests that are in the Photocopiable Materials section at the back of this Teacher's Book.
> **Extra Practice** 1B SB p97
> **Self-study DVD-ROM** Lesson 1B
> **Workbook** Lesson 1B p4

▷ REAL WORLD

1C In class
Student's Book p10–p11

Vocabulary the alphabet; things in your bag (1); *a* and *an*
Real World first names and surnames; classroom language

QUICK REVIEW This activity reviews *What's his/her name?* and the names of the students in the class. Pre-teach *I don't know.* Put students into pairs. Students take turns to ask the names of other students in the class, as shown in the examples. Point out that students can answer the questions with *His/Her name's ...* , as in the examples, or by just saying the person's name. If you have a multilingual class, ask students to practise the question *Where's he/she from?* as well. At the end of the activitiy, ask each student to tell the class the names of two people sitting near them.

The alphabet

1 **CD1▷ 15** **PRONUNCIATION** Focus students on the letters *Aa–Zz*. Teach *the alphabet* /ˈælfəbet/.

Play the recording. Students listen and practise the alphabet. Alternatively, model and drill the letters yourself.

Point out that the letters in pink are called *vowels* /vaʊəlz/ and the letters in blue are called *consonants* /ˈkɒnsənənts/. If the English script is new for your students, point out that each letter has a capital form (*A*, *B*, *C*, etc.) and a lower-case form (*a*, *b*, *c*, etc.). You can also point out that *z* is pronounced /ziː/ in American English.

> **EXTRA IDEAS**
>
> • If you have a class of false beginners, ask them to close their books and write down the English alphabet from memory. ✏ Check the answers by eliciting the alphabet from the class and writing it on the board. Then play **CD1▷ 15** and ask students to practise saying the letters.
> • If you have a monolingual class, highlight any differences between the English alphabet and the students' alphabet (extra letters, missing letters, the lack of accents, how particular letters are pronounced, etc.).

2 **CD1** 16 Play the recording (SB p107). Students listen and write the letters in their lower-case forms. There are two letters for each number. Play the recording again if necessary. Note that these pairs of letters have been chosen as they are often confused by learners of English.
Students compare answers in pairs. Check answers with the class.

1 u v 2 y i
3 g j 4 b v
5 a r 6 e i
7 b p 8 t d
9 u q 10 v w

> **EXTRA IDEAS**
> - Students work in pairs and take turns to say the letters of the alphabet in order.
> - For more on when we use capital letters in English, see **Reading and Writing Portfolio 1** and **2** on p52–p55 of the **face2face** Second edition Starter Workbook.

What's your first name?

3 **a** Focus students on photo A. Ask who is the teacher (Sally) and who is the student (Pablo). Point out that Pablo is a new student in the class.
Students do the exercise on their own, then compare answers in pairs.

b **VIDEO** 1.1 **CD1** 17 Play the video or audio recording (SB p107). Students listen and check their answers. Check answers with the class.
Note that all the *Real World* videos can be found on the **Teacher's DVD** at the back of this book. For more information on the Teacher's DVD, see p10. If you are not able to use video in your classroom, use the audio recording on the Class Audio CD instead. Note that the content of the videos and the audio recordings is identical.
Highlight the difference between *first name* and *surname*, and check students understand the verb *spell*. Note that this language is drilled in **5a**.
Also use the recording to teach *Thank you* and *Welcome* (*to the class*).

1c 2a 3b

4 **a** **VIDEO** 1.2 **CD1** 18 Play the video or audio recording (SB p107). Students watch or listen and write the names of two more students in Sally's class. Play the video or audio recording again if necessary.

b Students compare answers in pairs.
Ask students to spell the students' names and write them on the board.

1 Dorota Kowalska
2 Khalid Nazeer

5 **a** **CD1** 19 **PRONUNCIATION** Focus students on the example drill. Play the recording (SB p107). Students listen and practise.
Highlight the pronunciation of *first name* /ˈfɜːs neɪm/ and *surname* /ˈsɜːneɪm/. Note that we don't usually pronounce the *t* in *first name*. Repeat the drill if necessary.

b Students move around the room and ask three people the questions in **3a**. Students should write the names in their notebooks and check that they have spelt them correctly before moving on to talk to a different student. If students aren't able to move around the room, they should talk to three people sitting near them.
Ask a few students to tell the class the first names or surnames of other people in the class.

> **EXTRA IDEA**
> - If your students know each other well, give them role cards with new names on before they do **5b**.

Things in your bag (1)

6 **a** Focus students on photo B. Students do the exercise in pairs. Check answers with the class.
Point out that we can say *a mobile*, *a phone* or *a mobile phone*. Also teach students that we say *a cell* or *a cell phone* in American English.

a dictionary 3; an apple 2; a pen 7; a pencil 8;
a book 4; a notebook 5; an umbrella 9; a mobile 6

> **EXTRA IDEA**
> - If your students are all complete beginners, consider teaching this vocabulary yourself by bringing photos of the things in photo B or the items themselves to the class. Teach the words one by one, drilling each word in turn. You can then use **6a** for practice.

b **CD1** 20 **PRONUNCIATION** Play the recording. Students listen and practise. Highlight the pronunciation of *dictionary* /ˈdɪkʃənri/ and *pencil* /ˈpensəl/. Also check that students say the multi-syllable words with the correct stress. Highlight that *dictionary* is three syllables, not four. Repeat the drill if necessary.

7 Focus students on the speech bubbles and check they remember *What's number … ?*. Students do the exercise in new pairs.

> **EXTRA IDEA**
> - Ask students which things in photo B they have with them. If you have a strong class, teach other words for things that your students have with them, for example, *glasses*, *make-up*, *a bottle of water*, etc.

HELP WITH VOCABULARY *a* and *an*

Help with Vocabulary sections help students to explore and understand how vocabulary works, often by focusing on aspects of lexical grammar. Students should usually do the exercises on their own or in pairs before you check the answers with the class.

For more information on the **face2face** approach to Vocabulary, see p20. For **Teaching Tips** on Vocabulary, see p22.

8 Focus students again on the words in **6a**. Tell the class that these words are called *nouns*. Point out the pink and blue letters at the beginning of each word. Students do the exercise on their own. Check the answers with the class.

- We use *a* with nouns that begin with a **consonant** sound.
- We use *an* with nouns that begin with a **vowel** sound.

9 Students do the exercise on their own, then compare answers in pairs. Check answers with the class.

Point out that we also use *an* with 'adjective + noun' (*an English dictionary*, *an Italian bag*, etc.) if the adjective begins with a vowel sound.

2 a 3 an 4 a 5 an 6 a 7 an

Excuse me!

10 Focus students on the English class in photo C. Point out the teacher (Sally), Pablo (from photo A), Dorota and Khalid (from the recording in **4a**).
VIDEO 1.3 **CD1** 21 Play the video or audio recording (SB p107). Students watch or listen and do the exercise. Check answers with the class.

1b 2c 3a

REAL WORLD Classroom language

Real World sections introduce students to functional and situational language they will need in real-world situations. Students should usually do the exercises on their own or in pairs before you check the answers with the class.

For **Teaching Tips** on Speaking, see p22.

11 **VIDEO** 1.3 **CD1** 21 Focus students on the sentences in the box, then play the video or audio recording again. Students listen and tick the sentences when they hear them.

Check students understand the meaning of the sentences. We suggest that you teach this language as fixed phrases, rather than focus on the grammar of these sentences at this stage of the course.

Point out that we can say *Can you repeat that, please?* or *Can you say that again, please?*.

┌─ **EXTRA IDEA** ┐

- Write the sentences in **11** on cards and put them up around the classroom. Use these prompts in future lessons to remind students of this language when they are unsure what to say to you in class.

12 **CD1** 22 **PRONUNCIATION** Focus students on the sentences in **11**. Play the recording. Students listen and practise.
Play the recording again, pausing after each sentence for students to repeat individually.

13 **a** Students do the exercise on their own, then compare answers in pairs.
Check answers with the class.

2 mean
3 understand
4 repeat
5 sorry
6 know
7 What's
8 spell

b Students practise the conversations in pairs, taking turns to be the teacher (Sally). While they are working, monitor and correct any pronunciation mistakes you hear.
Finally, ask a few pairs to role-play the conversations for the class.

┌─ **EXTRA IDEA** ┐

- If you haven't taught the **Classroom Instructions** on SB p135 yet, ask students to learn these common instructions for homework and check they remember them next class.

┌─ **FURTHER PRACTICE** ┐

Ph **Class Activity** 1C Real names p128 (Instructions p114)
Extra Practice 1C SB p97
Self-study DVD-ROM Lesson 1C
Workbook Lesson 1C p6

VOCABULARY
1D AND SKILLS ▶ People and things
Student's Book p12–p13

Vocabulary people; things; plurals
Skills Listening: What's in your bag?

QUICK REVIEW This activity reviews spelling the alphabet. Students work on their own and write five English words they know. Students then complete the activity in pairs.

1 **a** Focus students on the picture. Students do the exercise on their own or in pairs. Check answers with the class.

b a man **c** a woman **d** a boy **e** a girl

b [CD1▶23] [PRONUNCIATION] Play the recording. Students listen and practise. Highlight the pronunciation of *woman* /'wʊmən/. Alternatively, model the words yourself and ask students to repeat chorally and individually.

2 **a** Focus students on the photo of Sally (the teacher from lesson 1C). Students do the exercise on their own or in pairs.
Check answers with the class. Alternatively, ask students to check their answers in [VOCABULARY 1.7 ▶] SB p114. You can also teach *a laptop* and *a tablet* (*computer*).
If your students don't have articles in their own language(s), highlight the use of *a* with the singular nouns in **1a** and **2a**.

a chair **1**; a table **6**;
a computer **3**; a camera **7**;
a watch **2**; a sandwich **5**

b [CD1▶24] [PRONUNCIATION] Play the recording. Students listen and practise. Highlight the pronunciation of *diary* /'daɪəri/, *chair* /tʃeə/ and *sandwich* /'sænwɪdʒ/.

c Students do the activity in pairs. Check answers with the class.

an umbrella, a bag, a pen, a book/books, an apple, a mobile (phone), a pencil, a dictionary

3 **a** Give students one minute to memorise all the things in the photo. You can set a time limit of two minutes for this stage of the activity.
Ask students to close their books. Students work on their own and write all the things in the picture they can remember.

b Students compare their answers in pairs and check their partner's spelling.
Students can then open their books and check if they have remembered all the things in the picture. Find out which students in the class remembered the most words.

HELP WITH VOCABULARY Plurals

4 Focus students on the pictures and the table. Use the pictures to teach *singular* and *plural*. Students do the exercise on their own by referring to the other words in the table. ✍ While they are working, draw the table on the board. Check answers with the class.

- **Answers** things, boys, sandwiches, babies
  ✍ Elicit the answers from students and write them in the table on the board. Use the table to highlight the following rules:
- We usually make nouns plural by adding *-s*: *chairs*, *tables*, *things*, *boys*, etc.
- If a noun ends in *-ch*, we add *-es*: *watches*, *sandwiches*, etc.
- If a noun ends in consonant + *y*, we change *-y* to *-ies*: *diaries*, *babies*, etc. Point out that if a noun ends in vowel + *y*, we simply add *-s* (*boy* → *boys*, etc.).
- A few common nouns have irregular plurals: *men*, *women*, *people*, etc.
- Note that we also add *-es* to words ending in *-s*, *-ss*, *-sh*, *-x* and *-z*: *bus* → *buses*, *class* → *classes*, etc. Point out these plurals when students meet words with these endings later in the course.
- Also highlight that we don't use *a* or *an* with plural nouns.

5 [CD1▶25] [PRONUNCIATION] Play the recording. Students listen and practise. Check that students say the *-es* /ɪz/ endings in *watches* and *sandwiches* correctly. Also highlight the pronunciation of *women* /'wɪmɪn/ and *people* /'piːpəl/. Repeat the drill if necessary.

6 Students do the exercise on their own, then compare answers in pairs. Check answers with the class.

2 cameras **3** countries **4** watches
5 men **6** computers **7** women
8 apples **9** dictionaries **10** people

7 Put students into pairs. Ask all students to turn to SB p96. Check they are all looking at the correct exercise.

a Focus students on the picture. Point out that students need to complete the words and write the number of people or things they can see in the picture, as in the example. Tell students that some of the things in the picture are hidden. Students do the exercise in their pairs. You can set a time limit of five minutes.

b Put two pairs together in groups of four. If this is not possible, ask students to work in new pairs. Students compare their answers and see who has found more things and people.

c Ask students to turn to SB p134. Students check their answers. Point out that each group of things or people is in a different colour in the picture. Check answers with the class.

> 3 tables; 5 men; 2 women; 10 books; 3 pens; 8 pencils; 7 apples; 4 bags; 6 mobiles

What's in your bag?

8 **a** Focus students on the photos of Linda, Bill and Caroline. Tell the class these people are in London.

CD1 ▶ 26 Play the recording (SB p107). Students listen and tick the things that are in the people's bags.

b Students compare answers in pairs.

c Play the recording again. Students listen, check their answers and write where the people are from. Check answers with the class.

> **LINDA** (books), a dictionary, a notebook, pens, a mobile (She's from London.)
> **BILL** a mobile, photos, a pen, an apple, sandwiches (He's from Boston, in the USA.)
> **CAROLINE** a camera, books, a notebook, a pencil, an umbrella (She's from Sydney, in Australia.)

9 Put students into groups of three or four. Students take turns to say what is in their bags and find out who has the same things. If some students don't have bags with them, ask them to say what is in their pockets. While they are working, monitor and help students with any new vocabulary they need.

Ask each student to tell the class one thing that they have in their bags. 🖊 Write any new vocabulary on the board and allow students time to copy it in their notebooks.

Finally, ask each group who has the same things in their bags.

┌─ **EXTRA IDEA** ┐

• Use the photocopiable worksheet **Vocabulary Plus** 1 Things in a room p167 (Instructions p162) in class or give it to your students for homework.

┌─ **FURTHER PRACTICE** ┐

Ph **Class Activity** 1D Pictures and words p129 (Instructions p115)
Ph **Vocabulary Plus** 1 Things in a room p167 (Instructions p162)
Extra Practice 1 SB p97
Self-study DVD-ROM Lesson 1D
Workbook Lesson 1D p7
Workbook Reading and Writing Portfolio 1 p52–p53
Ph **Progress Test** 1 p180

HELP WITH PRONUNCIATION /æ/ and /ə/

Help with Pronunciation sections are designed to help students hear and pronounce individual sounds that are often problematic for learners of English.

For more information on the **face2face** approach to Pronunciation, see p20. For **Teaching Tips** on Pronunciation, see p23.

1 **CD1** ▶ 27 Focus students on the phonemes /æ/ and /ə/, the pictures and the words. Play the recording. Students listen to the sounds and the words.

Point out that *a* in *bag* is pronounced with an /æ/ sound, and *o* and *er* in *computer* are pronounced with an /ə/ sound. Point out that *r* at the end of a word is not usually pronounced in British English (*computer, teacher, doctor,* etc.).

Note that the /ə/ sound is called 'the schwa' and is the most common sound in English.

Check students understand that /æ/ and /ə/ represent individual sounds and are not letters of the alphabet.

Point out that phonemic script is always written between two parallel lines (/ /) and should not be confused with standard written English.

Play the recording again. Students listen and practise. If students have problems producing the sounds, help them with the mouth position for each sound.

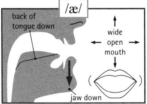 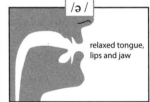

Point out that when we make the /æ/ sound, the mouth is wide open and the jaw down. When we make the /ə/ sound, the mouth is slightly open and the lips, tongue and jaw are relaxed. Also point out that they are both short sounds.

2 Focus students on the boxes. Point out that all the pink letters are pronounced /æ/ and all the blue letters are pronounced /ə/.

CD1 ▶ 28 Play the recording. Students listen and notice how we say the pink and blue letters.
Play the recording again. Students listen and practise.

3 **a** **CD1** ▶ 29 Play the recording. Students listen and read the sentences.

Play the recording again. Students listen and practise. Check they say the pink letters with an /æ/ sound and the blue letters with an /ə/ sound.

b Students practise the sentences in pairs.
Finally, ask students to say the sentences for the class.

┌─ **EXTRA IDEA** ┐

• Point out the chart of phonemic symbols on SB p134. Also tell students they can practise drills from the Student's Book on the Self-study DVD-ROM.

continue2learn

There is a *continue2learn* section at the end of each unit. The **Vocabulary, Grammar and Real World** section highlights where students can review and practise the language from the unit. The **Reading and Writing** section directs students to the Reading and Writing Portfolios in the **face2face** Second edition Starter Workbook. This portfolio contains 10 stand-alone reading and writing lessons that can be done either in class or at home.

For more on the **face2face** approach to writing, see page 20.

- Focus students on the *continue2learn* section on SB p13. Tell students that this section shows where they can review and practise the language taught in Unit 1.
- Ask students to turn to **Extra Practice 1 and Progress Portfolio 1** on SB p97. Students can do these exercises in class or for homework. For more information on the Extra Practice and Progress Portfolio sections, see p34.
- Also point out that **Language Summary 1** on SB p114–p115 contains all the key language taught in the unit, along with extra information, examples and tips. Note that if you are planning to give your students Progress Test 1 (see p000), you can tell the class that this test will only contain questions about the language that is included in Language Summary 1.
- If your students have the **face2face** Second edition Starter Workbook, point out that there are practice exercises for lessons 1A–1D in the Student's Book (WB p3–p7). If students haven't already done these exercises at the end of each lesson, they can do them at the end of the unit.
- Also remind students that the **face2face** Self-study DVD-ROM also contains a variety of practice exercises, class drills, class audio recordings and a review video for each unit. Note that the video on the Self-study DVD-ROM is a soap opera in 10 episodes, **not** the Real World videos. You can also point out that there is a grammar reference section, a word list, customisable tests and many other features. Encourage students to use the Self-study DVD-ROM at home after each lesson or unit.
- If your students need more practice in reading and writing, you can either do **Reading and Writing Portfolio 1** (WB p52–p53) in class or ask students to do it at home. They can check the answers in the Workbook or with you next class. Note that students are asked to do a piece of writing at the end of each lesson, which they hand to you next class for checking. For more information on how to use the Reading and Writing Portfolio in class, see the next section.

Reading and Writing Portfolio

- There is a 20-page Reading and Writing Portfolio section in the Starter Workbook. This section contains 10 double-page stand-alone lessons, one for each unit of the Student's Book, which are designed for students to do in class or at home.

The topics and content of these lessons are based closely on the *Common European Framework of Reference for Languages* (CEFR) reading and writing competences for level A1. At the end of this section there is a list of 'can do' statements that allows students to track their progress. For more information on the CEFR, see p14–p19.

- **Reading and Writing Portfolio 1** (WB p52–p53) can be used any time after you have completed unit 1 of the Student's Book.

Tips for using the Reading and Writing Portfolios in class

- Use the photos and illustrations to establish characters and context in each lesson.
- Go through the examples in each exercise with the class to check that students understand what to do.
- Ask students to compare answers in pairs or groups before checking answers with the class. The answers are in the Answer Key in the middle of the Workbook (pi–pviii).
- Go through the *Help with Writing* sections with the class and use the examples to highlight the relevant points. Note that all the examples in these sections come from the presentation texts.
- If you have a monolingual class, consider comparing the rules for writing in English with those of the students' language.
- The final activity of each lesson asks the students to do some personalised writing, using what they have learned from the lesson. These activities are preceded by a preparation stage, in which students are asked to decide what they are going to write by filling in a table, making notes, etc.
- Ask students to do the final writing activity on separate pieces of paper and collect them in at the end of the class. If you set the final writing activity for homework, collect the students' work at the beginning of the next class.
- When marking students' work, make sure you comment on examples of correct English, as well as highlighting errors. Also remember to praise successful communication and interesting ideas as well as correct language.
- Consider asking students to write a second draft of their work, incorporating your corrections and suggestions. These can be collected in and corrected again, or put up around the classroom for other students to read.
- Remember that writing in a new language is a difficult skill to acquire, particularly if the students' first language is very different from English. At Starter level, it is important to encourage and praise students so that they view writing as a valuable and interesting part of the learning process.
- At the end of each lesson, ask students to tick the things they can do in the **Reading and Writing Progress Portfolio** (Workbook p72). This will help students monitor the progress they are making in their writing.

Extra Practice

The *Extra Practice* sections in the back of the Student's Book provide further controlled practice of the language taught in the unit. They can be done in class, or students can do the exercises on their own for homework. There are exercises for each lesson (1A, 1B, etc.), which can also be done as 'fillers' if you finish the final activity of a lesson a few minutes early. For **Teaching Tips** on Reviewing and Recycling, see p23.

Here are some ideas for exploiting the Extra Practice sections in class.

Make it a competition

Ask students to do individual exercises in pairs or groups (for example, Exercise 1 on SB p97). Give students a time limit of two or three minutes. Check the answers with the class. The pair/group with the most correct answers wins.

Alternatively, put students into pairs and ask them to complete all the Extra Practice exercises. You can set a time limit of 15 or 20 minutes. Check the answers with the class and give one point for each correct answer. The pair with the most points wins. You may wish to give the winners a small prize at the end of the lesson!

Extension

After finishing an exercise, ask students to write similar sentences about themselves and people they know (for example, Exercise 2 on SB p103). Students can then compare sentences in pairs or in groups and check each other's work.

Word stress

After vocabulary exercises that focus on individual words (for example, Exercise 1 on SB p98), ask students to mark the stress on each word. ✏ Check the answers on the board, drilling problematic vocabulary as necessary.

Personalisation

Where appropriate, ask students to say how many of the sentences in an exercise are true for them (for example, Exercise 1 on SB p101), or ask students to tick vocabulary items that they like (for example, Exercise 1 on SB p103).

Role play

Put students into pairs to practise conversations (for example, Exercise 6 on SB p98). Students can then change roles and practise the conversation again. You can also ask them to memorise the conversation, close their books and practise the conversations from memory.

Extra Practice 1 SB p97

1A

1 1 your **3** my **4** you **5** You **6** you **7** I **8** you **9** I **10** your **11** your **12** you **13** you

2 2 two **3** three **4** four **5** five **6** six **7** seven **8** eight **9** nine **10** ten **11** eleven **12** twelve

3 2 Turkey **3** Russia **4** Egypt **5** Germany **6** China **7** Italy **8** Mexico **9** Brazil ↓ Australia

4 2 His **3** he **4** He **5** her **6** Her **7** she **8** She

1C

5 2 an apple **3** a dictionary **4** a notebook **5** a book **6** an umbrella **7** a pencil **8** a pen **9** a mobile

6 2 What's your first name? **3** How do you spell that? **4** What does bag mean? **5** What's this in English? **6** I'm sorry, I don't know. **7** How do you spell Egypt? **8** Can you repeat that, please? **9** I'm sorry, I don't understand.

1D

7a

W	O	V	B	O	Y	N	W
D	F	M	A	N	C	E	A
E	D	L	B	B	H	J	T
S	I	A	Y	G	A	R	C
S	A	N	D	W	I	C	H
H	R	G	A	W	R	A	K
J	Y	G	I	R	L	M	D
C	O	M	P	U	T	E	R
P	T	A	B	L	E	R	Z
I	E	L	W	O	M	A	N

7b men, sandwiches, girls, computers, tables, women, diaries, babies, chairs, cameras, watches

Progress Portfolio 1

The *Progress Portfolio* sections at the end of each Extra Practice section encourage students to reflect on what they have learned and help them decide which language areas they need to study again.

Note that the *I can ...* statements reflect communicative competences as set out in the *Common European Framework of Reference for Languages* (CEFR) for level A1. For more information on the CEFR, see p14 and the tables of competencies on p16–19.

a Students work through the list of *I can ...* statements on their own and tick the things they feel they can do. They can refer to Language Summary 1 SB p114–p115 if they wish.

Students can also work in pairs or groups and compare which statements they have ticked.

b Students work on their own, in pairs or in groups and decide which language areas they need to study again. Encourage students to use the Self-study DVD-ROM lessons 1A–D to help them improve in these areas. For photocopiable instructions on how to use the Self-study DVD-ROM, see p11–p13. There is also further practice on all key language taught in the Student's Book in the **face2face** Second edition Starter Workbook.

2A ▶ She's British
Student's Book p14–p15

Vocabulary nationalities
Grammar *be* (singular): positive and negative

QUICK REVIEW This activity reviews plurals. Students work on their own and write five singular words. Put students into pairs. Students complete the activity with their partner, as shown in the examples.

Nationalities

1 a Ask students which letters in the alphabet are vowels (*a, e, i, o, u*).
Students do the exercise on their own, then compare answers in pairs. Check answers with the class.

2 Brazil **3** Russia **4** the USA **5** Germany
6 Egypt **7** Australia **8** Mexico **9** Turkey
10 the UK **11** Spain **12** China

b Pre-teach *nationality* and elicit the plural form (*nationalities*). Students do the activity on their own or in pairs.
✎ Check answers with the class by writing the countries and nationalities on the board. Highlight that nationalities often end in *-n, -an, -ian, -ish* and *-ese* by underlining these endings on the board.
You can also point out that we usually describe people from Brazil, Colombia, Peru, Argentina, etc. as *South American*, not *American* (which is only used to refer to people from the USA).

b8 c1 d3 e4 f11 g6 h2 i10 j9 k12 l7

2 a CD1▶ 30 PRONUNCIATION Play the recording. Students listen and practise the countries and nationalities. Note that students should say both words together (*Italy, Italian*, etc.). Repeat the drill if necessary.
Point out that the same syllable is stressed in most nationalities (*Brazil, Brazilian*, etc.).
Highlight the different stress patterns in *Italy* → *Italian, Egypt* → *Egyptian* and *China* → *Chinese*.

b Students do the exercise in pairs, as shown in the speech bubbles.

c ✎ Write *I'm from* + country and *I'm* + nationality on the board. Elicit examples for each structure (*I'm from Italy. I'm Italian.*, etc.).
Focus students on the speech bubbles and teach the nationalities *Japanese, French* and *Colombian*. Model and drill these words with the class, highlighting the different stress pattern in *Japan* → *Japanese*.
Ask students to tell the class their nationalities.
✎ If you have students who have different nationalities from those already taught in the lesson, write the countries and nationalities on the board and drill the words with the class.

Around the world

3 a Pre-teach *a car*. Focus students on photos A–D. Students do the exercise in pairs.

b CD1▶ 31 Play the recording. Students listen and check their answers. Check answers with the class.

A British **B** German
C Brazilian **D** American

HELP WITH GRAMMAR
be (singular): positive

4 Pre-teach *positive*. Tell the class that all positive verb forms in the Student's Book are marked with a (+) sign.
Students do the exercise on their own, then compare answers in pairs. Check answers with the class.
Note that the verb *be* is particularly problematic for students whose languages don't have an equivalent verb. If possible, check if your students' language(s) have the verb *be*, as this will help you understand why students might be making mistakes.

- **Answers 1** 'm **2** 're **3** 's **4** 's **5** 's
- Check students understand the subject pronouns *I, you, he, she* and *it*. Point out that we use *it* for things (*a car, a book*, etc.).
- Point out that *'m, 're* and *'s* are parts of the verb *be*. Check students understand which part of *be* goes with each subject pronoun.
- Highlight that *'m, 're* and *'s* are the contracted forms of *am, are* and *is*. Point out that contractions are very common in spoken and written English. Tell students to use contracted forms when speaking and writing, particularly after *I, you, he, she* and *it*.

5 CD1▶ 32 PRONUNCIATION Focus students on the example drill. Play the recording (SB p107). Students listen and practise. Check that students pronounce the contractions correctly.
Repeat the drill if necessary, pausing for students to repeat chorally and individually.

6 **a** Students do the exercise on their own.

b Students do the exercise in pairs. Check answers with the class. Ask students to give reasons for the photos they chose.

> 1 's, 's, photo C 2 'm, 'm, photo A 3 's, photo D
> 4 's, photo A 5 's, photo B 6 'm, photo D

HELP WITH GRAMMAR
be (singular): negative

7 Check students understand *negative*. Tell the class that all negative verb forms in the Student's Book are marked with a (–) sign.

Students do the exercise on their own, then compare answers in pairs. Check answers with the class.

> - **Answers** 1 'm not 2 aren't 3 isn't 4 isn't 5 isn't
> - Point out that we use *not* to make a verb form negative.
> - Also highlight that *I'm not* is the contracted form of *I am not*, *aren't* is the contracted form of *are not* and *isn't* is the contracted form of *is not*. Remind students to use contracted forms when speaking and writing.
> - 🖉 Tell students that we can also say *you're not*, *he's not*, *she's not* and *it's not*, and write these forms on the board for students to copy.
> - Point out that we can't say *I amn't* as an alternative to *I'm not*.

┌─ **EXTRA IDEA** ─┐

- Ask students to turn to Language Summary 2, SB p116–p117. Point out the vocabulary section **VOCABULARY 2.1** and the grammar sections **GRAMMAR 2.1** and **GRAMMAR 2.2** from lesson 2A. Give students a few moments to read the sections so they can review what they have learned in the lesson. Remind students that all the new language from each lesson is included in the Language Summaries.

8 **CD1 ▶ 33** **PRONUNCIATION** Focus students on the example drill. Play the recording (SB p107). Students listen and practise the sentences in **7**. Check that students pronounce the contractions correctly.

True or false?

9 **a** Pre-teach the vocabulary in the box using examples that students are likely to know. Point out that we usually say *the capital*, not *the capital city* (*London is the capital of the UK.*, etc.).

Note that the aim of this box is to highlight which new words students need in order to do the exercise in **9b**.

b Focus students on photos 1 and 2, and the corresponding examples. Use these to teach students

true, *false* and *tick*. Drill these words with the class. Also point out that we use the pronoun *She* in the correct sentence in question 2, rather than repeating the name of the person (*Gisele Bündchen*). Students do the exercise in pairs.

c Students check their answers on SB p134. Check answers by asking students one question each around the class. Ask if any students got all the answers correct.

> 3 Leonardo DiCaprio isn't Italian. He's American. 4 Nissan isn't a Chinese company. It's a Japanese company. 5 ✓ 6 The White House isn't in New York. It's in Washington. 7 Prince William isn't Russian. He's British. 8 ✓ 9 Fiat isn't a French company. It's an Italian company. 10 ✓

Get ready … Get it right!

10 Focus students on the examples. Ask students if they think the sentences are true or false. The first sentence is true. The second sentence is false (BMW isn't a British company. It's a German company).

Put students into new pairs. Students work with their partner and write three true sentences and three false sentences. If necessary, direct students to **9b** for examples of the types of sentence they can write. While they are working, monitor and check their sentences for accuracy.

11 **a** Use the speech bubbles to teach *I think that's …* as a way to give your opinion, and the answers *Yes, you're right.* and *No, you're wrong.* Drill these phrases with the class.

Put two pairs together so that they are working in groups of four. If that isn't possible, organise the class into new pairs. Students take turns to read their sentences to the other pair or student, who must guess if the sentences are true or false. Tell students to keep a record of how many sentences they guess correctly. While they are working, monitor and correct any grammar or pronunciation mistakes you hear.

b Finally, ask students to tell the class two of their true sentences.

┌─ **FURTHER PRACTICE** ─┐

Ph **Vocabulary Plus** 2 Countries and nationalities p168 (Instructions p162)
Extra Practice 2A SB p98
Self-study DVD-ROM Lesson 2A
Workbook Lesson 2A p8

What's your job?
Student's Book p16–p17

Vocabulary jobs
Grammar *be* (singular): questions and short answers

QUICK REVIEW This activity reviews countries and nationalities. Students do the activity in pairs, as in the example. Remind students that they can check countries and nationalities in **VOCABULARY 2.1** SB p116. At the end of the activity, ask each pair to tell the class one person or thing they talked about.

Jobs

1 **a** Pre-teach *a job*. Focus students on pictures a–i. Students do the exercise in pairs. Early finishers can check their answers in **VOCABULARY 2.2** SB p116. Check answers with the class.

Point out that we say *an actor/a waiter* for men and *an actress/a waitress* for women (although nowadays *an actor* is often used for both men and women). All the other words can be used for both men and women. You can also teach students *a shop assistant*, *a policeman* and *a policewoman*.

Also highlight that we always use *a* or *an* with jobs: *He's a doctor. not ~~He's doctor.~~* This is particularly important if your students don't have articles in their own language(s), or if they don't use articles for jobs in their own language(s).

Draw students' attention to the **TIP** and point out that only the main stress is shown in the vocabulary boxes and the Language Summaries. We feel this is the simplest and most effective way to make sure students put the main stress in the correct place. For example, the main stress in *taxi driver* is on the first syllable of *taxi*, not on the first syllable of *driver* (which is also stressed).

> a doctor **e**; a teacher **c**; a sales assistant **a**;
> an actor/an actress **h**; a waiter/a waitress **i**;
> a taxi driver **d**; a musician **f**; a police officer **g**

b **CD1** 34 **PRONUNCIATION** Play the recording. Students listen and practise. Alternatively, model each sentence yourself and ask students to repeat chorally and individually.

Highlight the pronunciation of *manager* /ˈmænɪdʒə/ and *musician* /mjuːˈzɪʃən/. Also highlight the /ə/ sound at the end of most of the jobs, for example *doctor* /ˈdɒktə/, *actor* /ˈæktə/, *teacher* /ˈtiːtʃə/, etc.

c Use the speech bubbles to teach *What's his job?* and *What's her job?*. Drill the questions and answers with the class. Also teach and drill the question *What's your job?*.

Note that *What do you do?* is also a common question when asking about jobs. However, we feel at this stage of the course it is important to keep language as simple as possible. We suggest that you wait until students learn the Present Simple (in unit 4 of the Student's Book) before teaching this question.

Put students into new pairs. Students take turns to point to pictures a–i and ask questions about the people, as shown in the speech bubbles. Remind students of the phrase *I don't know.* before they begin.

> **EXTRA IDEAS**
>
> • If your students are all complete beginners, you may choose to present the vocabulary yourself first. Prepare flashcards for the jobs and hold them up in front of the class as you teach the words. The matching activity in **1a** can then be used as controlled practice.
>
> • ✍ If you have a strong class, teach the English words for students' jobs and write them on the board. You can also teach *I'm a housewife/househusband*, *I'm unemployed* and *I'm retired* /rɪˈtaɪəd/. Check students remember *What's your job?*. Students then move around the room and ask each other what their jobs are.

Photos of friends

2 **a** Pre-teach the vocabulary in the box, using examples, board drawings, pictures, translation, etc. Note that the aim of this box is to highlight which new words students need in order to understand the conversation they are about to hear.

Drill the words with the class. Point out that *married*, *single* and *beautiful* are all adjectives and are used with the verb *be* (*I'm married. He's single. It's beautiful.*, etc.).

b **CD1** 35 Focus students on the photo of Tina and Matt on SB p17 and point out photos 1–4 of Tina's friends. Play the recording (SB p107). Students listen and match the names in the box to photos 1–4. Check answers with the class.

> Sofia **4**; Marco **3**; Emma **1**; Gary **2**

c Play the recording again. Students listen and complete the table.
Students can compare answers in pairs. Check answers with the class.

	Gary	**Marco**	**Emma**	**Sofia**
country	Australia	Mexico	France	Italy
job	a doctor	a musician	a teacher	an actress

> **EXTRA IDEA**
>
> • Ask students to look at Audio Script **CD1** 35 SB p107. Play the recording again. Students listen, read and check their answers.

HELP WITH GRAMMAR
be (singular): *Wh-* questions

3 Check students understand *a question*. Point out that all question-form tables in the Student's Book are marked with a (?).
Students do the exercise on their own, then compare answers in pairs.
Check answers with the class.

- **Answers** 1 am 2 are 3 's 4 's 5 's 6 's 7 's
- Highlight the word order in questions with *be*: question word + *am/are/'s* + person or thing + ...
- Remind students that we use *Where* to ask about a place (Turkey, London, etc.) and *What* to ask about a thing (a name, a job, etc.).
- Point out that *Where's* = *Where is* and *What's* = *What is*. Encourage students to use contracted forms when speaking and writing.
- Point out that we don't use the contracted form of *am* or *are* in questions: *Where am I?* not ~~*Where'm I?*~~, *Where are you from?* not ~~*Where're you from?*~~, etc.
- Remind students that we can also make questions with *How*: *How are you?*, etc.

4 **a** **CD1▶ 36** **PRONUNCIATION** Play the recording. Students listen and practise. Check students pronounce the contractions *Where's* and *What's* correctly. Point out that *are* is usually pronounced /ə/ in questions, for example, *Where are /ə/ you from?*. Repeat the drill if necessary, pausing the recording after each question for students to repeat chorally and individually.

b Ask students to cover the table in **2c**. Focus students on the speech bubbles and drill the questions with the class. Also drill the equivalent questions with *she/her* (*What's her name?*, *Where's she from?*, *What's her job?*).
Students do the exercise in pairs.

Is he a musician?

5 **a** Students do the exercise on their own.

b Students compare answers in pairs. Check answers with the class.

2a 3b 4a 5 Students' answers 6 Students' answers

HELP WITH GRAMMAR *be* (singular): *yes / no* questions and short answers

6 Students do the exercise on their own, then compare answers in pairs. 🖉 While they are working, copy the table onto the board so you are ready to check students' answers.
Check answers with the class by eliciting students' answers and writing them in the correct place on the board.

- **Answers** See the table in **GRAMMAR 2.4 ▶** SB p117.
- Highlight the inverted word order in *yes/no* questions with *be*: *Am I ... ?*, *Are you ... ?*, *Is he ... ?*, etc.
- Point out that we don't usually answer these questions with just *Yes.* or *No.*, as this can sound impolite.
- Point out that we can also say *No, you're not.*, *No, he's not.*, *No, she's not.* and *No, it's not.*
- Highlight that we don't use contractions in positive short answers: *Yes, you are.* not ~~*Yes, you're.*~~, *Yes, I am.* not ~~*Yes, I'm.*~~, *Yes, he is.* not ~~*Yes, he's.*~~, etc.
- Also highlight that we don't usually use the uncontracted form in negative short answers: *No, you aren't.* not ~~*No, you are not.*~~, etc.

7 **CD1▶ 37** **PRONUNCIATION** Play the recording. Students listen and practise. Check that students pronounce the contractions correctly.
Play the recording again if necessary, pausing after each question or short answer for students to repeat individually.

8 **a** Students do the exercise on their own. Check answers with the class.

2 Is 3 Are 4 Are 5 Is 6 Are 7 Is 8 Is

b Students do the exercise in pairs. Remind students to use the correct short answers.

Get ready ... Get it right!

9 Put students into new pairs, student A and student B. Student As turn to SB p87 and student Bs turn to SB p92. Check they are all looking at the correct exercise.

a Focus students on the six photos. Tell the class that the people are all friends of Matt (the man in the photo on SB p17).
Students work on their own and write *yes/no* questions to check the information in blue, as in the example. Students are not allowed to look at each other's books. While they are working, monitor and check their questions for accuracy.

┌─ EXTRA IDEA ───────────────────────┐
- Ask students to check their *yes/no* questions with another student from the same group before they work with their partner in **b**.
└────────────────────────────────────┘

b Check students understand that some of the information in blue is correct and some is incorrect. Students work with their partners. Student As ask their questions from **a** and either tick the correct information or change the incorrect information for each person.

Encourage student Bs to use the correct short answers during the activity. While they are working, monitor and check students are doing the activity correctly.

c Students swap roles and student B in each pair asks his/her questions from **a**.

d Put students in pairs with another student of the same group. Students compare answers by saying sentences about the people, as in the example.
Finally, ask students to tell the class about each person in turn.

FURTHER PRACTICE

Ph **Class Activity** 2B New identities p115 (Instructions p130)
Extra Practice 2B SB p98
Self-study DVD-ROM Lesson 2B
Workbook Lesson 2B p9

▷ REAL
2C WORLD ▷ Personal information
Student's Book p18–p19

Vocabulary titles; greetings
Real World email addresses; personal information questions

QUICK REVIEW This activity reviews jobs. Students work on their own and write four jobs. Pre-teach *mime* by miming a job (for example, a musician) and asking students what the job is. Put students into pairs. Students take turns to mime the jobs on their list and guess their partner's jobs.

Good morning!

1 **a** Check students remember *married* and *single*. Point out that Brown, King and Roberts are common surnames in the UK.
Students do the exercise on their own. Check answers with the class.
Point out that *Ms* can be used for married and single women.

1c 2a 3b

b **CD1** ▶ **38** **PRONUNCIATION** Focus students on the example. Play the recording (SB p108). Students listen and practise. Highlight the pronunciation of *Mr* /ˈmɪstə/, *Mrs* /ˈmɪsɪz/ and *Ms* /məz/. Repeat the drill if necessary.

2 **a** Focus students on pictures A–D. Ask students who the man is in all four pictures (Mr Brown). Students do the exercise on their own or in pairs.

EXTRA IDEA

• If you have a class of complete beginners, teach the words *morning, afternoon, evening* and *night* before asking students to do **2a**.

b **CD1** ▶ **39** Play the recording (SB p108). Students listen and check their answers. Check answers with the class.
Point out that *Good morning, Good afternoon* and *Good evening* mean *Hello* and that *Good night* means *Goodbye*. Tell the class that we also say *Good night* before going to bed.
Highlight that *Good morning, Good night*, etc. are more formal than *Hello/Hi* and *Goodbye/Bye*. Also point out that we often respond to *Good morning*, etc. by repeating the same phrase.
Use picture C to teach *sir* /sɜː/ (a polite way to address a man you don't know) and the female equivalent, *madam* /ˈmædəm/.
PRONUNCIATION Play the recording again, pausing after each sentence or phrase for students to repeat chorally and individually. Check that students sound polite and interested.

A Good morning B Good afternoon (x2)
C Good evening (x2) D Good night (x2)

c Students practise the conversations in pairs. Ask a few pairs to role-play the conversations for the class.

REAL WORLD Email addresses

3 Focus students on the email address and the speech bubble. Point out that we say *dot* (.) and *at* (@) when we say email addresses.

4 **a** Focus students on the business card, mobile phone and email. Students work in pairs and try to say email addresses 1–4.

b **CD1** ▶ **40** Play the recording. Students listen and check their answers.

5 **a** **CD1 41** **PRONUNCIATION** Focus students on the example drill. Play the recording (SB p108). Students listen and practise. Check they say @, .co.uk, .com, .net and .org correctly. Repeat the drill if necessary.

b Focus students on the speech bubbles. Drill the question *What's your email address?*.

Ask students to write down their email addresses and give them time to work out how to say them in English. If necessary, teach students that we also say *hyphen* (-) and *underscore* (_).

Also check students know how to say the part of their email address that indicates their country (.uk, .es, .ja, etc.). Note that we usually say country email addresses letter by letter (*dot u-k, dot e-s, dot j-a,* etc.), while we say .com, .net, .org, etc. as single words.

Students move around the room and ask three people for their email addresses. Alternatively, they can ask three people sitting near them. Students write each person's email address, then check that they have written each address correctly.

> **EXTRA IDEAS**
>
> - In some classes it may not be appropriate for students to give each other their real email addresses. If this is the case in your class, write fictitious email addresses on cards and give them to your students before doing **5b**.
> - Alternatively, ask each student to choose a famous fictional character or celebrity and invent an email address for him or her (james.bond007@gmail.com, etc.). They can then pretend to be that character or celebrity when they do **5b**.

The City Gym

REAL WORLD
Personal information questions

6 Check students remember *vowels* (a, e, i, o, u) and highlight the vowels in blue in sentence 1.

Students do the exercise on their own or in pairs. Check answers with the class. Note that these sentences are drilled later in the lesson in **8**.

> - **Answers** 2 What's your surname? 3 What's your nationality? 4 What's your address? 5 What's your mobile number? 6 What's your email address?
> - Check students remember *What's ... ? = What is ... ?*.
> - Remind students of the personal information question *What's your home number?*.
> - You can also teach the question *What's your work number?* if you think this will be useful for your students.

7 **a** Focus students on the photo of Karen and Peter and pre-teach *a gym*. Also draw students' attention to Peter's business card on SB p18. Ask students where Peter works (The City Gym) and what his job is (he's a manager).

VIDEO 2 **CD1 42** Play the video or audio recording (SB p108). Students watch or listen and tick the sentences in **6** when they hear them. Ask students how many sentences they ticked.

Note that all the Real World videos can be found on the **Teacher's DVD** at the back of this book.

b Focus students on form A and pre-teach *a new member* (a person who joins the gym for the first time). Ask students who is the new member in the photo (Karen).

Play the video or audio recording again. Students watch or listen and complete the form. Play the video or audio recording again if necessary.

c Students compare answers in pairs. Check answers with the class.

Highlight *L11 7HR* in Karen's address and teach *a postcode* (US: *a zip code*).

surname Wendell **nationality** British **address** 7 Hatherley Road, Liverpool L11 7HR **mobile number** 07854 864247 **email address** k.wendell9@gmail.com

> **EXTRA IDEA**
>
> - Ask students to look at Audio and Video Script **VIDEO 2** **CD1 42** SB p108. Play the recording again. Students listen, read and underline all the personal information questions.

8 **CD1 43** **PRONUNCIATION** Play the recording (SB p108). Students listen and practise. Establish that intonation is very important in English and that the correct intonation pattern can help students to sound polite. Repeat the drill if necessary, focusing on polite intonation.

9 **a** Put students into pairs. If possible, ask students to work with someone they don't know very well.

Students take turns to interview their partner and fill in form B. Remind students to use the questions in **6** when they are the interviewer.

Also remind students of the questions *How do you spell that?* and *Can you repeat that, please?* before they begin.

> **EXTRA IDEA**
>
> - If your students know each other well, or if you feel it is inappropriate for your students to give each other their personal details, use **Class Activity** 2C The City Gym p131 as an alternative to **9a** (see Procedure A, Instructions p116).

b Students work in their pairs and check that all the information on their partner's form is correct. Finally, you can ask one or two pairs to role-play their conversations for the class.

┌─ **EXTRA IDEAS** ─────────────────────────┐

• When students have finished **9a**, put them into new pairs. Students ask questions with *he/his* and *she/her* about the person his/her partner has just interviewed (*What's his/her first name?*, *What's his/her surname?*, etc.).

• Alternatively, **Class Activity** 2C The City Gym p131 can also be used to practise *he/his* and *she/her* questions (see Procedure B, Instructions p116).

┌─ **WRITING** ─────────────────────────┐

Ask students to imagine they are new members at The City Gym. Students write a conversation between Peter and themselves, using the personal information questions in **6** and their own answers.

┌─ **FURTHER PRACTICE** ─────────────────────┐

Ph **Class Activity** 2C The City Gym p131 (Instructions p115)
Extra Practice 2C SB p98
Self-study DVD-ROM Lesson 2C
Workbook Lesson 2C p11

VOCABULARY
2D AND SKILLS ▶ How old is she?
Student's Book p20–p21

Vocabulary numbers 13–100
Real World *How old … ?*
Skills Listening: five conversations

QUICK REVIEW This activity reviews numbers 0–12. Students do the first part of the activity on their own. Put students into pairs. Students check their partner's spelling and then say the numbers. Students can check spelling in **VOCABULARY 1.1** ▶ SB p114.

1 **CD1▶ 44** **PRONUNCIATION** Play the recording. Students listen and practise the numbers. Note that stress is dealt with in **3a–c**.

Point out the irregular spelling of *thirteen* and *fifteen*.

2 **a** Students do the exercise on their own or in pairs. Check answers with the class.

Point out that we can also say *one hundred*, but that *a hundred* is more common.

40 forty	**50** fifty	**60** sixty	**70** seventy
80 eighty	**90** ninety	**100** a hundred	

b 🖊 Remind students of word stress by writing some multi-syllable words on the board and asking the class which syllable is stressed.
CD1▶ 45 **PRONUNCIATION** Play the recording. Students listen and practise. Highlight the pronunciation of *thirty* /ˈθɜːti/ and *forty* /ˈfɔːti/.

HELP WITH LISTENING
Numbers with *-teen* and *-ty*

This *Help with Listening* section helps students to hear the difference between numbers that end in *-teen* and those that end in *-ty*.

3 **a** **CD1▶ 46** Play the recording. Students listen and notice the stress on the numbers. Point out that we usually stress the *-teen* syllable in numbers 13–19 and the first syllable in numbers 20–100.

We appreciate that this stress rule for numbers ending in *-teen* is somewhat simplistic, as there are times when we naturally stress the first syllable (for example, when counting or when the number is followed by a noun). However, we feel that at this level it is more helpful to give students a clear rule that will avoid confusion and be correct most of the time (for example, when talking about ages later in the lesson).

b Students do the exercise on their own before comparing answers in pairs.

c **CD1▶ 47** Play the recording. Students listen and check their answers.
🖊 If necessary, write the numbers on the board and ask students which syllable is stressed in each number.

seventeen ninety fifty thirteen
thirty nineteen seventy fifteen

4 **CD1▶ 46** **CD1▶ 47** **PRONUNCIATION** Play both recordings again. Students listen and practise. Alternatively, model the numbers yourself in order and ask students to repeat chorally and individually. Check that students stress the numbers correctly.

Note that the *th* sound /θ/ (as in *thirty*, *thirteen*, etc.) is dealt with in the *Help with Pronunciation* section at the end of unit 4.

5 **a** Focus students on the examples. Point out that we use a hyphen (-) in these numbers.

Students do the exercise on their own, then compare answers in pairs.

✍ Check the answers by writing the numbers (*23*, etc.) on the board and asking students how to write the words (*twenty-three*, etc.).

Point out that we usually put the main stress on the final syllable in compound numbers (*twenty-óne*, *twenty-twó*, etc.).

23 twenty-three 24 twenty-four 25 twenty-five
26 twenty-six 27 twenty-seven 28 twenty-eight
29 twenty-nine

┌─ **EXTRA IDEA** ┐
- ✍ Write a few other numbers between 31 and 99 on the board and ask students how we say them.

b Students work in pairs and take turns to say the numbers.

Check students' pronunciation by going round the class and asking them to say one number each.

6 **a** Students work on their own and write four numbers.

b Students do the exercise in new pairs.

┌─ **EXTRA IDEA** ┐
- Use **Class Activity** 2D Hear a number, say a number p132 (Instructions p116).

7 **a** Focus students on the photo. Students do the exercise on their own or in pairs. Note that the aim of this box is to highlight which new words students need in order to understand the conversation they are about to hear.

Check answers with the class. Model and drill the vocabulary with the class if necessary.

a girl 5; a house 1; a cat 3; a dog 4

b **CD1** ► 48 Tell students they are going to listen to five conversations about the people, animals or things in the photo. Play the recording (SB p108). Students listen and fill in the gaps with the correct numbers. Play the recording again if necessary.

Students compare answers in pairs. Check answers with the class.

Note that in the UK and many other countries, we often think of one 'human year' as being equivalent to seven 'dog years'.

a 13 b 100 c 9 d 21 e 7 (or 49 'dog years')

8 **a** Students do the exercise on their own or in pairs.

b **CD1** ► 49 Focus students on the speech bubbles in **8a**. Play the recording. Students listen and check their answers. Check answers with the class.

PRONUNCIATION Play the recording again. Students listen and practise.

Point out that we usually use *How old is/are … ?* to ask about age (not ~~How many years … ?~~ or ~~What age is/are … ?~~).

Highlight that we use the verb *be* to talk about age, not *have*: *I'm twenty-six.* not ~~I have twenty-six.~~

Also highlight that we don't usually say *years old* for people: *Emily's nine.*, *I'm thirty.*, etc., and that we don't say ~~I'm thirty years.~~

Explain that in the UK and other English-speaking countries, asking people how old they are is often considered impolite, particularly if you don't know them very well.

You can also teach the noun *age* /eɪdʒ/, but point out that we don't say ~~What age are you?~~.

2 is 3 old 4 are 5 I'm

9 Focus students on the photo. Ask them to cover **7** and **8**. Students do the activity in pairs.

10 **a** Put students into new pairs. Focus students on the photos and the ages in the box.

Students work with their partner and try to guess how old each person is. Before they begin, use the speech bubbles to remind students that we say *I think …* when we want to give our opinion.

b Students check their answers on SB p134.

Finally, ask each pair how many they got right and find out which pair got the most correct answers.

Amybeth 24; Richard 58; Lucinda 22
Adela 47; Dagmar 76
Joe 13; Alexander 16
Luke 35; Jessica 41; Maggie 71
Salvador 3; Alec 5; Belle 2
Jean 80; Don 87; Chris 51

┌─ **EXTRA IDEA** ┐
- Before asking students to check their answers to **10a** on SB p134, put students into groups of four or six and ask them to compare their ideas.

┌─ **FURTHER PRACTICE** ┐
Ph Class Activity 2D Hear a number, say a number p116 (Instructions p132)
Extra Practice 2 SB p98
Self-study DVD-ROM Lesson 2D
Workbook Lesson 2D p12
Workbook Reading and Writing Portfolio 2 p54–p55
Ph Progress Test 2 p181

HELP WITH PRONUNCIATION /ɪ/ and /iː/

1 **CD1▶ 50** Focus students on the phonemes /ɪ/ and /iː/, the pictures and the words. Play the recording. Students listen to the sounds and the words. Point out that *i* in *six* is pronounced with an /ɪ/ sound and *ee* in *nineteen* is pronounced with an /iː/ sound.

Play the recording again. Students listen and practise. If students are having problems, help them with the mouth position for each sound.

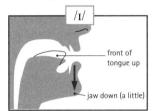
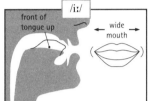

Point out that /ɪ/ is a short sound and /iː/ is a long sound (as indicated by the ː symbol). Also highlight that the mouth is wide when saying the /iː/ sound. You can tell students that the letter *e* is also pronounced /iː/.

2 **CD1▶ 51** Focus students on the boxes. Point out that the pink vowels are pronounced /ɪ/ and the blue vowels are pronounced /iː/. Play the recording. Students listen and notice how we say the pink and blue vowels.

Play the recording again. Students listen and practise.

3 **a** Focus students on the words in the box. Go through the examples with the class. Students do the exercise on their own.

✍ While students are working, write the words on the board ready for checking in **3c**.

b Students compare answers in pairs. Tell students to say the words to each other when comparing answers.

c **CD1▶ 52** Play the recording. Students listen and check their answers.

✍ Check the answers by eliciting the correct sound for each of the vowels in bold and writing it on the board under the vowel, as shown in the Answer Key below.

Play the recording again. Students listen and practise the words. Check they pronounce the vowels in **bold** correctly.

Finally, ask students to say the words for the class.

sandwiches	teacher	think	married	isn't	read
/ɪ/	/iː/	/ɪ/	/ɪ/	/ɪ/	/iː/

musician	assistant	me	Spanish	Japanese	sixteen
/ɪ/	/ɪ/	/iː/	/ɪ/	/iː/	/iː/

▶ continue2learn

Focus students on the **continue2learn** section on SB p21. See p33 of this book for ideas on how to use this section in class.

Extra Practice 2 SB p98

See p34 for ideas on how to use this section in class.

2A
1 2 Mexican **3** Italian **4** British **5** Chinese
6 Brazilian **7** American **8** Egyptian **9** Spanish
10 Turkish **11** Russian **12** German
2 1 's 2 aren't; 're 3 isn't; 's 4 'm not; 'm 5 's; isn't

2B
3 2 a musician 3 a doctor 4 a waitress 5 a sales
assistant (a shop assistant) 6 a waiter 7 an actor
8 a taxi driver (a cab driver) 9 a police officer
(a policewoman)
4 2 Where are you from? 3 What's your job?
4 Where's he from? 5 What's his job?
6 What's her name? 7 What's her job?
5a 2 Is 3 Are 4 Am 5 Are 6 Is
5b 2 No, he isn't. / No, he's not. 3 Yes, I am.
4 No, you aren't. / No, you're not. 5 No, I'm not.
6 Yes, she is.

2C
6 2 What's your surname? 3 What's your
nationality? 4 What's your address? 5 What's
your mobile number? / What's your phone
number? 6 What's your email address?

2D
7 14 fourteen 15 fifteen 16 sixteen 17 seventeen
18 eighteen 19 nineteen 21 twenty-one
33 thirty-three 47 forty-seven 56 fifty-six
64 sixty-four 72 seventy-two 89 eighty-nine
95 ninety-five 100 a hundred
8 2 's 3 is 4 's 5 are 6 'm

Progress Portfolio 2

See p34 for ideas on how to use this section in class.

3A ▶ Two cities
Student's Book p22–p23

Vocabulary adjectives (1); word order
with adjectives; *very*
Grammar *be* (plural): positive, negative,
questions and short answers

QUICK REVIEW This activity reviews numbers 1–100. Students do the activity in pairs. If you have a small class, you can do the activity by asking students to count in threes and fours round the class.

Adjectives (1)

1 **a** Focus students on the pictures and use the example (*good* and *bad*) to teach the meaning of *adjective* and *opposite*. Tell students that each pair of words are opposites.

Students do the exercise on their own or in pairs. Early finishers can check their answers in Language Summary 3 **VOCABULARY 3.1** ▶ SB p118. Check answers with the class.

Note that *nice* is a very general positive adjective that can mean *good, friendly, enjoyable, beautiful, comfortable, delicious*, etc. The opposite of *nice* therefore depends on the context.

hot/cold **e**; big/small **c**; new/old **g**; expensive/cheap **f**; beautiful/ugly **b**; friendly/unfriendly **a**; nice **h**

b **CD1 ▶ 53** **PRONUNCIATION** Play the recording. Students listen and practise. Alternatively, model the words yourself and ask students to repeat chorally and individually. Check that students copy the word stress correctly. Repeat the drill if necessary.

EXTRA IDEA
- After doing **1b**, students work in pairs and take turns to test each other on the adjectives. One student says an adjective, for example *hot*, and his/her partner says the opposite, for example *cold*.

HELP WITH VOCABULARY
Word order with adjectives; *very*

2 **a** Ask students to read the rules about adjectives and the examples. ✎ Alternatiely, write the example sentences on the board and go through the rules with the class, highlighting the following points.

- Adjectives go after *be*: *Your watch is nice.* not *Your watch nice is.*
- Adjectives go before nouns: *It's a new car.* not *It's a car new.*
- Also highlight that the adjective comes after the article *a* (*It's a new car*) and that we use *an* when the adjective begins with a vowel (*It's an old car*).
- Adjectives are **not** plural with plural nouns. *They're good friends.* not *They're goods friends.*
- Also highlight the word order in questions: *Are you cold?, Is he friendly?*, etc.

b Students do the exercise on their own. Go through the following points with the class.

- Use the pictures to check students understand the meaning of *very*.
- Highlight that we put *very* before adjectives: *It's **very** hot.*
- Point out that we say *It's (very) hot/cold.* to talk about the weather. Highlight *It* at the beginning of the sentence and point out that we say *It's hot.* not *Is hot.*, etc.

3 Students do the exercise on their own, then compare answers in pairs. Check answers with the class. Highlight the word order in each answer.

2 He's a very good actor. **3** It's an expensive camera. **4** His friends are very nice. **5** She's a good musician. **6** Her house is very beautiful. **7** It's a very cold night. **8** Your children are very friendly.

An email to friends

4 **a** Students do the exercise in pairs. Note that these words are cognates in many languages, so students may already know what they mean as they have the same or similar words in their own language. Note that the aim of this box is to highlight which new words students need in order to understand the conversation they are about to hear.

b Check the meaning of any words in **4a** that students don't know using pictures, drawings, translation, etc. Model and drill the words with the class. Point out that *restaurant* /ˈrestrɒnt/ is two syllables, not three. Also highlight that although there is usually an accent on *café* in English, we stress the first syllable, not the second.

c Check students understand *an email* by referring to email A. Point out that the stress on *email* is on the first syllable, not the second.

Ask who the people in the photo are (Alice and Mike). Students read email A and find out where Alice and Mike are (in Istanbul, Turkey).

Teach the new words *and, but, here* and *now* in the email. Note *and* and *but* are practised further in **Reading and Writing Portfolio 3** on p56–p57 of the **face2face** Second edition Starter Workbook.

Highlight that *people* is always plural in English: *the people are friendly* not *the people is friendly*.

You can also point out that we often end emails to friends or family with *Love* and then our name(s).

5 Go through the two examples with the class and check they understand what to do. Students do the exercise on their own before comparing answers in pairs. Check answers with the class.

3 The people are **friendly**. 4 ✓ 5 Alice and Mike are in a **small** hotel. 6 ✓ 7 The rooms are very **big**.

HELP WITH GRAMMAR
be (plural): positive and negative

6 Students do the exercise on their own or in pairs. Check answers with the class.

- **Answers** We**'re** in a new hotel. They**'re** very big. We **aren't** in the hotel now. They **aren't** very expensive.
- Point out that *are* is the plural form of *be* (as well as the singular *you* form).
- Check students understand *we* and *they*. Point out that we can use *they* for people and things.
- Tell students that *you* is singular and plural: *You're a student. You're students.* Also remind students that there is no polite form of *you* in English.
- Highlight that *we're*, *you're* and *they're* are contracted forms of *we are*, *you are* and *they are*.
- Also point out that we don't contract *are* after a name or a noun: *Alice and Mike are in Moscow.* not ~~*Alice and Mike're in Moscow.*~~ and *The rooms are nice.* not ~~*The rooms're nice.*~~
- Check students remember that *aren't* is the contracted form of *are not*.
- Tell students that we can also say *we're not*, *you're not* and *they're not*.

7 **CD1▸ 54** **PRONUNCIATION** Play the recording. Students listen and practise the sentences in **6**. Check that students pronounce the contractions correctly. Alternatively, model each sentence yourself and ask students to repeat chorally and individually.
You can also point out that the pronunciation of *you're* and *your* is the same /jɔː/.

HELP WITH LISTENING Contractions

This *Help with Listening* section helps students to understand contractions in natural spoken English.

8 **a** Use the examples (*I'm, we're, aren't*, etc.) to teach students what a contraction is. Give students time to read sentences 1–6. Check students understand that the missing words in each sentence are contractions, as shown in the example in 1.
CD1▸ 55 Play the recording (SB p108), pausing after each sentence to allow students time to write. Students listen and fill in the gaps with the correct contractions.
Play the recording again if necessary.

b Students compare answers in pairs.

✎ Check answers with the class by writing the sentences on the board and asking students to tell you the missing contractions. Ask students which contractions are negative (*aren't* and *isn't*).

1 We **aren't** from Italy, **we're** from Spain.
2 It**'s** a new hotel, but it **isn't** very nice.
3 He**'s** a doctor and he **isn't** married.
4 You **aren't** Australian, **you're** American.
5 I**'m** a manager and **she's** a musician.
6 They**'re** actors, but they **aren't** very good.

9 **CD1▸ 55** **PRONUNCIATION** Play the recording again. Students listen and practise. Check they are pronouncing the contractions correctly. Repeat the drill if necessary, pausing after each sentence for students to repeat chorally and individually.

Where are they?

10 Focus students on email B. Ask who the people in the photo are (Liz and Steve). Students do the exercise on their own, then compare answers in pairs. Check answers with the class.

2 're 3 's 4 are 5 aren't 6 're 7 are 8 isn't 9 's

HELP WITH GRAMMAR
be (plural): questions and short answers

11 Students do the exercise on their own or in pairs.
✎ While they are working, copy the table onto the board so you are ready to check students' answers. Check answers with the class by eliciting students' answers and writing them in the correct place on the board.

- **Answers** See the table in **GRAMMAR 3.2▸** SB p119.
- Highlight the inverted word order in *yes/no* questions: *Are they … ?, Are you … ?*, etc.
- Point out that we can also say *No, we're not., No, you're not.* and *No, they're not.*
- Also point out that we don't usually answer these questions with just *Yes.* or *No.* as this can sound impolite.
- Highlight that we don't usually use contractions in positive short answers: *Yes, you are.* not ~~*Yes, you're.*~~, etc.
- Also highlight that we don't usually use the uncontracted form in negative short answers: *No, you aren't.* not ~~*No, you are not.*~~, etc.
- Highlight the word order in *Wh-* questions. Point out that we don't contract *Where are*: *Where are you?* not ~~*Where're you?*~~

┌─ **EXTRA IDEA** ─
- Ask students to turn to Language Summary 3, SB p119. Focus students on **GRAMMAR 3.1▸** and **GRAMMAR 3.2▸**. Give students time to study the grammar tables, read the **TIPS** and ask you any questions.

12 **CD1▸ 56** **PRONUNCIATION** Play the recording. Students listen and practise. Repeat the drill if necessary.

Get ready … Get it right!

 Put students into pairs, student A and student B. Student As turn to SB p88 and student Bs turn to SB p93. Check they are all looking at the correct exercise.

a Students do the exercise on their own. Check answers with the class. Only check the verb forms so that students don't hear the questions they are about to be asked. Note that the answers are the same for student As and student Bs.

Student A/Student B
2 Are **3** Are **4** 's **5** Are **6** Is

b Students do the exercise on their own. They can make notes of the answers if necessary.

c Students work with their partners. Student As ask their questions about Alice and Mike from **a**. Encourage student Bs to use short answers where appropriate (*Yes, they are.*, *No, they aren't.*, etc.). Student A then tells his/her partner how many of his/her answers are correct. While they are working, monitor and correct any mistakes you hear.

d Students swap roles so that student Bs ask their questions about Liz and Steve from **a**. Check answers with the class if necessary. Finally, ask the class how many students answered all the questions correctly.

Student A 1 They're in Istanbul. **2** Yes, they are. **3** No, they aren't. **4** It's near the Blue Mosque. **5** Yes, they are. **6** No, it isn't. / No, it's very hot.
Student B 1 They're in Cairo. **2** Yes, they are. **3** Yes, they are. **4** It's near the Egyptian museum. **5** Yes, they are. **6** No, it isn't.

EXTRA IDEA

- Ask your students to bring in photos of their family to the next class, so that they can be used during the *Get ready … Get it right!* speaking activity in lesson 3B.

WRITING

Do **Reading and Writing Portfolio 3** *See you soon!* (Workbook p56–p57). This can be done in class or for homework. For more information on how to use the Reading and Writing Portfolios in class, see p33.

FURTHER PRACTICE

Ph **Class Activity** 3A Where are they? p133 (Instructions p116)
Extra Practice 3A SB p99
Self-study DVD-ROM Lesson 3A
Workbook Lesson 3A p13

3B ▶ Brothers and sisters
Student's Book p24–p25

Vocabulary family
Grammar possessive *'s*; subject pronouns (*I, you*, etc.) and possessive adjectives (*my, your*, etc.)

QUICK REVIEW This activity reviews adjectives. Students work on their own and write four adjectives. Tell students to choose adjectives they learned in lesson 3A. Students complete the activity in pairs, as shown in the examples. Ask each pair to tell the class one or two things for the adjectives they chose.

Our family

 CD1 57 Focus students on the photo of the Cooper family. Play the recording. Students listen and read speech bubbles 1–4. Play the recording again if necessary.
Note that students are often asked to 'listen and read' in the Student's Book. At this level we feel it is very useful for students to listen and read at the same time, as this helps them to 'tune in' to English and to connect what they hear with how it is written.

2 **a** Focus students on the table. Go through the headings with the class. Check they understand the male and female symbols in the column headings and teach the meaning of *both*. Students do the exercise in pairs.
 While they are working, draw the table, including the words (*father*, etc.) on the board.
Check answers with the class by eliciting the missing words and writing them in the correct places in the table on the board.
Point out that *dad* and *mum* are informal words for *father* and *mother*. You can also teach *kids*, which is an informal word for *children*, and *a boyfriend/ a girlfriend*.

Highlight that the singular form of *parents* is *a parent* and that the plural of *a wife* is *wives*, not ~~wifes~~. Also highlight that the plural of *a child* is irregular (*children*).

You can also point out that your *parents* are your mother and father only, and that other family members who are not part of your immediate family (aunts, uncles, etc.) are called *relatives*.

men/boys 👤	women/girls 👤	both 👤👤
father (**dad**)	mother (**mum**)	parents
son	daughter	children (singular: child)
husband	**wife**	
brother	sister	

b **CD1 ▶ 58** **PRONUNCIATION** Play the recording. Students listen and practise the words. Highlight the pronunciation of *parents* /ˈpeərənts/. Point out that the stress on all the two-syllable words in the table is always on the first syllable. Also highlight the /ʌ/ sound in *mother* /ˈmʌðə/, *mum* /mʌm/, *son* /sʌn/, *husband* /ˈhʌzbənd/ and *brother* /ˈbrʌðə/. Note that this sound is practised further in the *Help with Pronunciation* section in this unit.

> ⌐ **EXTRA IDEAS** ⟩
>
> • If you have a class of complete beginners, consider teaching the family vocabulary yourself at the beginning of the lesson. ✏ Draw the Cooper family tree on the board (father: Nick, mother: Fiona, son: Kevin, daughter: Anne). Then use the relationships between the people to teach the vocabulary in **bold** in the speech bubbles. You can then use **2** for practice.
> • ✏ Alternatively, draw your own family tree and use this to teach the family vocabulary. You can also bring in photos of your family to show the class.

3 Students do the exercise on their own before comparing answers in pairs. Check answers with the class.

2 son 3 mother 4 daughter
5 father 6 sister 7 parents

HELP WITH GRAMMAR Possessive *'s*

4 Go through the rule and the **TIP** with the class. Highlight the following points.

• We use a name or a noun for a person + *'s* for the possessive. For example, we say *Fiona is Nick's wife.* not ~~Fiona is the wife of Nick.~~, and *It's my sister's car.* not ~~It's the car of my sister.~~ Use the second example to highlight that we use *'s* for things we have, as well as for family relationships.

• Check students understand that we can use *'s* with other nouns for people: *It's my **teacher's** car.* *It's his **friend's** camera.*, etc. Note that we can use the possessive *'s* with some other nouns (*It's the **world's** biggest animal.*, etc.), but at Starter level we feel it is easier for students to focus only on nouns for people.

• Point out that *'s* can mean *is* or the possessive: *Anne's my sister.* (*'s* = *is*) *Kevin is Nick's son.* (*'s* = possessive)

• Point out that for plural nouns, the apostrophe (') is after the *-s*: *It's my parents' house.*

• Also highlight that when there are two names, the *'s* goes after the second name only: *They're Kevin and Anne's parents.* not ~~They're Kevin's and Anne's parents.~~

• You can tell students that when a name ends in an /s/ sound, the *'s* is pronounced as an extra syllable /ɪz/, for example *Luis's* /luːˈiːsɪz/, *Chris's* /ˈkrɪsɪz/, etc.

5 **CD1 ▶ 59** **PRONUNCIATION** Play the recording (SB p108). Students listen and practise the sentences in **3**. Check that students pronounce the possessive *'s* in each sentence correctly.

Students might ask why we don't contract *is* in these sentences (*Nick's Fiona's son.*, etc.). You can point out that writing *'s* twice in short sentences such as these looks rather unnatural, but is still correct.

6 Focus students on the example. Students do the exercise on their own. Check answers with the class.

2 Fiona is Nick's wife. 3 Kevin is Fiona's son.
4 Anne is Nick's daughter. 5 Kevin is Anne's brother.
6 Anne and Kevin are Nick and Fiona's children.

Our grandchildren

7 **a** Focus students on the photo of Sid and Mary. Tell the class that they are Kevin and Anne's grandparents.

Students work on their own and complete the table with the words in the box.

Check answers with the class. Point out that the singular of *grandchildren* is *a grandchild*.

👤	grandfather	**grandson**
👤	grandmother	granddaughter
👤👤	**grandparents**	grandchildren

b **CD1 ▶ 60** **PRONUNCIATION** Play the recording. Students listen and practise. Point out that the stress on these words is always on the first syllable, and that we don't pronounce the *d* in *grand-*: *grandfather* /ˈɡrænfɑːðə/, etc.

8 **a** **CD1** **61** Tell the class they are going to listen to Mary talk about her family. Play the recording (SB p108). Students listen and put the people in the order she talks about them.
Check answers with the class.

> Anne 4; Fiona 2; Kevin 5; Nick 3

b Give students time to read questions 1–6. Play the recording again. Students listen and answer the questions. Check answers with the class.

> 2 She's a teacher. 3 She's 43. 4 He's a doctor.
> 5 Yes, she is. 6 He's 12.

HELP WITH GRAMMAR
Subject pronouns (*I*, *you*, etc.) and possessive adjectives (*my*, *your*, etc.)

9 **a** Focus students on the four example sentences from the recording. Point out the words in blue and pink in these sentences. Students complete the table on their own or in pairs.
✎ While students are working, draw the table on the board so that you are ready to check their answers. Check answers with the class.

> - subject pronouns: **I**, you, **he**, she, **it**, we, they
> - possessive adjectives: **my**, your, his, **her**, its, **our, their**

b Focus students on the box. Use the examples to check students understand the difference between a verb and a noun.
Students do the exercise on their own or in pairs. Check answers with the class.

> family **N**; listen **V**; read **V**; cat **N**

c Go through the rules with the class. Use the examples to highlight that we use subject pronouns with verbs (*I'm*, *you listen*, *they read*, etc.) and possessive adjectives with nouns (*my sister*, *your family*, *their cat*, etc.).
Point out that *you* and *your* are both singular and plural. Also point out that verbs in English always need a subject: *It's my bag.* not *~~Is my bag.~~*, etc.
If it's relevant for your students, point out that nouns in English have no gender and that we use *it* or *its* to refer to a thing: *It's a very nice **photo**.* etc.

10 Students do the exercise on their own, then compare answers in pairs.
Check answers with the class. Highlight that *their* is pronounced the same as *they're* /ðeə/.
You can also use question 3 to point out that we usually use *his* or *her* to refer to animals if we know what gender they are, and *it* if we don't.

> 2 They, their 3 our, His 4 My, your
> 5 you, his 6 Her, she

Get ready … Get it right!

11 Students write a list of people in their family. Tell students to write only the names of family members that they have learned in the lesson (not uncles, aunts, cousins, etc.).

> **EXTRA IDEAS**
> - If you asked your students to bring in photos of their family at the end of the previous lesson, they can use these photos instead of writing the names of their family. Teach students to say *This is …* when they point to a person in the photo (*This is Lucas. He's my brother.*, etc.).
> - Students can draw their family tree instead of writing a list of names in **11**. ✎ You can demonstrate this by drawing your own family tree on the board before they begin. You can also use your family tree to elicit the questions in the speech bubbles in **12a**.

12 **a** Use the speech bubbles to remind students of the questions *How old is he?*, *What's his job?* and *Is he married?*. Elicit the corresponding questions with *she* (*How old is she?*, etc.).
Put students into pairs. If possible, ask students to work with someone they don't know very well.
Students take turns to tell their partner who the people are on their list. Their partner asks questions about each person, as shown in the speech bubbles. While students are working, monitor and correct any mistakes you hear.

b Finally, ask each student to tell the class about one person in their partner's family, as shown in the speech bubble.

> **WRITING**
> Students write a short description of their family. Ask students to include a family tree, and/or some photos of family members. Their descriptions can be collected in the next class and put around the room for other students to read.

> **FURTHER PRACTICE**
> **Ph** Class Activity 3B Barry and Wendy's family p134–p135 (Instructions p117)
> **Extra Practice** 3B SB p99
> **Self-study DVD-ROM** Lesson 3B
> **Workbook** Lesson 3B p14

Eat in or take away?
Student's Book p26–p27

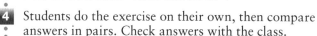

Vocabulary food and drink (1)
Real World money and prices;
How much … ?; in a café

QUICK REVIEW This activity reviews family vocabulary and possessive *'s*. Students do the first part of the activity on their own. Put students into pairs. Students take turns to tell their partner about their friends and family. Encourage students to ask questions about the people if possible. At the end of the activity, you can ask a few students to tell the class about their partner's family.

Money and prices

1 **a** Pre-teach *money* /ˈmʌni/ and *price* /praɪs/. Drill these words with the class.

Students do the exercise on their own, then compare answers in pairs. Check answers with the class.

Check students understand the symbols £ (*pounds*), $ (*dollars*), € (*euros*), p (*pence*) and c (*cents*). Point out that in the UK it is much more common to say *ten p* than *ten pence*, although both are correct. Also point out that we often miss out the currency words (*pounds, euros*, etc.) in prices with both pounds and pence or euros/dollars and cents if the context is clear (*ten fifty, five ninety-nine*, etc.). However, we always say the currency when there are no pence or cents (*ten pounds, fifty euros, twelve dollars*, etc.).

Also teach students how to say the currency from their country/countries in English if appropriate.

2b 3e 4c 5a 6d

b **CD1▶ 62** **PRONUNCIATION** Play the recording. Students listen and practise the prices. Check that students pronounce *p* /piː/, *euros* /ˈjʊərəʊz/ and *cents* /sents/ correctly. Repeat the drill if necessary.

2 **a** Students do the exercise in pairs.

b **CD1▶ 63** Play the recording (SB p108). Students listen and check their answers.

PRONUNCIATION Play the recording again. Students listen and practise the prices.

a seventeen pounds b seventy p c a hundred dollars d twenty-one euros e thirty-five cents f twenty-one dollars fifty g three euros seventy-five h seven pounds sixty

3 **a** **CD1▶ 64** Tell students that they are going to listen to five conversations. Play the recording (SB p108). Students listen and write the prices. Play the recording again if necessary.

b Students compare answers in pairs. Check answers with the class.

1 £25 2 $64 3 70p 4 £48.50 5 €95

REAL WORLD *How much … ?*

4 Students do the exercise on their own, then compare answers in pairs. Check answers with the class.

- **Answers** 1 is 2 is 3 are 4 are
- Point out that we use *How much is … ?* for singular nouns and *it*, and *How much are … ?* for plural nouns and *they*.
- You can teach students *this* (in question 1). Note that *this, that, these* and *those* are taught in lesson 4C.

5 **CD1▶ 65** **PRONUNCIATION** Play the recording. Students listen and practise the questions in **4**. Alternatively, model and drill the questions yourself.

Can I help you?

6 **a** Focus students on the Café Pronto price list. Teach the words *food* and *drink*.

Students work on their own or in pairs and match the food and drink on the price list to photos 1–10. Check answers with the class.

Point out that the Italian words *cappuccino* and *espresso*, and the French word *croissant*, are very common in English, particularly in coffee shops and cafés. You can also teach other Italian words for types of coffee that often appear on café price lists, for example *a latte* /ˈlæteɪ/ (coffee made with hot milk), *an Americano* /əmerɪˈkɑːnəʊ/ (black coffee), *a mocha* /ˈmɒkə/ (coffee with chocolate), etc.

Teach students that we can also say *a white coffee* (with milk) and *a black coffee* (without milk).

Point out that we can say *a mineral water* or *a bottle of mineral water* and that we can say *a coffee/tea* or *a cup of coffee/tea*.

1 a cheese and tomato sandwich 2 a tea
3 a mineral water 4 an orange juice 5 a cappuccino
6 a croissant 7 a tuna salad 8 an espresso
9 an egg sandwich 10 a coffee

┌─ **EXTRA IDEA** ─┐

- Give students one minute to remember all the things on the Café Pronto price list. Ask students to close their books. Students work in pairs and write down all the food and drink items they can remember.

b **CD1▶ 66** **PRONUNCIATION** Play the recording (SB p108). Students listen and practise the food and drink on the price list. Highlight the pronunciation of *cappuccino* /kæpʊˈtʃiːnəʊ/, *orange juice* /ˈɒrɪndʒ dʒuːs/, *croissant* /ˈkwæsɒ/ and *sandwich* /ˈsænwɪdʒ/. Play the recording again, pausing after each word so that students can repeat individually.

c Ask students to cover the price list. Students do the exercise in pairs, as shown in the speech bubbles.

7 Focus students on the speech bubbles and drill these examples with the class.
Students do the exercise in new pairs. While they are working, monitor and correct students' pronunciation if necessary.

8 **a** Focus students on the photo of Café Pronto on SB p27. Use the people in the photo to teach *an assistant* and *a customer*.
VIDEO ▶ 3 **CD1** ▶ 67 Play the video or audio recording (SB p108). Students watch or listen and tick what the two customers order on the price list. Note that all the Real World videos can be found on the **Teacher's DVD** at the back of this book.
Students compare answers in pairs. Check answers with the class.

> **1** an orange juice and a cheese and tomato sandwich
> **2** two cappuccinos, a croissant and an egg sandwich

b Play the video or audio recording again. Students listen and write how much each customer spends. Check the answers with the class.

> **1** £4.55 **2** £8.60

REAL WORLD In a café

9 Focus students on the conversation. Check they understand that the assistant says the sentences in the yellow boxes and the customer says the sentences in the red boxes. Point out that the language in brackets can change, depending on what the customer orders. Note that the language that students need to learn for **productive** use is always in the **red** boxes in these flow charts.
Students do the exercise on their own, then compare answers in pairs. Check answers with the class.

• **Answers** 2 please 3 thanks 4 away 5 in 6 very
• Check students understand all the sentences in the conversation. Highlight the difference between *eat in* (eat in the café) and *take away* (take the food and eat it somewhere else).
• You can point out that we say *take away* in British English and *to go* in American English.
• You can also teach *Of course.* as an alternative to *Sure.*

10 **a** **CD1** ▶ 68 **PRONUNCIATION** Play the recording (SB p109). Students listen and practise the sentences in **9**. Encourage students to copy the polite intonation. Play the recording again, pausing after each sentence for students to repeat chorally and individually.

b Put students into pairs, student A and student B. Student As are assistants and student Bs are customers. Students practise the conversation in **9** with their partner. After students have practised the conversation a few times, ask them to change roles.

> ┌─ **EXTRA IDEA** ┐
> • Before students work in pairs, practise the conversation in 'open pairs'. See **Teaching Tips** on drilling on p23.

11 **a** Put students into new pairs. Focus students on the Café Pronto price list on SB p26.
Students take turns to be the customer and order food and drink. The assistant must work out how much to charge the customer. You can ask students to cover the conversation in **9** before they begin.

b Finally, ask a few pairs to role-play a conversation in Café Pronto for the class.

> ┌─ **FURTHER PRACTICE** ┐
> **Extra Practice** 3C SB p99
> **Self-study DVD-ROM** Lesson 3C
> **Workbook** Lesson 3C p16

VOCABULARY
3D AND SKILLS ▶ Food I like
Student's Book p28–p29

Vocabulary food and drink (2); *love, like, eat, drink, a lot of*
Skills Listening: Fiona's family; Reading and Listening: food and drink I like

QUICK REVIEW This activity reviews money and prices. Students work on their own and write four prices, as in the examples. Students complete the activity in pairs.

1 **a** Focus students on the photo. Students do the exercise on their own or in pairs. Check answers with the class. Note that many of these words

(*milk, tea, rice, fruit*, etc.) are uncountable nouns. However, we feel that asking students to differentiate between countable and uncountable nouns would be unnecessarily complicated at Starter level. Note that countable and uncountable nouns are dealt with thoroughly in **face2face** Second edition Elementary.

> milk 6; tea 2; sugar 14; meat 11; fish 9; orange juice 5; eggs 13; cheese 12; bread 7; pasta 15; rice 10; vegetables 4; fruit 1; chocolate 16; water 8

b [CD1► 69] [PRONUNCIATION] Play the recording. Students listen and practise. Alternatively, model the words yourself and ask students to repeat chorally and individually.

Highlight the pronunciation of *orange juice* /ˈɒrɪndʒ dʒuːs/, *vegetables* /ˈvedʒtəbəlz/, *fruit* /fruːt/ and *chocolate* /ˈtʃɒklət/. Point out that *vegetables* is three syllables, not four, and that *chocolate* is two syllables, not three.

┌─ **EXTRA IDEAS** ───────────────────────────┐

● If you have a class of complete beginners, consider teaching this vocabulary yourself at the beginning of the lesson. Prepare flashcards of the food and drink items and teach the words one by one. You can then use the matching activity in **1a** for practice.

● If you have a strong class, use **Vocabulary Plus** 3 Food and drink p169 (Instructions p163) in this lesson or give this worksheet to students for homework.

└──┘

2 **a** Give students one minute to remember all the words for food and drink in the photo. Students are not allowed to write anything down.

b Ask students to close their books. Put students into pairs. Students say all the words for food and drink in the photo they can remember. Alternatively, ask them to write down the words in their pairs.

Ask one pair to tell you all the words for food and drink they can remember and write them on the board. Ask other students to tell you any missing words until you have all 16 words from **1a**.

3 Focus students on pictures A–D. Students do the exercise on their own, then compare answers in pairs. Check answers with the class.

Check students understand the new verbs *like*, *love*, *eat* and *drink*. We suggest you treat these verbs as lexical items at this stage and avoid eliciting any negative sentences during the lesson. Note that the Present Simple is taught in units 4 and 5.

Also check students understand *a lot of*: *I drink a lot of coffee.*, *I eat a lot of rice.*, etc.

2A 3D 4C

4 [CD1► 70] [PRONUNCIATION] Play the recording. Students listen and practise the sentences in **3**. Highlight the vowel sound in *love* /lʌv/.

5 **a** Ask students to look at the photo of Fiona and her family in lesson 3B on SB p24. Ask the class what they remember about the family.

[CD1► 71] Focus students on the vocabulary box in **1a**. Play the recording (SB p109). Students listen and tick the food and drink that Fiona talks about. Students can compare answers in pairs. Check answers with the class.

coffee tea meat fish eggs pasta chocolate

b Give students time to read sentences 1–7. Play the recording again. Students listen and choose the correct words. Play the recording again if necessary.

c Students compare answers in pairs. Check answers with the class.

2 coffee 3 tea 4 fish 5 eggs 6 pasta 7 chocolate

6 **a** Pre-teach the vocabulary in the box using pictures, translation, etc. Note that the aim of this box is to highlight which new words students need in order to understand the texts they are about to read.

Model and drill the words with the class. Note that the stress on *ice cream* can be on either word.

b Focus students on the photos and the texts. Students do the exercise on their own, then compare answers in pairs. Check answers with the class.

2 Ed and Mei 3 Zoe and Ed 4 Zoe and Ben
5 Mei and Ben 6 Ed and Mei 7 Zoe and Ben

7 **a** [CD1► 72] Play the recording. Students listen and underline all the food words.

b Students compare answers in pairs. Check answers with the class.

ZOE	coffee, water, rice, pasta, salads, vegetables, cheese, ice cream
ED	coffee, milk, chocolate biscuits, meat, fish, fruit, vegetables, bread, egg and tomato sandwiches
MEI	tea, coffee, rice, fish, vegetables, apples, oranges, cheese sandwiches, chocolate biscuits
BEN	fruit, vegetables, meat, fish, rice, pasta, salads, fruit juice, chocolate ice cream

8 **a** Students do the exercise on their own. While students are working, check their sentences for accuracy and help with any new vocabulary.

b Teach the phrase *Me too*. Students work in groups and take turns to say their sentences. Students say which of their partners' sentences are also true for them, for example: **A** *I love chocolate.* **B** *Me too.* Finally, ask each group to tell the class about food and drink they love, like, etc., for example: *Karla and I love chocolate.*

┌─ **FURTHER PRACTICE** ──────────────────────┐

[Ph] **Class Activity** 3D From start to finish p136 (Instructions p117)

[Ph] **Vocabulary Plus** 3 Food and drink p169 (Instructions p163)

Extra Practice 3 SB p99

Self-study DVD-ROM Lesson 3D

Workbook Lesson 3D p17

Workbook Reading and Writing Portfolio 3 p56–p57

[Ph] **Progress Test** 3 p182

└──┘

HELP WITH PRONUNCIATION /ɒ/ and /ʌ/

1 **CD1** 73 Focus students on the phonemes /ɒ/ and /ʌ/, the pictures and the words. Play the recording. Students listen to the sounds and the words. Point out that *o* in *coffee* is pronounced with an /ɒ/ sound and *u* in *umbrella* is pronounced with an /ʌ/ sound.

Play the recording again. Students listen and practise. If students have problems producing the sounds, help them with the mouth position for each sound.

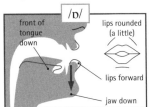
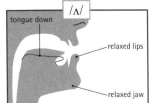

Point out that we round the lips when we say /ɒ/. Also highlight that the lips are relaxed when we say /ʌ/.

2 Focus students on the boxes. Point out that the pink vowels are pronounced /ɒ/ and the blue vowels are pronounced /ʌ/.

CD1 74 Play the recording. Students listen and notice how we say the pink and blue vowels.

Play the recording again. Students listen and practise.

3 **a** Go through the example with the class. Students do the exercise in pairs. Ask students to cover the words in **2** before they begin. Encourage students to say all the words when comparing answers.

b **CD1** 75 Play the recording. Students listen and check their answers.

Note that all the words with an /ɒ/ sound are said by a man and all the words with an /ʌ/ sound are said by a woman.

Play the recording again. Students listen and practise the words. Check they pronounce the vowels in bold correctly.

Finally, ask each student to say one group of three words for the class. If necessary, correct their pronunciation and ask them to say the words again.

2 doctor **3** country **4** love **5** number **6** husband

> **EXTRA IDEA**
>
> • Remind students that there is a chart of the phonemic symbols on SB p134 and that they can practise the *Help with Pronunciation* drills at home on the Self-study DVD-ROM.

---

continue2learn

Focus students on the **continue2learn** section on SB p29. See p33 of this book for ideas on how to use this section in class.

Extra Practice 3 SB p99

See p34 for ideas on how to use this section in class.

3A
1 **2** small; big **3** cold; hot **4** ugly; beautiful
   5 cheap; expensive **6** good; bad
2 **2** 's **3** isn't / 's not **4** is **5** are **6** 're **7** are **8** aren't
3a **2** Is the school cheap? **3** Is the teacher very good? **4** Are the students friendly?
   5 Where's the hotel? **6** Are the rooms very big?
3b **2** No, it isn't. / No, it's not. **3** Yes, she is.
   4 Yes, they are. **5** It's near the school.
   6 No, they aren't. / No, they're not.

3B
4 **2** sister **3** grandfather **4** father **5** mother
   6 grandmother **7** son **8** husband **9** daughter
   10 parents
5 **2** his **3** their **4** She; my **5** he **6** our **7** they
   8 We; his

3C
6 **2** coffee **3** sandwich **4** Eat **5** take **6** Take
   7 else **8** all **9** Thank **10** much **11** welcome

3D
7a **2** fruit **3** eggs **4** fish **5** vegetables **6** rice
   7 chocolate **8** pasta **9** tea **10** meat **11** bread
   12 sugar

Progress Portfolio 3

See p34 for ideas on how to use this section in class.

Vocabulary phrases with *like, have, live, work, study*

Grammar Present Simple (*I, you, we, they*): positive and negative

Phrases with *like, have, live, work, study*

1 a Focus students on the vocabulary box, the pictures and the example. Point out that *like* and *football* go together to make the phrase *like football*. Check students understand the other verbs (*have, live, work, study*) if necessary.

Students do the exercise on their own or in pairs. Early finishers can check their answers in Language Summary 4 **VOCABULARY 4.1** ▶ SB p120.

Check answers with the class. Check students understand all the new vocabulary, including the verbs, referring to the pictures if necessary. Point out that collocations (words that go together) are very important for students learning English and encourage students to make a note of other collocations when they meet them.

Point out that we can say *in the centre of the city* or *in the city centre*. However, when we use the name of the city, we say *I live in the centre of London.* not ~~*I live in London centre*~~.

Highlight the prepositions in the phrases *work for a (Spanish) company* and *work in (an office)*.

Also use the **TIP** to highlight that we say *a flat* in British English and *an apartment* in American English.

You can also teach students *live in a (big/small) house* and *work at home* (not ~~*work in my house*~~). Highlight that we use *a house* to refer to the type of building, whereas we use *home* to refer to the place where you live.

b like **rock music**
c have **two children**
d have **a car**
e live **in a flat**
f live **in the centre of the city**
g work **for a Spanish company**
h work **in an office**
i study **English**
j study **languages**

b **CD2** **1** **PRONUNCIATION** Play the recording. Students listen and practise the phrases. Highlight the pronunciation of *work* /wɜːk/, *company* /ˈkʌmpəni/, *office* /ˈɒfɪs/ and *languages* /ˈlæŋɡwɪdʒɪz/. Repeat the drill if necessary.

Life in Mexico

2 a **CD2** **2** Focus students on the photo of Carmen and the speech bubble. Play the recording. Students listen, read and find out who Cesar, Marissa and Teresa are.
Check answers with the class.

Cesar is Carmen's husband. Marissa and Teresa are Carmen and Cesar's daughters.

b Students do the exercise on their own.

c Students compare answers in pairs. Check answers with the class.

2 Mexican **3** Mérida **4** three
5 is **6** are **7** Italian

HELP WITH GRAMMAR Present Simple (*I, you, we, they*): positive and negative

3 a Students do the exercise on their own. Check answers with the class.

- **Answers** You <u>study</u> English. We <u>live</u> in a very nice flat. They <u>like</u> rock music.
- Point out that these verbs are in the Present Simple.
- Use the four example sentences to highlight that the Present Simple positive is the same for *I, you, we* and *they* (and is the same as the infinitive form). However, we suggest you simply call the infinitive 'the verb' at this level to avoid overloading students with grammatical terms.

b ✍ Draw the table on the board and write in the example sentences. Note that in grammar tables the auxiliary verbs are shown in blue and the main verbs are shown in pink. This approach, which is used throughout the Student's Book, helps visual learners to understand the word order of positive sentences, negatives and question forms in English. Go through the following points with the class.

- Use the examples to highlight the word order: *I/you/we/they* + *don't* + verb + ...
- Point out that *don't* is the contracted form of *do not* and that we usually use this form when writing and speaking.
- Establish that the auxiliary *do* has no meaning, but is used to make the negative form of the Present Simple with *I/you/we/they*.
- Also point out that we use *don't* in negatives with *I*, *you*, *we* and *they* for all verbs except *be*. ✍ If necessary, write these sentences on the board for comparison: *I'm not a teacher.* *You aren't French.* *We aren't in this class.* *They aren't from the USA.*
- With a strong class you can teach students that *I*, *you*, *we* and *they* in the example sentences are called 'the subject', and that in positive sentences the subject always comes before the verb.

c Students do the exercise on their own. Check answers with the class.

- Focus students on the table on the board. Elicit which words in sentences 1 and 2 from **3c** go in each column and complete the table (see the table in GRAMMAR 4.1 ▸ SB p121).
- Use the sentences in the table to check students understand the word order in Present Simple negatives.

4 CD2 ▸ 3 PRONUNCIATION Play the recording. Students listen and practise the sentences in **3**. Check that students pronounce *don't* /dəʊnt/ correctly in each sentence. Repeat the drill if necessary.

Life in the USA

5 **a** Focus students on the photo of Richard and the speech bubble. Check students understand that a (+) sign indicates a positive verb form and a (−) sign indicates a negative verb form. Students do the exercise on their own, then compare answers in pairs.

b CD2 ▸ 4 Play the recording. Students listen and check their answers. Check answers with the class.

> 2 live 3 have 4 don't live 5 live 6 work
> 7 like 8 don't like 9 study 10 like

┌─ EXTRA IDEA ─┐

- Put students into pairs, A and B. Ask student As to look at the text about Carmen and student Bs to look at the text about Richard. Students underline all the phrases from **1a** they can find in their texts. Students then work with their partner, swap books and check their partner's answers.

6 **a** Check students understand what to do by focusing on the example and asking individual students whether the positive or negative sentence is true for them.
Students do the exercise on their own.

b Students work in pairs and take turns to say their sentences to each other. Students also decide how many of their true sentences are the same.
Ask each pair to tell the class two sentences that are true for both students, for example, *We don't work in an office.*, *We like Italian food.*, etc.

┌───┐

Get ready ... Get it right!

7 Focus students on the examples and check they remember *true* and *false*.
Students do the exercise on their own. While they are working, check their sentences for accuracy and help with any new vocabulary.

┌─ EXTRA IDEA ─┐

- ✍ Demonstrate the activity by writing three true and three false sentences about you on the board, using language from **1a**. Students work in pairs and guess which sentences are false. Students can then do **7** on their own.

8 Drill the sentences in the speech bubbles to remind students of the language they need to do the exercise.
Put students into new pairs, A and B. Student As say their sentences from **7**. Student Bs decide if they are true or false. When they have finished, students change roles.
At the end of the activity, ask if any students guessed all six of their partner's sentences correctly.
Finally, ask each student to tell the class one of their partner's true sentences.

└───┘

┌─ WRITING ─┐

Students write a paragraph about themselves using the language from the lesson. Ask students to include a photo of themselves. The students' work can be collected in next class and put up around the room for other students to read.

┌─ FURTHER PRACTICE ─┐

Extra Practice 4A SB p100
Self-study DVD-ROM Lesson 4A
Workbook Lesson 4A p18

QUICK REVIEW This activity reviews the Present Simple positive and negative. ✏ Write the prompts (*I have …* , *I don't have …* , etc.) on the board. Students work on their own and write four sentences about themselves. Put students into pairs. Students say their sentences to their partner and decide if any are the same, as shown in the example.

Free time activities

1 **a** Teach the phrase *free time activities* (things you do when you're not working or studying). Point out that the singular of *activities* is *an activity*.
Students do the exercise in pairs. Alternatively, use the pictures to teach the phrases yourself, then use the matching activity for practice. Check answers with the class.
Highlight the different phrases with *go*: **go to** *concerts*, **go to** *the cinema*, **go** *shopping*, **go out** *with friends*. Point out *the* in go to **the** *cinema* (not ~~go to cinema~~).
Also highlight the capital letters in *TV* and *DVD* and point out that *TV* stands for *television*.
Point out that we can say *video games* or *computer games*. You can also tell students that we can say *eat out* or *go out to eat*.

> go to the cinema 3; go shopping 2; go out with friends 4; play tennis 6; watch TV or DVDs 1; play video games 8; eat out 5

b **CD2** 5 **PRONUNCIATION** Play the recording. Students listen and practise. Check that students stress the phrases correctly. Note that only the main stress in words and phrases is shown in vocabulary boxes and the Language Summaries.
Play the recording again, pausing after each phrase for students to repeat individually.

┌─ **EXTRA IDEA** ─────────────────────
│
│ • If you have a strong class, consider using **Vocabulary Plus** 4 Free time activities p170 (Instructions p163) at this stage of the lesson.
│
└────────────────────────────────────

2 **a** Focus students on the example sentences. Point out the preposition *in* in the first sentence (*I play tennis **in** my free time.*).
Use the second sentence to teach the meaning of *a lot* (*I watch TV **a lot**.*).
Students work on their own and write four sentences about their free time using phrases from the lesson. Before they begin, tell the class that these sentences can be positive or negative (*I **don't go** to concerts.*).

b Students work in pairs and take turns to say their sentences, making a note of any that are the same. Ask each pair to tell the class any sentences that are the same for both students.

An online interview

3 **a** Teach students the words in the vocabulary box, using pictures, mime, synonyms or translation. Note that the aim of this box is to highlight which new words students need in order to understand the text they are about to read.

b Focus students on the web page on SB p33 and the photo of rock band Big Noise. Tell the class that the woman's name is Ruby Connor and the man on the far right with the red guitar strap is her brother, Phil. **CD2** 6 Play the recording. Students listen, read and find three things that Ruby and Phil do in their free time. Check answers with the class.

> listen to (a lot of rock) music, go out with friends (a lot), watch (a lot of) DVDs, go to concerts, eat out (a lot)

4 **a** Students do the exercise on their own, as shown in the example.

b Students compare answers in pairs. Check answers with the class.

> 2F 3T 4T 5F 6F 7F 8T

HELP WITH GRAMMAR Present Simple (*I, you, we, they*): questions and short answers

5 **a** ✏ Draw the table on the board and write in the example questions. Go through the following points with the class.

• Use the examples to highlight the word order: question word + *do* + *I/you/we/they* + verb + … .
• Establish that the auxiliary *do* has no meaning, but is used to make the question form of the Present Simple with *I*, *you*, *we* and *they*.
• Also point out that we use the auxiliary *do* with all verbs except *be*. ✏ If necessary, write the following questions with *be* on the board for comparison: *Where am I? Where are **you** from? Where are **we**? Where are **they** from?*.

b Students do the exercise on their own. Check answers with the class.

• Focus students on the table on the board. ✏ Elicit which words in questions 1 and 2 from **5b** go in each column and complete the table (see the table in **GRAMMAR 4.2** SB p121).

- Use these questions to further highlight the word order in *Wh-* questions. Point out that Present Simple questions are the same for *I*, *you*, *we* and *they*.
- Use the second and fourth questions in the table to highlight that we sometimes use a noun after *What* ... : *What music do you like?*, *What food do you like?*, etc.
- You can also teach students the question *What do you do?* = *What's your job?*: **A** *What do you do?* **B** *I'm a doctor.*

c Students do the exercise on their own or in pairs. Check answers with the class.

- **Answers Do** you like London? Yes, I do. No, I **don't**. **Do** you go to concerts? Yes, we **do**. No, we **don't**. **Do** they like Chinese food? Yes, they **do**. No, they **don't**.
- Highlight the word order in the *yes/no* questions: *Do + I/you/we/they* + verb + ...
- Point out that we use *do* or *don't* in the short answers, but we don't repeat the verb: *Yes, I do.* not ~~Yes, I like.~~ or ~~Yes, I do like.~~

6 **a** Go through the example with the class. Point out that all the questions are about Ruby and Phil Connor.

Students do the exercise on their own.

Check answers with the class. You can point out that in question 4 *do* is both the auxiliary and the main verb.

2 Do ... have 3 Do ... like 4 do ... do 5 Do ... go 6 Do ... go 7 Do ... like 8 Do ... eat

b Students do the exercise in pairs. You can ask students to cover the interview before they begin. Remind students to use the correct short answers where appropriate. They can check their answers on the web page about Ruby and Phil Connor if necessary. Check answers with the class.

1 In Camden, in London. 2 No, they don't. 3 No, they don't. 4 They listen to music, go out with friends, watch DVDs, go to concerts and eat out. 5 Yes, they do. 6 No, they don't. 7 Yes, they do. 8 Yes, they do.

HELP WITH LISTENING
Questions with *do you*

This *Help with Listening* section helps students to understand Present Simple questions with *do you* ... ?.

7 **a** **CD2 7** Focus students on sentences 1–4. Play the recording. Students listen, read and notice how we say *do you* in Present Simple questions.

Highlight the pronunciation of *do you* /dəjə/ and point out that these words are usually pronounced in their weak forms in natural spoken English.

While it is not essential for students at this level to use the weak form themselves, it is important that they understand it when they are asked questions in the Present Simple.

Note that *do you* can also be pronounced /djə/ or /dʒə/, but we rarely use the strong form /du: ju:/. The alternative weak form /djə/ is practised in **face2face** Second edition Elementary.

b **CD2 8** Play the recording (SB p109). Students listen and write the questions. Play the recording again if necessary, pausing after each sentence to give students time to write.

c Students compare questions in pairs and check if they are the same.

Check answers by eliciting each question and writing it on the board. You can leave these questions on the board so that they can be used in **8b**.

Encourage students to use weak forms when speaking and highlight them when appropriate in future classes.

1 Do you go to the cinema? 2 What food do you like? 3 Where do you go shopping? 4 Do you play video games?

8 **a** **CD2 9** **PRONUNCIATION** Play the recording (SB p109). Students listen and practise. Encourage students to copy the pronunciation of *do you*. Play the recording again, pausing after each question and short answer for students to repeat individually.

b Put students into pairs, student A and student B. Student As ask the questions in **7a**. Student Bs ask the questions in **7b** that are on the board. Remind students to give their own answers.

Avoid doing any whole-class feedback at the end of the activity, as this would require *he* and *she* forms of the Present Simple. These forms are taught in unit 5.

Get ready ... Get it right!

9 Put students into new pairs, student A and student B. If possible, put students in pairs with somebody they don't know very well.

Student As turn to SB p86 and student Bs turn to SB p91. Check they are all looking at the correct exercise.

a Focus students on the examples. Students do the exercise on their own.

Avoid checking the questions with the whole class so that students don't hear the questions that they are about to be asked.

Student A 2 Do you watch a lot of DVDs? 3 Do you live in a house or a flat? 4 Do you like Italian food? 5 Do you have an old computer?
Student B b Do you play tennis or football? c Do you work in an office? d Do you like Chinese food? e Do you have a new mobile phone?

b Students work with their partner. Student As ask questions 1–5. Remind student Bs to use *Yes, I do.* or *No, I don't.* when answering the questions.

c Students swap roles so that student B asks questions a–e.

Again, avoid doing any class feedback on the answers themselves, as this would require students to use *he* and *she* forms of the Present Simple. Instead, students can ask you one question each. Give your own answers if possible.

> **EXTRA IDEA**
>
> • 🖊 After students have written the questions in **a**, they guess whether their partner is going to answer *yes* or *no* to each question. When students ask their questions in **b** and **c**, they check how many of their guesses are correct. At the end of the activity, ask if any students guessed all five answers correctly.

> **WRITING**
>
> Students imagine they are famous rock stars and write a short interview with a journalist, similar to the Big Noise interview on SB p33. They can add photos or illustrations if they wish.

> **FURTHER PRACTICE**
>
> **Ph** **Class Activity** 4B Find two people p137 (Instructions p118)
>
> **Ph** **Vocabulary Plus** 4 Free time activities p170 (Instructions p163)
>
> **Extra Practice** 4B SB p100
> **Self-study DVD-ROM** Lesson 4B
> **Workbook** Lesson 4B p19

▷ REAL
4C WORLD ▷ Buying things
Student's Book p34–p35

Vocabulary things to buy; *this, that, these, those*
Real World in a shop

QUICK REVIEW This activity reviews Present Simple *yes/no* questions with *you*. Check students remember the meaning of *both*. Students do the activity in pairs, as shown in the examples. At the end of the activity, ask a few pairs to tell the class one or two things they both do.

Things to buy

1 **a** Focus students on pictures 1–10. Students do the exercise in pairs. Check answers with the class. Check students understand *a birthday* and teach the phrase *Happy birthday!* as shown on the card (picture 7).

a newspaper **4**; a map **3**; a postcard **5**; a birthday card **7**; a box of chocolates **10**; tissues **2**; sweets **9**; batteries **8**; chewing gum **6**

> **EXTRA IDEA**
>
> • If you have a class of complete beginners, consider teaching these words yourself by bringing the items to the class. Hold up each item in turn and tell students the word in English. You can then use the matching activity in **1a** for practice.

b **CD2 ▶ 10** **PRONUNCIATION** Play the recording. Students listen and practise. Check they stress the words correctly and highlight the pronunciation of *birthday* /ˈbɜːθdeɪ/, *chocolates* /ˈtʃɒkləts/ and *tissues* /ˈtɪʃuːz/.

Point out that *batteries* /ˈbætriz/ is usually pronounced as two syllables, not three. Note that the stress on *magazine* can also be on the first syllable. Point out that the plural of *box* is *boxes* and that the singular of *batteries* is *a battery*.

c Students do the activity in pairs.

HELP WITH VOCABULARY
this, that, these, those

2 Focus students on photos A–D and the *How much … ?* questions in the speech bubbles. Ask where the people are (in a shop). Check students remember *a customer* and *an assistant*. Point out that the things each customer wants to buy are highlighted with a red arrow on the photos.

Students work on their own or in pairs and write the words in bold in the questions in the table.

🖊 While they are working, draw the blank table on the board.

Check answers with the class and highlight the following points.

- Focus students on the table on the board. Check students understand *here* and *there*. Elicit which words go in each column and complete the table.

	here ↓	there →
singular	this	that
plural	these	those

- Point out that we use *this/these* for something close to us and *that/those* for something further away.
- Check students understand that we use *this/that* for singular nouns and *these/those* for plural nouns.
- Point out that *this*, *that*, *these* and *those* go before a noun: *How much is **this** map?*, ***These** bags are beautiful.*, etc.

3 | CD2 ▶ 11 | PRONUNCIATION | Focus students on the example drill. Play the recording (SB p109). Students listen and practise. Highlight the /ɪ/ sound in *this* /ðɪs/ and the /iː/ sound in *these* /ðiːz/, which students studied in the *Help with Pronunciation* section in unit 2. Repeat the drill if necessary.

4 | Students do the exercise on their own, then compare answers in pairs. Check answers with the class.

1 these **2** That **3** those **4** this

Anything else?

5 | **a** Ask students to close their books. Tell the class that they are going to watch or listen to two conversations in a shop.

VIDEO ▶ 4 CD2 ▶ 12 Play the video or audio recording. Students listen and write down what the two customers buy. Note that all the Real World videos can be found on the **Teacher's DVD** at the back of this book.

Students can compare answers in pairs. Check answers with the class.

Customer 1 a map (of London), batteries, sweets
Customer 2 two birthday cards, a big box of chocolates

b Ask students to open their books again. Give students time to read the conversations. Avoid dealing with any new language at this stage.

Play the video or audio recording again. Students watch or listen and write the prices in the conversations.

Students compare answers in pairs. Check answers with the class.

1 £5.75 **2** £2.99
3 £9.34 **4** £1.79
5 £8.75 **6** £12.33

REAL WORLD In a shop

6 | **a** Focus students on the conversations. Point out that the language in brackets can change, depending on what the customer buys.

Students do the exercise on their own by referring to the conversations in **5b**.

Check answers with the class.

- **Answers 2** much **3** have **4** else **5** all **6** are **7** lot
- Check students understand the new words and phrases: *Yes, they're over there.*, *They're (£1.79) each.* and *Here you are.*
- Point out that we say *Thanks a lot.* or *Thanks very much.* Also remind students of other ways to say thank you: *Thanks.*, *Thank you.* and *Thank you very much.* You can point out that *Thanks* is more informal than *Thank you.*

b Students do the exercise on their own. Check answers with the class.

- **Answers 1** Do you have any (maps of London)? **2** Can I have (these cards and that box of chocolates), please? **3** How much is (this map)? How much are (these birthday cards)?
- Check students understand the phrases *Do you have … ?*, *Can I have … ?* and *How much … ?*. Point out that we use *Can I have … ?* to ask for things.
- We suggest that at this stage of the course you teach *any* as part of the phrase *Do you have any … ?* and point out that *any* is followed by a plural noun (*maps*, etc.). Note that *a/an*, *some* and *any* are studied in unit 6.

7 | CD2 ▶ 13 | PRONUNCIATION | Play the recording (SB p109). Students listen and practise the sentences in the flow chart in **6a**. Encourage students to copy the polite intonation and highlight the pronunciation of *London* /ˈlʌndən/. If necessary, play the recording again, pausing after each sentence for students to repeat individually.

8 | Students practise the conversations in **5b** in pairs, taking turns to be the customer. Encourage the customers to use polite intonation when asking for things. While they are working, monitor and correct students' pronunciation as necessary.

⌐ EXTRA IDEA ⌐

- Ask each pair to choose one of the conversations from **5b**. Students decide who is the customer and who is the assistant. Students practise the conversation until they can remember it. Ask students to close their books and practise the conversation again. Ask two or three pairs to role-play their conversations for the class.

9 | Students work in the same pairs. Student As turn to SB p88 and student Bs turn to SB p93. Check they are all looking at the correct exercise.

a Pre-teach *spend* (*money*). Ask students to look at photos a–d. Allow students time to read the information about their roles and point out the prompts in the box.

Students role-play the conversation in their pairs. Student A in each pair starts the conversation by saying *Excuse me. Do you have any batteries?*.

b Students swap roles so that student B in each pair is the customer and student A is the sales assistant. Again, draw students' attention to the prompts in the box before they begin.

At the end of the activity, ask students how much they spent (student A: £17.90, student B: £12.50).

10 a Students do the activity in new pairs. Encourage students to use vocabulary from **1a** and phrases from **6a** in their conversations. While they are working, check their conversations for accuracy and correct any mistakes you hear.

b Students practise their conversations until they have memorised them.

c Put two pairs together so that they are working in groups of four. Pairs then take turns to role-play their conversations. Students listen to the other pair's conversation and find out what the customer buys and how much he or she spends. Students can ask the other pair to repeat the conversation if necessary. Finally, ask two or three pairs to role-play their conversations for the class.

> **FURTHER PRACTICE**
>
> **Ph** **Class Activity** 4C Shopping bingo p138 (Instructions p118)
> **Extra Practice** 4C SB p100
> **Self-study DVD-ROM** Lesson 4C
> **Workbook** Lesson 4C p21

VOCABULARY
4D AND SKILLS ▷ What time is it?
Student's Book p36–p37

Vocabulary days of the week; time words
Real World telling the time; talking about the time
Skills Reading and Listening: days and times

QUICK REVIEW This activity reviews things to buy. Students do the first part of the activity on their own. They can write things that are in the shop in lesson 4C, or their own ideas. Put students into pairs. Students complete the activity with their partner.

1 a **CD2 ▷ 14** **PRONUNCIATION** Focus students on the days of the week. Play the recording. Students listen and practise. Alternatively, model and drill the days yourself. Point out that *Wednesday* /ˈwenzdeɪ/ is two syllables, not three. Also point out that the stress on each day is on the first syllable.

b Students do the exercise in pairs, as shown in the speech bubbles.

c Students do the exercise in the same pairs. Check answers with the class. Model and drill *today*, *tomorrow* and *the weekend*. Note that *weekend* can be stressed on either the first or the second syllable.

2 a Students do the exercise in pairs. Alternatively, teach the words yourself first and use this exercise for practice.

b **CD2 ▷ 15** Play the recording. Students listen and check their answers.
PRONUNCIATION Play the recording again. Students listen and practise. Highlight the pronunciation of *minute* /ˈmɪnɪt/ and the silent *h* in *hour* /aʊə/.
Teach students that 30 minutes = *half an hour*, 15 minutes = *quarter of an hour* and 18 months = *a year and a half*.

You can also point out that we say *two and a half hours* not ~~two hours and a half~~.

2 a minute **3** an hour **4** a day **5** a week **6** a month

c Students do the exercise on their own before checking in pairs. Check answers with the class.

b minutes **c** hours **d** week **e** year **f** months

3 a Pre-teach *time* and *a clock*. You can also teach students the difference between *a clock* and *a watch*. Students do the exercise in pairs. Check answers with the class. Point out that we can say *quarter past/to …* or *a quarter past/to …* .

quarter to seven **D**; quarter past six **B**; six o'clock **A**

b Tell students that we can say times in two ways. Students do the exercise with their partner. Check answers with the class.
Also highlight that we can say *(a) quarter past (six)* or *(six) fifteen*, but not ~~fifteen past (six)~~.

six thirty **C**; six forty-five **D**; six fifteen **B**

> **EXTRA IDEA**
>
> • If you have a class of complete beginners, consider teaching the time yourself first by using a large clock with movable hands. ✎ Alternatively, draw clock faces on the board. You can then use **3** and **4** for practice.

4 Students do the exercise on their own or in pairs. Check answers with the class.

Tell students that we can also say these times as *six fifteen*, *six twenty-five*, etc. Although this alternative form is probably easier for students to use than the *past/to* form, it is important that they understand both ways of telling the time when they hear them.

Point out that we say *six oh five* for 6.05, not ~~six five~~ or ~~six zero five~~.

You can also highlight that in American English 6.05 = *five after six*, 6.10 = *ten after six*, etc.

2a 3h 4b 5g 6f 7e 8d

5 **CD2** 16 **PRONUNCIATION** Play the recording. Students listen and practise the times in **3a** and **4**. Note that the times are recorded in logical order (*six o'clock*, *five past six*, etc.).

Highlight the pronunciation of *quarter* /ˈkɔːtə/ and *half* /hɑːf/. Also highlight that we don't pronounce the *t* in *five past* /pɑːs/ *six*, etc., and that we use the weak form of *to* in *five to* /tə/ *six*, etc.

Repeat the drill if necessary, pausing after each time for students to repeat individually.

6 **a** **CD2** 17 Tell students that they are going to listen to five conversations. Play the recording (SB p109). Students listen and write the times.

b Students compare answers in pairs. Play the recording again, pausing after each conversation to check students' answers.

1 twenty to three 2 half past eight 3 six o'clock
4 quarter to twelve 5 two thirty

7 **a** Focus students on pictures 1 and 2. Students do the exercise on their own.

b **CD2** 18 Play the recording. Students listen and check their answers.
PRONUNCIATION Play the recording again, pausing after each sentence for students to repeat chorally and individually. Encourage students to copy the polite intonation in the questions.

Check students understand that we use *What time is it, please?* to ask the time. Also teach and drill the alternative question *What's the time, please?*, etc.

Also point out that we use *at* for times: *It's **at** half past eight*.

Teach students that we use *a.m.* for times 0.00–12.00 and *p.m.* for times 12.00–24.00. Also point out that *a.m.* and *p.m.* are sometimes written without the full stops (*am, pm*).

1 **WOMAN** Excuse me. **What** time is **it**, please?
  MAN It's twenty **to** three.
2 **WOMAN** What **time** is your English class?
  MAN It's **at half** past eight.

8 Put students into new pairs, student A and student B. Student As turn to SB p89 and student Bs turn to SB p94. Check they are all looking at the correct exercise.

a Focus students on the film times. Use the speech bubbles to teach *What time is ... on?* and the response *It's on at ...* . You can point out that we also use these phrases to talk about TV programmes. Students take turns to ask the times of the films and fill in the gaps on the timetable. Students are not allowed to look at their partner's book. While they are working, monitor and correct students' pronunciation if necessary.

b Students compare times with their partner and check that they are correct.

9 **a** Teach the words in the box, using examples, drawings, translation, etc. Note that the aim of this box is to highlight which new words students need in order to understand the text they are about to read.
Model and drill the words with the class, highlighting the pronunciation of *Europe* /ˈjʊərəp/ and *flight* /flaɪt/.

b Students read the text about days and times around the world and choose the correct answers.

c Students compare answers in pairs.

d **CD2** 19 Play the recording. Students listen and check their answers. Check answers with the class. Finally, ask the class how many answers they got right.

b Friday and Saturday c 32 d morning
e afternoon f Friday 13th g Tuesday 13th
h 7 hours i 11½ hours j Sundays
k Tuesdays l Thursdays

FURTHER PRACTICE

Ph **Class Activity** 4D Time dominoes p139
(Instructions p118)
Extra Practice 4 SB p100
Self-study DVD-ROM Lesson 4D
Workbook Lesson 4D p22
Workbook Reading and Writing Portfolio 4 p58–p59
Ph **Progress Test** 4 p183

HELP WITH PRONUNCIATION /θ/ and /ð/

1 Tell students that there are two different ways to pronounce *th*. Focus students on the phonemes /θ/ and /ð/, the pictures and the words.

CD2 20 Play the recording. Students listen to the sounds and the words. Point out that *th* in *three* is pronounced with a /θ/ sound and *th* in *mother* is pronounced with a /ð/ sound.

Play the recording again. Students listen and practise. If students are having problems producing the sounds, help them with the mouth position for each sound.

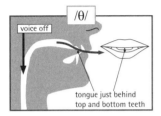 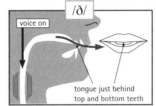

Point out that the mouth position is the same for both sounds, with the tip of tongue just between the top and bottom teeth. However, when we say the /θ/ sound, there is no voice from the throat and you can feel the air from your mouth on your hand. When we say the /ð/ sound, there is voice from the throat.

You can ask your students to place their fingers and thumb on their throats. When they say the /ð/ sound, they will feel vibration in the throat.

Another useful tip is to ask them to place their index finger on their lips, as if they were making a *shhh* sound. When saying both *th* sounds, the tip of the tongue should touch the side of the finger.

2 **CD2 21** Focus students on the boxes. Play the recording. Students listen and notice how we say *th* in both sets of words.

Play the recording again. Students listen and practise.

3 **a** **CD2 22** Play the recording. Students listen and read the sentences.

Play the recording again. Students listen and practise. Repeat the drill if necessary, pausing after each sentence for students to repeat chorally and individually.

b Students practise the sentences in pairs.

Finally, ask students to say the sentences for the class. If necessary, correct their pronunciation and ask them to say the sentences again.

▶ continue2learn

Focus students on the **continue2learn** section on SB p37. See p33 of this book for ideas on how to use this section in class.

Extra Practice 4 SB p100

See p34 for ideas on how to use this section in class.

4A

1 2 study 3 work 4 have 5 like 6 study 7 live 8 have 9 live 10 work

2 2 You don't like Mexican food. 3 I don't have a new phone. 4 I'm not from the USA. 5 We aren't musicians. / We're not musicians. 6 We don't live in Australia. 7 Tim and Joe aren't brothers. 8 They don't work in London. 9 She isn't / She's not a sales assistant.

4B

3 go shopping; watch DVDs; play video games; eat out; watch TV; go to the cinema; go out with friends; play tennis

4 2 Do you go to concerts? 3 What music do they like? 4 Where do you live? 5 Do they watch TV a lot? 6 Do you like Chinese food? 7 Do we have a class today? 8 What do you do in your free time?

4C

5 2 a map 3 sweets 4 batteries 5 a magazine 6 a birthday card 7 chewing gum 8 tissues 9 a box of chocolates

6 2 Do 3 they're 4 are 5 They're 6 these 7 else 8 this 9 that's 10 Here 11 Thanks

4D

7 Sunday 7; Thursday 4; Saturday 6; Friday 5; Tuesday 2; Wednesday 3

8 b twenty to four c quarter past seven d half past one e quarter to five f nine o'clock

Progress Portfolio 4

See p34 for ideas on how to use this section in class.

5A ▶ A typical day
Student's Book p38–p39

Vocabulary daily routines
Grammar Present Simple (*he, she, it*):
positive and negative

morning	have breakfast, leave home, start work
afternoon	have lunch, finish work, (get home)
evening	get home, have dinner, (go to bed)
night	go to bed, sleep

Daily routines

1 a Focus students on pictures 1–10 of Carol's routine. Use the pictures to teach the phrase *daily routine* /ˈdeɪli ruːˈtiːn/.

Students do the exercise on their own or in pairs. Early finishers can check their answers in Language Summary 5 **VOCABULARY 5.1** ▶ SB p122. Check answers with the class.

Point out that we usually say *have breakfast/lunch/dinner* not **eat breakfast/lunch/dinner**.

Also point out that *get home* means *arrive home*, and that we say *go to bed* not ~~go to the bed~~.

Highlight that *work* in the phrases *start work* and *finish work* is a noun, not a verb.

If your students are at school or university, teach them the phrases *start/finish school, start/finish university* and *start/finish classes* as alternatives to *start/finish work*.

> go to bed **9**; leave home **3**; get home **7**;
> start work **4**; finish work **6**; have breakfast **2**;
> have lunch **5**; have dinner **8**; sleep **10**

> **EXTRA IDEA**
>
> • Teach the words/phrases in **1a** yourself first by telling the students about your daily routine. Alternatively, make your own flashcards of your daily routine and use these to teach the words/phrases. You can then use the matching activity in **1a** for practice.

b **CD2▶ 23** **PRONUNCIATION** Play the recording. Students listen and practise. Alternatively, model the sentences yourself and ask students to repeat chorally and individually. Highlight the pronunciation of *breakfast* /ˈbrekfəst/, *lunch* /lʌntʃ/ and *work* /wɜːk/. You can also compare the vowel sounds in *leave* /liːv/ and *live* /lɪv/, which students studied in the *Help with Pronunciation* section in unit 2.

Repeat the drill if necessary, pausing after each phrase for students to repeat individually.

Note that only the main stress in each phrase is shown in vocabulary boxes and in the Language Summaries.

c Check students remember *morning, afternoon, evening* and *night*.

Students do the exercise in pairs. Check answers with the class. Note that some phrases may match with more than one time of day.

2 a Focus students on the speech bubbles. Remind students that we use *at* with times and use the first pair of speech bubbles to teach the phrase *at the same time*. Tell students to talk about their routine in the week, not at the weekend, and to make a note of things they both do at the same time.
Students do the activity in new pairs.

b Students tell the class things that they and their partner do at the same time, as in the speech bubble.

Carol's routine

3 a Pre-teach the words in the box using examples, board diagrams, translation, etc. Note that the aim of this box is to highlight which new words students need in order to understand the text they are about to read.

Model and drill the words with the class. Highlight the pronunciation of *university* /juːnɪˈvɜːsəti/ and point out the different stress patterns in *midday* and *midnight*.

b Focus students on pictures 1–10 on SB p38 and the photo of Carol on SB p39. Check students remember that the pictures are of Carol's routine. Students read the text and fill in the gaps with the correct times. Tell students to write the times in numbers, not words, as shown in the example.

c **CD2▶ 24** Play the recording. Students listen and check their answers. Check answers with the class.

> b 7.45 c 8.15 d 9.00 e 12.45 f 5.30 g 6.15 h 7.30

HELP WITH GRAMMAR Present Simple
(*he, she, it*): positive and negative

4 a ✎ Focus students on the four example sentences in the Student's Book or write them on the board. Point out that the verbs in blue are in the Present Simple. Ask students to complete the rule.
Check students understand that in Present Simple positive sentences with *he, she* and *it* we add *-s* or *-es* to the verb.

b Focus students on the table. Point out that the first column of the table shows the spelling rules for the *he, she, it* positive form of the Present Simple, and that the second column gives some examples.
Students do the exercise on their own by referring back to the verbs in bold in the text about Carol.
✎ While students are working, draw the table from **4b** on the board. Check answers with the class.

- • Focus students on the table on the board. Elicit which verbs go in each row and complete the table (see the table in **GRAMMAR 5.1** SB p123).
- • Go through the spelling rules with the class by asking students to tell you the endings on each verb in the second column. Underline these endings on the board.
- • Point out that *have* is irregular and that we say *has*, not ~~haves~~.
- • Use the examples and the context to highlight that we use the Present Simple to talk about daily routines.
- • Note that verbs ending in *-ss*, *-sh*, *-x* or *-zz* (*miss*, *wish*, *fix*, *buzz*, etc.) also add *-es* in the *he*, *she*, *it* form of the Present Simple. However, as students haven't met any of these verbs yet, we suggest that you highlight these *he*, *she*, *it* forms in future lessons when they occur.

c Focus students on the sentences in the table. Go through the following points with the class.

- • Use the sentences to highlight the word order: *he/she/it* + *doesn't* + verb + … .
- • Point out that *doesn't* is the contracted form of *does not* and that we usually use this form when writing and speaking.
- • Also highlight that there is no *-s* or *-es* on the main verb in the Present Simple negative: *She doesn't like mornings.* not ~~She doesn't likes mornings~~.
- • Use the **TIP** to highlight that the negative is the same for *he*, *she* and *it*: *He doesn't have a car. It doesn't start today.*
- • Also point out that we use *doesn't* in negatives with *he*, *she*, *it* for all verbs except *be*. If necessary, write these sentences on the board for comparison: *He isn't a doctor. She isn't Italian. It isn't expensive.*

5 **CD2 25** **PRONUNCIATION** Play the recording. Students listen and practise. Check that students pronounce *doesn't* /ˈdʌzənt/ correctly. Repeat the drill if necessary.

6 **a** Students do the exercise on their own, then compare answers in pairs.
 Check the answers by writing each verb on the board and then writing the *he*, *she*, *it* form next to it.

2 plays **3** starts **4** finishes **5** has **6** studies **7** loves **8** goes **9** eats **10** watches **11** drinks **12** reads

b **CD2 26** **PRONUNCIATION** Play the recording (SB p109). Students listen and practise. Note that students should repeat both the verb and its *he*, *she*, *it* form together (*like*, *likes*, etc.), not separately. Ask students which *he*, *she*, *it* forms have the sound /ɪz/ at the end (*finishes* /ˈfɪnɪʃɪz/, *studies* /ˈstʌdɪz/, *watches* /ˈwɒtʃɪz/). Highlight the endings of these words on the board. Repeat the drill if necessary.

Tom's routine

7 **a** Focus students on the photo of Tom. Ask the class who he is (Carol's brother). Students do the exercise on their own. Early finishers can compare answers in pairs.

b **CD2 27** Play the recording. Students listen and check their answers. Check answers with the class. Highlight that answer 14 is a plural negative form, and that answers 15 and 16 are plural positive forms, therefore do not end in *-s* or *-es*.
Ask students what Carol and Tom do on Mondays.

2 doesn't work **3** gets up **4** doesn't have **5** has **6** goes **7** leaves **8** starts **9** finishes **10** doesn't eat **11** has **12** gets **13** watches **14** don't work **15** have **16** talk
On Mondays Carol and Tom have lunch together and talk about the week.

EXTRA IDEA
- • Put students into pairs, student A and student B. Student As write two true and two false sentences about Carol. Student Bs write two true and two false sentences about Tom. Ask students to close their books. Students take turns to say their sentences to each other. Students say if their partner's sentences are true or false.

Get ready … Get it right!

8 Put students into new pairs, student A and student B. Student As turn to SB p89 and student Bs turn to SB p94. Check they are all looking at the correct exercise.

a Focus students on column A of the table. Students do the exercise on their own, as in the example.
If necessary, check the answers with the class. Only check the words they need to fill in the gaps, so that students don't hear the questions they are about to be asked.

Student A **2** Do, watch **3** Do, have **4** Do, drink **5** Do, sleep
Student B **b** Do, have **c** Do, go **d** Do, work **e** Do, eat

b Students work with their partners. Student As ask questions 1–5 and put a tick or a cross in column B of the table. Remind student Bs to use short answers (*Yes, I do.* and *No, I don't.*). Student Bs can also give more information if possible.

c Students swap roles so that student B in each pair is asking his/her partner questions a–e. Remind student Bs to put ticks and crosses in column B of the table and student As to use short answers.

d Student As work in pairs with another student A and student Bs work in pairs with another student B. Students take turns to tell their new partner about their partner in **b** and **c**. Check that students use the *he, she, it* forms of the verbs.

Finally, ask each student to tell the class one or two things about their first partner.

FURTHER PRACTICE

Ph **Class Activity** 5A My partner's life p140 (Instructions p119)
Extra Practice 5A SB p101
Self-study DVD-ROM Lesson 5A
Workbook Lesson 5A p23

WRITING

Students write about their daily routine in the week, using phrases from **1a** and their own ideas. Tell them not to write about their weekend routines, as this is the topic of lesson 5D.

5B ▶ Where does she work?
Student's Book p40–p41

Vocabulary time phrases with *on, in, at*
Grammar Present Simple (*he, she, it*): questions and short answers

QUICK REVIEW This activity reviews daily routines and the Present Simple. Put students into pairs. Students do the activity in their pairs, as shown in the examples. At the end of the activity, ask a few students to tell the class one or two things about their partner.

Time phrases with *on, in, at*

1 **a** Focus students on the tables. Point out the prepositions *on, in, at* and the examples.
Students do the exercise on their own or in pairs. Early finishers can check their answers in **VOCABULARY 5.2** SB p122.

✍ While students are working, draw the tables on the board. Check answers with the class by saying each phrase in the box and asking students which table it goes in.

Use the tables to highlight the following patterns: we use *on* with days of the week (*Sunday*, etc.) and parts of particular days (*Tuesday morning*, etc.); we use *in* with *the morning, the afternoon* and *the evening* (but we say *at night* not ~~in the night~~); we use *at* with times (*at six o'clock, at midday*, etc.).

Point out that we say **in the week** and **at the weekend**. You can also highlight that in American and Australian English we say **on the weekend**.
Remind students that *midday* = 12.00 and *midnight* = 24.00.

Tell the class that when we talk about our routines, we can use the singular or plural form of days, parts of days and *the weekend*: *I play football on Friday/Fridays. He works on Wednesday evening/evenings. They eat out at the weekend/weekends*. etc.

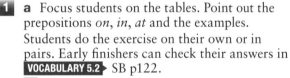

on (Sunday), Monday, Tuesday morning, Friday afternoon, Saturday evening
in (the morning), the afternoon, the evening, the week
at (six o'clock), half past ten, midday, midnight, night, the weekend

b **CD2** 28 **PRONUNCIATION** Play the recording. Students listen and practise. Point out that we say the weak form of *at* /ət/ with time phrases. Repeat the drill if necessary.

EXTRA IDEA

• Students work in pairs and test each other on the prepositions. One student says a word or phrase from the box in **1a**, for example *Monday*, and his/her partner says the phrase with the correct preposition, for example *on Monday*.

2 **a** Students do the exercise on their own before comparing their answers in pairs. Check answers with the class.

1 at **2** at, in **3** on **4** at, on **5** in **6** on **7** at, at, in **8** at, on

b Students do the exercise on their own. While they are working, monitor and check their sentences for accuracy.

c Students work in pairs and take turns to say their sentences.
Ask each student to tell the class one of their sentences.

Lunch on Monday

3 **a** Focus students on the photo. Ask students what they remember about Carol and Tom from lesson 5A. Don't tell students anything about Nadine /næˈdiːn/ at this stage.

Give students time to read sentences 1–5. Check students understand *other people* in question 5.
CD2 29 Play the recording (SB p109). Students listen and choose the correct words in the sentences. Students compare answers in pairs. Check answers with the class.

2 doesn't work 3 Italian 4 Germany 5 two

b Give students time to read questions 1–6. Play the recording again. Students listen and answer the questions.

c Students compare answers in pairs. Check answers with the class.

2 She works in a/the mobile phone shop with Carol. 3 She's a student at the university. 4 She lives near the university. 5 Yes, she does. 6 She plays tennis and she goes to the cinema a lot.

HELP WITH GRAMMAR Present Simple (*he*, *she*, *it*): questions and short answers

4 **a** ✍ Draw the table on the board and write in the example questions. Highlight the following points.

- Use the example questions to highlight the word order:
  question word + *does* + *he/she/it* + verb + ...
- Highlight that the auxiliary *does* has no meaning, but is used to make the question form of the Present Simple with *he*, *she* and *it*.
- Point out that there is no -*s* on the main verb in Present Simple questions: *Where does Nadine work at the weekend?*, not ~~*Where does Nadine works at the weekend?*~~
- Also point out that Present Simple questions are the same for *he*, *she* and *it*.
- Highlight that we use the auxiliary *does* with all verbs except *be*: *Where is he?*, etc.

b Students do the exercise on their own. Check answers with the class.

- ✍ Focus students on the table on the board. Elicit which words in questions 1 and 2 from **4b** go in each column and complete the table (see the table in **GRAMMAR 5.2** SB p123).
- Use these example questions to further highlight the word order.
- You can also teach the question *What does he/she do?* = *What's his/her job?*.

c Students do the exercise on their own or in pairs. Check answers with the class.

- **Answers** *Does* he know Nadine? Yes, he **does**. No, he doesn't. *Does* she like Manchester? Yes, she does. No, she **doesn't**.
- Highlight the word order in the *yes/no* questions: *Does* + *he/she/it* + verb + ...
- Remind students that there is no -*s* or -*es* on the main verb in Present Simple questions: *Does she work at home?* not ~~*Does she works at home?*~~.
- Also point out that we don't use the main verb (*know*, *like*, etc.) in short answers: **A** *Does he know her?* **B** *Yes, he does.* not ~~*Yes, he knows.*~~ or ~~*Yes, he does know.*~~

d Students do the exercise on their own. Check answers with the class.

- We use *does* in questions with *he*, *she* and *it*.
- We use *do* in questions with *I*, *you*, *we* and *they*.

> **EXTRA IDEA**
>
> - If you have a class of false beginners, ask students to do **4a–d** in pairs. Students can then check their answers in **GRAMMAR 5.2** SB p123. Check answers with the class and highlight the bullet points in **4a–d**.

5 **CD2** 30 **PRONUNCIATION** Play the recording. Students listen and practise. Play the recording again if necessary, pausing after each question or short answer for students to repeat individually.

HELP WITH LISTENING Sentence stress (1)

This *Help with Listening* section introduces students to the concept of sentence stress.

6 **a** **CD2** 31 Play the recording. Students listen and notice the sentence stress on the six example questions. Point out that we stress the important words (the words that carry the meaning).

b Play the recording again. Students listen and read the questions. Ask the class if *does* is stressed in questions (it isn't).

Note that students whose languages have different stress patterns from English can often find it difficult to tune in to the way sentences are stressed. We suggest you use every opportunity to work on sentence stress with your class when drilling, and as follow-up activities to listening texts.

> **EXTRA IDEA**
>
> - With a strong class, use the questions in **6a** to point out what types of word we usually stress, such as question words (*What*, etc.), names (*Tom*, etc.), verbs (*live*, etc.) and nouns (*week*, etc.). You can also highlight grammatical words such as articles (*the*, *a*, *an*), prepositions (*with*, etc.) and pronouns (*she*, etc.) that are usually unstressed in natural spoken English.

7 a **CD2 31** **PRONUNCIATION** Play the recording again. Students listen and practise. Check they copy the sentence stress correctly. Repeat the drill if necessary, asking students to repeat the questions chorally and individually.

b Students do the exercise in pairs, as shown in the speech bubbles. While students are working, monitor and check they are saying the questions with the correct stress.

8 Students work in the same pairs, student A and student B. Student As turn to SB p89 and student Bs turn to SB p94. Check they are all looking at the correct exercise.

a Check students understand that the woman in the pictures is Nadine. Students do the exercise on their own.
Check answers with the class if necessary. Only check the words they need to fill in the gaps, so that the students don't hear the questions they are about to be asked. Note that the answers are the same for student A and student B.

Student A/Student B
2 does/Does she, on
3 Does/does she, on
4 Does/does she, at
5 Does she, on

b Students work with their partner. Student A in each pair asks questions 1–5. Student B looks at pictures a–e and answers his/her partner's questions. Remind student Bs to use short answers (*Yes, she does., No, she doesn't.*) where appropriate.

Student A
1 8.45
2 She plays tennis.
3 No, she doesn't.
4 Yes, she does.
5 Yes, she does.

c Students swap roles so that student B in each pair asks questions 1–5. Student A looks at pictures a–e and answers his/her partner's questions. Remind student As to use the correct short answers where appropriate.
If necessary, check answers with the class.

Student B
1 11.30
2 Yes, she does.
3 She goes to the cinema.
4 8.00
5 No, she doesn't.

Get ready ... Get it right!

9 a Put students into new pairs. If possible, ask students to work with someone they don't know very well.
Pre-teach *my best friend*, *male* and *female*. Students tell their partner their best friend's name and if this friend is male or female. Note that this stage is included so that students will know whether to write questions with *he* or *she* in **9b**.

b Students do the exercise on their own. Before they begin, point out that they can write questions about the topics in the box and the things in the photos, as shown in the example questions, or use their own ideas.

10 a Students work with their partner. One student in each pair asks all his/her questions about his/her partner's best friend. Encourage students to ask more questions if possible. When he/she has finished, students swap roles and the other student asks all his/her questions.

b Finally, ask each student to tell the class two things about their partner's best friend.

> **EXTRA IDEA**
>
> • Bring in a photo of your best friend and show it to the class. Students work in pairs and write five questions to ask you about your best friend. Students then take turns to ask you questions about him/her.

> **WRITING**
>
> Students write a profile of their best friend. Encourage students to include a photo of him or her if possible. These can be collected in next class and displayed around the classroom for other students to read.

> **FURTHER PRACTICE**
>
> **Ph** **Class Activity** 5B A writer's week p141–p142 (Instructions p119)
> **Ph** **Vocabulary Plus** 5 Jobs p171 (Instructions p164)
> **Extra Practice** 5B SB p101
> **Self-study DVD-ROM** Lesson 5B
> **Workbook** Lesson 5B p24

▶ REAL
5C WORLD **An evening out**
Student's Book p42–p43

Vocabulary food and drink (3)
Real World in a restaurant

QUICK REVIEW This activity reviews Present Simple questions and ways of telling the time. Go through the instructions and the examples with the class. Students do the activity in pairs. At the end of the activity, ask a few pairs to tell the class three things they both do at the same time of the day.

What's on the menu?

1 **a** Focus students on the restaurant menu. Teach students *menu* /'menjuː/ and check they remember *restaurant* /'restrɒnt/. Model and drill these words with the class. Remind students that *restaurant* is two syllables, not three. You can also teach the meaning of *sunrise*, which is the name of the restaurant.

Students work in pairs and match the food and drink on the menu to photos 1–10. Early finishers can check their answers in **VOCABULARY 5.3** SB p122. Check answers with the class.

Check students understand all the new vocabulary, referring to the photos if necessary.

Use the menu to teach *main course* /'meɪn kɔːs/ and *dessert* /dɪ'zɜːt/. You can also teach *a starter*, which is eaten before the main course.

Highlight the difference between *still mineral water* (without bubbles) and *sparkling mineral water* (with bubbles). In restaurants in the UK it is also very common to ask for *tap water*, which is always clean, drinkable and free!

1 burger and chips **2** mushroom pizza **3** vegetable lasagne **4** chicken salad **5** fruit salad **6** chocolate ice cream, strawberry ice cream, vanilla ice cream **7** apple pie and cream **8** coffee, tea **9** a bottle of still mineral water, a bottle of sparkling mineral water **10** orange juice

b **CD2 32** **PRONUNCIATION** Play the recording (SB p109). Students listen and practise. Highlight the pronunciation of *chicken* /'tʃɪkɪn/, *vegetable* /'vedʒtəbəl/, *lasagne* /lə'zænjə/, *burger* /'bɜːgə/, *chocolate* /'tʃɒklət/ and *orange juice* /'ɒrɪndʒ dʒuːs/. Also point out that we can stress either word in *ice cream*. Repeat the drill if necessary.

> **EXTRA IDEA**
> • If you have a monolingual class, teach students how to say common main courses, desserts and drinks that are found in restaurants in the students' country.

2 Use the speech bubbles to remind students that we use *How much … ?* to ask about prices. Students do the activity in new pairs. Tell students to ask about three different combinations of food and drink.

Are you ready to order?

3 **a** Focus students on the photo of The Sunrise Restaurant. Ask students who the customers are (Martin and Louise) and who they are talking to (the waiter).
VIDEO 5 **CD2 33** Play the video or audio recording (SB p110). Students listen and tick the food and drink on the menu the customers order. Play the recording again if necessary. Note that all the Real World videos can be found on the **Teacher's DVD** at the back of this book.

Note that part of this conversation is reproduced in the **REAL WORLD** section in **4a** SB p43. However, we suggest you don't draw students' attention to this and treat this stage as a 'pure' listening activity. Alternatively, you can ask students to close their books and write down what the customers order in their notebooks.

b Pre-teach *the bill*. Students compare answers in pairs and then work out the customers' bill.
Check answers with the class.

With a strong class you can also teach *(leave) a tip* at this point in the lesson. You can also tell the class that customers in the UK usually leave a tip of about 10% in restaurants.

The customers ordered the chicken salad, the mushroom pizza, an orange juice, a bottle of sparkling mineral water, the apple pie (and cream), and two coffees.
The bill is £28.90.

REAL WORLD In a restaurant

4 **a** Focus students on the conversations. Check students understand that the sentences in the yellow boxes are said by the waiter and the sentences in the red boxes are said by the customers.
VIDEO 5 **CD2 33** Play the video or audio recording again. Students watch or listen and tick the customers' sentences when they hear them. Ask students if they ticked all the sentences.

You can also ask students what Martin and Louise decide to do next weekend (go to Cambridge). Their visit to the Cambridge tourist information office is featured in lesson 6C.

Check students understand all the vocabulary in the flow chart and point out that we can use *the* or *a* when we order food in a restaurant: *Can I have the/a chicken salad, please?*.

b Students do the exercise on their own before comparing answers in pairs.
Check answers with the class and go through the points on the next page.

- **Answers 1** Can I have (the chicken salad), please? And can I have (the mushroom pizza)? **2** And can we have (a bottle of mineral water)? Can we have the bill, please? **3** What would you like to drink? Would you like a dessert?
- Check students understand that we use *Can I/we have … ?* to ask for things and *Would you like … ?* to ask people what they want.
- At this level, we suggest you teach *Can I/we have … ?* and *Would you like … ?* as fixed phrases, rather than explore the grammar of *can* and *would*.

5 **a** CD2▶34 PRONUNCIATION Play the recording. Students listen and practise. Check that students sound polite when practising questions with *Can I/we have … ?* and *Would you like … ?*. Play the recording again if necessary, pausing after each sentence for students to repeat individually.

b Put students into groups of three. If you have extra students, have one or two pairs and ask one student in each pair to play the roles of both customers.

Students practise the conversations in **4a** in their groups, taking turns to be the waiter or waitress.

6 **a** Students do the activity in the same groups. Before they begin, remind students to use language from **4a** and the food and drink on the menu. Also ensure that both customers take turns in speaking in the students' conversations.

b Students in each group decide who is the waiter or waitress and who are the customers. Students then practise their conversation until they remember it.

c Each group role-plays their conversation for the class. Students listen to the other groups' conversations and find out what they order. Finally, the class can decide which group's conversation is the best.

┌─ **FURTHER PRACTICE** ─────────────────────┐
Extra Practice 5C SB p101
Self-study DVD-ROM Lesson 5C
Workbook Lesson 5C p26
└──┘

VOCABULARY
5D AND SKILLS ▶ A day off
Student's Book p44–p45

Vocabulary frequency adverbs and phrases with *every*
Skills Reading and Listening: our Sunday routine; Listening: I love Sundays

QUICK REVIEW This activity reviews food and drink vocabulary. Ask students to close their books. Check students remember The Sunrise Restaurant in lesson 5C. Students work in pairs and make a list of all the food and drink on the menu they can remember. Students compare lists with another pair, then check on SB p42. Ask if any pairs remembered all the food and drink on the menu.

1 **a** Focus students on the diagram and point out 100% and 0% at each end. Use the diagram to teach the meaning of *always* and *never*. Point out that *never* has a negative meaning.
Students work on their own and write *sometimes*, *usually* and *not usually* on the line.
Check answers with the class. Note that the word order of frequency adverbs is dealt with in **4**.

always **usually** **sometimes** **not usually** never

b Teach students the meaning of *every day* by using an example about yourself, for example, *I watch TV every day*. Students do the exercise on their own. Check answers with the class.
Point out that we use *every* with time words: *every day*, *every week*, etc. Highlight that we say *every day* not *every days*.

every year 4; every month 3; every week 2

c Students do the exercise on their own or in pairs, as shown in the examples. ✎ Check answers with the class by eliciting students' ideas and writing correct phrases on the board.

Possible answers (every morning), every afternoon, every evening, every night, (every Sunday), every Friday evening, every six weeks, every four years, etc.

d CD2▶35 PRONUNCIATION Play the recording (SB p110). Students listen and practise. Highlight the pronunciation of *usually* /ˈjuːʒəli/ and point out that *every* is two syllables, not three.
Note that this recording includes the words and phrases in **1a**, **1b** and the possible answers given above for **1c**.

2 **a** Pre-teach the words in the box using examples, mime, translation, etc. Note that the aim of this box is to highlight which new words students need in order to understand the texts they are about to read and listen to.
Model and drill the new words with the class, highlighting the pronunciation of *early* /ˈɜːli/, *tired* /taɪəd/ and *busy* /ˈbɪzi/.

b Focus students on the photos of Ian and Becky and the speech bubbles. Tell the class that they are going to read and listen to Ian and Becky's Sunday routines.

Teach the phrase *a day off* (= a day when you don't work or study), which is the title of the lesson.

CD2 36 Play the recording. Students read, listen and find out what Ian and Becky always do together on Sundays.

Check the answer with the class (Ian and Becky always have dinner at The Sunrise Restaurant on Sundays).

3 **a** Go through the instructions and the examples with the class. Students do the exercise on their own.

b Students compare answers in pairs. Check answers with the class. Use sentence 7 to highlight that *She has breakfast in bed **every Sunday**. = She **always** has breakfast in bed **on Sundays**.*

3 He gets home at about **12.30**. **4** ✓
5 He **sometimes** sleeps for an hour or two.
6 Becky works in a hotel every **Saturday**.
7 ✓ **8** Her sister lives in the **USA**. **9** The Sunrise Restaurant **isn't usually** busy on Sundays.

HELP WITH VOCABULARY
Frequency adverbs and phrases with *every*

4 ✎ While students are doing **3a**, write the examples from the rules in **4** on the board. Focus students on the sentences on the board and highlight the blue and pink words. Alternatively, focus students on the rules in the Student's Book. Go through the following points with the class.

- Frequency adverbs go after the verb *be*: *I'm **always** tired on Sundays. It's **not usually** very busy.*
- Frequency adverbs go before other verbs: *I **never** have breakfast. I **usually watch** sport on TV.*
- Highlight that with other verbs we say *I don't usually …* , *He doesn't usually …* , etc. not ~~I not usually …~~ , ~~He not usually …~~ , etc.
- Phrases with *every* are usually at the end of the sentence: *I work in a hotel **every Saturday**., I play football **every Sunday morning**.*
- Point out that we can use the singular or plural form of days, parts of days or *the weekend* when we are talking about daily routines and habits: *I'm always tired on Sunday/Sundays. I play tennis in the afternoon/afternoons. I go out a lot at the weekend/weekends.*, etc.
- Remind students that we don't use a plural noun after *every*: *every Saturday*, etc. not ~~every Saturdays~~, etc.
- Also note that there is a lot of flexibility regarding the position of these adverbs (for example, *sometimes* can go at the beginning of a sentence, but *always* can't). However, at this level we feel that students only need the simplified rules given in the Student's Book.

┌─ **EXTRA IDEA** ─
- Students look at the texts about Ian and Becky again and underline all the examples of frequency adverbs and phrases with *every*. Students work in pairs, compare answers and notice the word order.

5 **a** Students do the exercise on their own, as shown in the example.

b Students compare sentences in pairs and decide which sentences are true for them. Check answers with the class. Ask students to tell the class which sentences are true for them.

2 I sometimes eat out at the weekend. **3** I'm always very busy in the week. **4** I don't usually work on Saturdays. **5** I never get up early at the weekend. **6** I'm usually tired on Mondays.

6 **a** Focus students on the photo. Ask students who Amy is (Becky's sister) and where she lives (in California, in the USA). Check students understand that Bruce is Amy's friend, not her husband.

CD2 37 Give students time to read the bulleted prompts, then play the recording. Students listen and tick the things that Amy and Bruce talk about. Students can compare answers in pairs.
Check answers with the class.

Amy and Bruce talk about: breakfast, phone calls, homework, lunch, DVDs

b Give students time to read sentences 1–6, then play the recording again. Students listen and choose the correct answers.
Students can compare answers in pairs. Check answers with the class.

2 husband **3** coffee **4** 30 **5** Thursdays **6** Lucas's

HELP WITH LISTENING Sentence stress (2)

This *Help with Listening* section reviews sentence stress in the context of a real-life conversation.

7 **a** **CD2 38** Focus students on the example sentences, then play the recording. Students listen and notice the sentence stress. Remind students that we stress the important words (the words that carry the meaning).

b Ask students to look at Audio Script **CD2 37** SB p110. Play this recording again. Students listen and follow the sentence stress.
Note that while 'listening and following' might seem a rather passive activity to the teacher, the students are probably working very hard as they try to match what they hear with the words on the page. We feel this type of task helps students to tune in to the rhythm of the language, which will increase students' confidence and their ability to understand natural spoken English.

8 **a** Students do the exercise on their own. Remind students to write sentences about their Sunday routine only, and to use a frequency adverb or a phrase with *every* in each sentence.

b Put students into pairs. Students take turns to say their sentences. Their partner guesses if the sentences are true or false.

Finally, ask students to tell the class one or two of their partner's true sentences.

> **EXTRA IDEA**
>
> - ✏️ Demonstrate this activity first by writing two true sentences and two false sentences about your Sunday routine on the board in random order. Students guess which sentences are true and which are false.

> **WRITING**
>
> Students write a description of their Sunday routines. Alternatively, you can ask them to write about their weekend routines, including Saturday.

> **FURTHER PRACTICE**
>
> **Ph** **Class Activity** 5D Always, sometimes, never p143 (Instructions p120)
>
> **Extra Practice** 5 SB p101
>
> **Self-study DVD-ROM** Lesson 5D
>
> **Workbook** Lesson 5D p27
>
> **Workbook** Reading and Writing Portfolio 5 p60–p61
>
> **Ph** **Progress Test** 5 p184–p185 (note that this is a two-page test with a listening section)

HELP WITH PRONUNCIATION /w/ and /v/

1 Focus students on the phonemes /w/ and /v/, the pictures and the words.

CD2 39 Play the recording. Students listen to the sounds and the words.

Play the recording again. Students listen and practise. If students are having problems, help them with the mouth position for each sound.

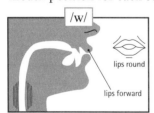
/w/
lips round
lips forward

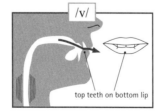
/v/
top teeth on bottom lip

Highlight that we round the lips to make the /w/ sound, then relax and open them as we push air out of the mouth.

Point out that we make the /v/ sound by placing the top teeth on the bottom lip and pushing air through the space. Also highlight that both of these sounds are voiced (there is vibration in the throat).

2 **CD2** 40 Focus students on the boxes. Play the recording. Students listen and notice how we say *w* and *v* in these words.

Play the recording again. Students listen and practise.

3 **a** **CD2** 41 Play the recording. Students listen and read the conversation.

Play the recording again, pausing after each sentence for students to repeat chorally and individually.

b Students practise the conversation in pairs.

Finally, ask a few pairs to role-play the conversation for the class.

continue2learn

Focus students on the **continue2learn** section on SB p45. See p33 of this book for ideas on how to use this section in class.

Extra Practice 5 SB p101

See p34 for ideas on how to use this section.

5A
1 2 have 3 leave 4 start 5 have 6 finish 7 get 8 have 9 go 10 sleep
2 2 lives 3 works 4 doesn't like 5 goes 6 watches 7 studies 8 has 9 doesn't have 10 talk 11 don't see 12 works

5B
3 2 in 3 on 4 at 5 in 6 at 7 in 8 at 9 in 10 on 11 at 12 at
4 2 does 3 do 4 does 5 does 6 do 7 do
5a 2 Does your sister like fish? 3 Do they go to concerts? 4 Does he work in a shop? 5 Does your dad have a car? 6 Do you like rock music?
5b 2 No, she doesn't. 3 No, they don't. 4 Yes, he does. 5 No, he doesn't. 6 Yes, I do. / Yes, we do.

5C
6 2 order 3 have 4 would 5 drink 6 juice 7 Would 8 dessert 9 strawberry 10 course
7 2 mushroom pizza 3 chicken salad 4 apple pie and cream 5 fruit salad 6 bottle of mineral water

5D
8 3 Lisa's brother is **always** busy. 4 My dad **usually** gets up early. 5 ✓ 6 We go shopping **every week**. 7 ✓ 8 I don't **usually** work on Wednesday afternoons.

Progress Portfolio 5

See p34 for ideas on how to use this section in class.

QUICK REVIEW This activity reviews frequency adverbs and the Present Simple. Students do the first part of the activity on their own. Put students into pairs. Students take turns to say their sentences. At the end of the activity, ask a few students to tell the class one thing about their partner's Saturday routine.

Places in a town or city (1)

1 **a** Teach *a town* and check students remember *a city*. Highlight the title of the lesson and teach the phrase *my home town*. Point out that we use this phrase to talk about the place where we live, even if we live in a city.

Students do the exercise on their own or in pairs. Check answers with the class. Check students understand all the new vocabulary.

Point out that we use *a station* to mean *a train station*. Teach students that we say *go to museums* but *go to **the** theatre*. You can compare these phrases to *go to concerts* and *go to **the** cinema*, which the students learned in lesson 4B.

You can also teach students that *a shopping centre* is called *a mall* /mɑːl/ in American English.

a museum **8**; a theatre **3**; a shopping centre **9**;
a park **1**; a river **5**; a station **2**; a bus station **7**;
an airport **6**

> ### EXTRA IDEAS
>
> - When students have finished the matching activity in **1a**, they can check their answers in Language Summary 6 **VOCABULARY 6.1** ▶ SB p124. Alternatively, ask early finishers to check their answers in the Language Summary before you check the answers with the class.
> - If you have a strong class, teach other words for places in a town or city, for example, *an art gallery, a department store, a car park, a library, a hospital, a mosque, a church, a temple, an underground station, a bar, a pub*, etc.

b **CD2** **43** **PRONUNCIATION** Play the recording. Students listen and practise. Alternatively, model and drill the words yourself and ask students to repeat chorally and individually. Highlight the pronunciation of *building* /ˈbɪldɪŋ/, *museum* /mjuːˈziːəm/ and *theatre* /ˈθɪətə/. Point out that the main stress on *shopping centre* and *bus station* is on the first word, not the second. Repeat the drill if necessary. For **Teaching Tips** on drilling, see p23. Note that only the main stress is shown in the vocabulary boxes and Language Summaries.

c Tell students to cover the words in **1a**. Students do the activity in pairs, as shown in the speech bubbles.

My city

2 **a** Pre-teach the words in the box using examples, definitions, translation, etc. Note that the aim of this box is to highlight which new words students need in order to understand the text they are about to read and listen to.

Drill the words with the class, highlighting the pronunciation of *famous* /ˈfeɪməs/ and *mile* /maɪl/.

b Focus students on the photos of Bath, a famous city in England. Drill *Bath* /bɑːθ/ and *England* /ˈɪŋɡlənd/ with the class.

Students do the exercise on their own or in pairs. Check answers with the class and teach any new words. Note that the photo on SB p47 is of the Roman Baths Museum in Bath.

Possible answers buildings, a park, a river, a bridge, flowers, a museum, hot springs, tourists, etc.

3 **a** **CD2** **44** Focus students on the photo of Susan and the speech bubble, then play the recording. Students listen and read. Ask students if Susan likes living in Bath. (Yes, she does.)

b Go through the examples with the class. Students do the exercise on their own before comparing answers in pairs. Check answers with the class. Note that *Thermae* is pronounced /ˈθɜːmeɪ/.

3 Susan goes to the Thermae Bath Spa every **Sunday**.
4 ✓ **5** The Jane Austen Centre is a **museum**. **6** ✓
7 There are trains to London every **half an hour /
thirty minutes**. **8** ✓

HELP WITH GRAMMAR
a, some, a lot of; there is / there are: positive

4 **a** Focus students on pictures A–C. Students do the exercise on their own. Check answers with the class.

- **Answers 1**C **2**A **3**B
- Check students understand the difference between *some* (more than one, but not a large number) and *a lot of* (a large number).
- Point out that we use *a* or *an* with singular nouns (*a person, an airport*, etc.). We use *some* and *a lot of* with plural nouns (***some** people, **some** museums, **a lot of** restaurants*, etc.).
- Also point out that we use *some* and *a lot of* in positive sentences.
- Teach the alternative form *lots of* and tell students that we often use this form when speaking or in informal writing: *There are **lots of** people in the park*.
- Note that *any* is taught in lesson 6B.

b Students do the exercise on their own. Check answers with the class.

- **Answers SINGULAR** There*'s* **a** big new shopping centre. There*'s* **an** airport in Bristol. **PLURAL** There <u>are</u> **five** theatres. There <u>are</u> **some** very nice parks. There <u>are</u> **a lot of** old buildings.
- Focus students on the words in **bold** in the example sentences and highlight that we use *there's* with *a* or *an* and *there are* with *some*, *a lot of* or a number (*five*, etc.).
- Point out that *there's* is the contracted form of *there is*.
- Also highlight that we write *there are* not ~~*there're*~~.
- We use *there is/there are* to say that things exist in a place. Students sometimes confuse *there is/there are* with *it is/they are*. ✐ If this is a problem for your students, write *There's a park. It's very big.* and *There are two restaurants. They're expensive.* on the board to highlight the difference.
- You can also highlight that *there*, *they're* and *their* all have the same pronunciation /ðeə/.
- Note that the negative and question forms of *there is/there are* are taught in lesson 6B.

⌐ **EXTRA IDEA** ⌐

- Students read about Bath again and underline all the examples of *there's* and *there are* in the text. Students compare answers in pairs and notice if these phrases are followed by *a*, *an*, *some*, *a lot of* or a number.

5 **a** Point out that sentences 1–8 are also about Bath. Pre-teach *a five-star hotel*.
Students do the exercise on their own.

b **CD2▶ 45** Play the recording. Students listen and check their answers. Check answers with the class. Play the recording again. Students listen and notice how we say *there's* /ðeəz/ and *there are* /ðeərə/, as shown in the examples. Also point out that *there's* and *there are* aren't usually stressed.

2 are 3 's 4 are 5 's 6 are 7 's 8 are

c **PRONUNCIATION** Play the recording again, pausing after each sentence for students to repeat chorally and individually. Repeat the drill if necessary.

6 **a** Students do the exercise on their own.

b Students compare answers in pairs. Check answers with the class.
Students then work with their partner and discuss which sentences are true for the town or city they are in now. Ask students to tell the class some of their true sentences.

2 three 3 some 4 a 5 some 6 an
7 a lot of 8 an 9 some 10 a

Get ready … Get it right!

7 Give students a few moments to think of a town or city they know well, but not the town or city they are in now. If you have a monolingual class, encourage students to think of towns or cities in other countries or regions if possible.
Students do the exercise on their own, as shown in the examples. Tell students to write at least six sentences if possible.
While they are working, check their sentences for accuracy and help students with any new vocabulary.
Tell students to memorise their sentences so that they can do **8a** without referring to their written work.

8 **a** Put students into pairs. If possible, students should work with someone who doesn't know their town or city.
Students take turns to tell their partner about the town or city they chose in **7**.

b Students tell the class two things about their partner's town or city.
Finally, ask students if they would like to visit their partner's town or city. Ask them to give reasons for their answers if possible.

⌐ **EXTRA IDEA** ⌐

- If your students haven't visited any other towns or cities, ask them to write three true sentences and three false sentences with *there's/there are* about the town or city they are in now. Students take turns to say their sentences to each other. Students say if they think their partner's sentences are true or false.

⌐ **WRITING** ⌐

Students write a description of their home town (or city), or another town or city they know well. They can include photos if they wish. Remind students to use language from **1a** and **4** in their descriptions.

⌐ **FURTHER PRACTICE** ⌐

Extra Practice 6A SB p102
Self-study DVD-ROM Lesson 6A
Workbook Lesson 6A p28

6B ▶ **Are there any shops?**
Student's Book p48–p49

Vocabulary places in a town or city (2)
Grammar *there is / there are*: negative,
yes / no questions and short answers; *any*

QUICK REVIEW This activity reviews *there is/there are* and places in a town or city. ✏ Write these prompts on the board: *There's a/an … , There are some … , There are a lot of … , There are (three) …* . Students do the activity in pairs. Tell students to say at least five sentences each. At the end of the activity, ask a few students to tell the class one or two of their sentences.

Places in a town or city (2)

1 **a** Students do the exercise in pairs. Early finishers can check their answers in **VOCABULARY 6.2** ▶ SB p124. Check answers with the class.

Point out the possessive *'s* in *chemist's* and tell students that the person is called *a chemist*. Also point out that we say *a pharmacy* /ˈfɑːməsi/ in American English.

Check students understand the difference between *a bus stop* and *a bus station*, and *a supermarket* and *a market*.

Highlight that we say *in* or *at* with *shops*: *You buy food in/at a supermarket.*, etc.

a bank **1**; a market **8**;
a chemist's **2**; a post office **9**;
a supermarket **6**; a bus stop **5**;
a square **7**; a cashpoint/an ATM **4**

b **CD2▶ 46** **PRONUNCIATION** Play the recording. Students listen and practise. Highlight the pronunciation of *chemist's* /ˈkemɪsts/ and *square* /skweə/. Also highlight that the main stress on *post office* and *bus stop* is on the first word, not the second. Repeat the drill if necessary.

c Ask students to close their books. Students work with their partner and write down all the places in the town or city they can remember. Tell students that these can be words from **1a** and those from lesson 6A, and any other words or phrases they know. You can set a time limit of one or two minutes.
✏ Ask one pair to tell you their words and write them on the board. Ask other pairs to suggest additional words and add them to the list until you have all the vocabulary taught in **1a** and lesson 6A on the board.

┌─ **EXTRA IDEA** ─┐

- If you have a strong class, teach other words for shops, for example, *a baker's, a butcher's, a department store, a bookshop, a newsagent's, a kiosk*, etc. Then ask students to work in pairs and discuss what people buy at each place: *You buy bread in a baker's., You buy meat in a butcher's.*, etc.

Welcome to my home

2 **a** Focus students on the photo of Susan and Isabel. Ask students where Susan lives (in Bath). Tell the class that Susan's friend Isabel has come to stay with her.
CD2▶ 47 Play the recording (SB p110). Students listen and put the things in the order that Susan and Isabel talk about them. Check answers with the class.

shops **2**; banks **3**; trains and buses **4**; restaurants **5**

b Give students time to read sentences 1–7 and check students remember *a mile*. Play the recording again. Students listen and choose the correct words.

c Students compare answers in pairs. Check answers with the class.

2 some 3 post office 4 two miles
5 ten 6 bus stop 7 in the centre

HELP WITH GRAMMAR
there is / there are: negative, *yes / no* questions and short answers; *any*

3 **a** Students do the exercise on their own. Check answers with the class.

- **Answers** 1 There **isn't** a station near here.
  2 There **aren't** any good restaurants near here.
- Use the example sentences to highlight the singular negative form *there isn't* and plural negative form *there aren't*.

b Students do the exercise on their own. Check answers with the class.

- **Answers** Is there a bank? Yes, there is. No, there **isn't**. Are there any shops? Yes, there **are**. No, there **aren't**.
- Highlight the inverted word order in the questions: *Is there … ?/Are there … ?*.
- Also point out that we don't contract *there is* in short answers: *Yes, there is.* not ~~*Yes, there's.*~~
- Note that *Wh-* questions with *there is/there are* are not very common, and are therefore not taught at this level.

c Students do the exercise on their own. Check answers with the class.

- We use ***any*** in negatives and questions with *there are*.
- ✏ Elicit the sentences with *any* from **3a** and **3b**, and write them on the board: *There aren't any good restaurants near here*. *Are there any shops?*. Highlight the position of *any* in these sentences.

- Also remind students that we can use *some* in positive sentences with *there are*: *There are some very nice restaurants in the centre.*
- Note that it is also possible to use *some* in questions with *there is/there are*. However, at this level we feel it is important to give students a simple rule that always produces correct sentences.
- Also note that students don't study the use of *some* and *any* with uncountable nouns at this level. This is dealt with in **face2face** Second edition Elementary.

HELP WITH LISTENING Linking (1)

This *Help with Listening* section introduces consonant–vowel linking in sentences.

4 Focus students on sentences 1–6. Point out the consonants in blue and the vowels in pink.

CD2▶ 48 Play the recording. Students listen and notice the linking between the consonant sounds and the vowel sounds.

Use the examples to highlight that when a word ends in a consonant sound and the next word begins with a vowel sound, we usually link them together so that they sound like one word. Point out that it is the initial and final sounds that are important, not the spelling. For example, *there are* links together, even though *there* ends in the letter *e*.

5 **CD2▶ 49** **PRONUNCIATION** Play the recording (SB p110). Students listen and practise the sentences in **4** and the short answers. Check students copy the stress and linking correctly. Play the recording again, pausing after each sentence for students to repeat individually.

6 **a** Tell students that prompts 1–8 are about places near Susan's flat. Use the examples to point out that a tick means students write a positive sentence and a cross means they write a negative sentence.

Students do the exercise on their own.

b Students compare answers in pairs. Check answers with the class.

3 There's a market. 4 There aren't any museums.
5 There's a park. 6 There isn't a square. 7 There aren't any nice cafés. 8 There are a lot of old houses.

7 Students work in the same pairs, student A and student B. Student As turn to SB p86 and student Bs turn to SB p91. Check they are all looking at the correct exercise.

a Students do the exercise on their own. Check answers with the class. Only check the words they need to fill in the gaps, so that students don't hear the questions they are about to be asked. Note that these answers are the same for student As and student Bs.

Student A/Student B 2 Are, any
3 Is, a 4 Are, any 5 Is, a

b Students work with their partners. Student A in each pair asks questions 1–5 from **a**. Student Bs answer the questions without looking at the Student's Book. When student A has asked all five questions, he/she says how many answers were correct. Before they begin, point out that the answers to student A's questions are in brackets in **a**.

c Students swap roles so that student Bs are asking student As their questions 1–5 from **a**.

At the end of the activity, find out how many students answered all five questions correctly.

Get ready … Get it right!

8 Focus students on the map and point out the places in the bubbles.

Students do the exercise on their own. Remind students to use *Is there a … ?*, *Are there any … ?* and the places in the bubbles in their questions, as shown in the examples.

9 **a** Focus students on the speech bubbles and teach the phrase *It's (five) minutes away.* = It's (five) minutes from my home.

Put students into pairs. If possible, ask students to work with someone they don't know very well. Students take turns to ask their questions from **8**.

Tell students to begin their conversations with *Where do you live?* before asking their questions. Also remind students to use correct short answers (*Yes, there is.*, *No, there isn't.*, etc.) where appropriate and to give more information if possible.

Tell students that they must make notes on their partner's answers, as they will need this information in **9b**. Students can put ticks and crosses next to each question to indicate a positive or negative answer, and write down any other interesting information they hear.

Early finishers can ask each other about the other places on the map they haven't already talked about.

b Put students into new pairs. Students tell their new partner about places near their first partner's home, as shown in the speech bubble. Remind students to refer to their notes from **9a** and to begin each conversation by saying where their first partner lives.

Finally, ask students to tell the class about one interesting place near their first partner's home.

┌─ **EXTRA IDEA** ─┐

- Use **Vocabulary Plus** 6 Rooms and furniture p172 (Instructions p164) in class or give it to students for homework. Note that this worksheet also practises *there is/there are*.

FURTHER PRACTICE

Ph **Class Activity** 6B London Road p144–p145 (Instructions p120)
Ph **Vocabulary Plus** 6 Rooms and furniture p172 (Instructions p164)
Extra Practice 6B SB p102
Self-study DVD-ROM Lesson 6B
Workbook Lesson 6B p29

▷ REAL
6C WORLD

Tourist information
Student's Book p50–p51

Vocabulary things in your bag (2)
Real World at a tourist information centre

QUICK REVIEW This activity reviews places in a town or city and *there is/there are*. Ask students to close their books. Students do the first part of the activity on their own. Put students into pairs to compare lists. Students then discuss which of the places on both lists are near their school (or the building where they are now). At the end of the activity, ask a few students to tell the class about some places near the school.

EXTRA IDEAS

- Before students do **1c**, ask your class what else they have in their bags and teach them how to say any new words in English. Words that students might find useful are *glasses*, *a driving licence*, *a tablet computer*, *a debit card*, *make-up*, etc.
- Use **Class Activity** 6C What's in your bag? p146 (Instructions p120) to practise the new vocabulary from **1a** and the things in your bag from lesson 1C.

Things in your bag (2)

1 **a** Students do the exercise in pairs. Early finishers can check their answers in **VOCABULARY 6.3** SB p124. Check answers with the class. Point out that men usually have *wallets* and women usually have *purses*.

> a purse **2**; keys **4**; money **11**; a credit card **10**;
> a passport **6**; an ID card **9**; a guide book **7**;
> a map **1**; a camera **3**; a laptop **5**

EXTRA IDEA

- If you have a class of complete beginners, consider teaching these words yourself by bringing the items (or photos of the items) to the class. Hold up each item in turn and tell students the word in English. You can then use the matching activity in **1a** for practice.

b **CD2** **50** **PRONUNCIATION** Play the recording. Students listen and practise. Alternatively, model the words yourself and ask students to repeat chorally and individually. Highlight the pronunciation of *purse* /pɜːs/, *money* /ˈmʌni/ and *guide book* /ˈɡaɪd bʊk/ and check students stress *an ID card* correctly. Repeat the drill if necessary.

c Put students into new pairs. Use the speech bubbles to teach the phrase *I have … with me*. Students take turns to say which things in **1a** they have with them.

When is it open?

2 **a** Pre-teach the words in the box using examples, pictures, board drawings, translation, etc. Note that the aim of this box is to highlight which new words students need in order to understand the conversation they are about to hear.

Point out that *open* is an adjective and a verb: *That shop is **open**.*, *The school **opens** at eight.* Also highlight that *closed* is an adjective (*This shop is **closed**.*) and the verb is *close* /kləʊz/: *What time does the school **close**?*

Ask students what other things people can *book* (a hotel, a train ticket, a holiday, etc.). Check students understand that *a walking tour* is when you walk from place to place with a guide, as shown in photo A SB p50.

Model and drill the new vocabulary, highlighting the pronunciation of *tourist* /ˈtʊərɪst/ and *tour* /tʊə/. Point out that *closed* /kləʊzd/ is one syllable, not two.

b Focus students on the photo on SB p51. Check that students remember Martin and Louise, who were customers in The Sunrise Restaurant in lesson 5C. Remind the class that they decided to go to Cambridge for the weekend at the end of their meal. Tell students that it is now the weekend and Martin and Louise are at the tourist information centre in Cambridge.

VIDEO ▸ 6 CD2 ▸ 51 Focus students on photos A–C, then play the video or audio recording (SB p110). Students watch or listen and put the photos in the order they hear about them. Note that all the Real World videos can be found on the **Teacher's DVD** at the back of this book.
Check answers with the class.

> 1B 2C 3A

3 **VIDEO ▸ 6 CD2 ▸ 51** Give students time to read sentences 1–6, then play the video or audio recording again. Students watch or listen and choose the correct answers.
Students compare answers in pairs. Check answers with the class.

> 2 11.30 3 closed 4 five
> 5 11; 1 6 £17.50

REAL WORLD
At a tourist information centre

4 Focus students on the conversations. Check students understand that the assistant says the sentences in the yellow boxes and the tourists say the sentences in the red boxes.
Students do the exercise on their own. Check answers with the class.

- **Answers** 2 have 3 open 4 closed 5 map
  6 book 7 start
- Point out the prepositions in *It's open from (11.30) a.m. to (5) p.m.* and check students understand that this means it opens at 11.30 a.m. and closes at 5 p.m.
- Highlight that we use *Where's the … ?* to ask where a place is (*Where's the Fitzwilliam Museum?*, etc.).
- Also point out that we use *in* with names of streets or roads (*It's in Trumpington Street.*).
- Check students understand *show* in *Can you show me on this map?*. Point out that we use *Can you* + verb … ? to ask people to do things for us.
- Point out the difference between *Here it is.* (when we show someone where a place is on a map) and *Here you are.* (which we use when we give something to someone).
- Also check students remember that *It's about (five) minutes away.* = It's about (five) minutes from here.
- Check students understand *per person* by asking how much it is for two people to go on the walking tour of Cambridge (£35).
- Note that the question *When is (Kettle's Yard art gallery) open?* asks about both opening and closing times. The question *When/What time does the (art gallery) open?* only asks about the opening time.

5 a **CD2 ▸ 52 PRONUNCIATION** Play the recording. Students listen and practise the sentences in **4**. Check they copy the polite intonation in the questions. Point out the importance of sounding polite in these types of situation, and that a flat intonation pattern will make students sound bored or rude.
Play the recording again, pausing after each sentence for students to repeat individually.

b Put students into pairs. Students practise the conversations in **4**, taking turns to be the tourist. Ask students to practise the conversations two or three times before they change roles.
Ask a few confident pairs of students to role-play the conversations for the class. Students don't have to leave their seats.

> **EXTRA IDEA**
> - Before students practise the conversations in pairs, ask students to practise in 'open pairs' (see **Teaching Tips** on drilling on p23).

6 a Students do the exercise on their own. You can ask students to cover the conversations in **4** before they begin.
Early finishers can compare answers in pairs.

b **CD2 ▸ 53** Play the recording. Students listen and check. Check answers with the class.

> 2 When 3 from 4 to 5 Is it 6 on
> 7 where's 8 in 9 map 10 Here it is.
> 11 afternoon 12 of 13 here you are
> 14 book 15 at 16 day 17 are 18 person

c Students practise the conversations in **6a** in pairs, taking turns to be the tourist.

7 a Students do the activity in new pairs. Remind students to use language from **4** before they begin writing their conversations. If you have an extra student, have one group of three with two tourists.
If your town or city doesn't have many places of interest, students can imagine the conversation is in their capital city, another town or city they know, or an imaginary town or city.
While they are working, monitor and check students' conversations for accuracy.

> **EXTRA IDEA**
> - Bring to class some tourist maps of your town or city, or print out copies from the internet. Give a copy of a map to each pair to help them think of ideas for their conversations.

b Ask one student to be the tourist and the other student to be the assistant at the tourist information centre. Students practise the conversations in their pairs until they can remember them.
While they are working, monitor and help students with any pronunciation problems.

c Students work in groups of four with another pair. Each pair takes turns to role-play their conversations. Students listen to the other pair's conversation and decides what the tourist asks about. Students can check their ideas at the end of each role-play. Finally, ask a few pairs to role-play their conversations for the class.

FURTHER PRACTICE

Ph **Class Activity** 6C What's in your bag? p000 (Instructions p000)
Extra Practice 6C SB p102
Self-study DVD-ROM Lesson 6C
Workbook Lesson 6C p31

VOCABULARY
6D AND SKILLS ▶ It's my favourite
Student's Book p52–p53

Vocabulary clothes, colours, *favourite*
Skills Listening: my clothes; Reading: my favourite places

QUICK REVIEW This activity reviews vocabulary for things in your bag. Students do the activity in pairs, as shown in the examples. 🖊 At the end of the activity, write *We both have …* on the board and then ask each pair to tell the class one or two things they both have with them.

1 **a** Pre-teach and drill *clothes* /kləʊðz/. Point out that *clothes* is one syllable, not two. You can also point out that many native speakers pronounce this word the same as *close* /kləʊz/.

Focus students on the photos. Students do the exercise in pairs. Early finishers can check their answers in **VOCABULARY 6.4** ▶ SB p124. Check answers with the class.

Point out that *trousers* and *jeans* are always plural and we can't say *a trouser* or *a jean*.

Also point out that *shoes*, *trainers* and *boots* are usually plural, but that we can say *a shoe*, *a trainer* and *a boot* when we refer to only one.

Teach students *a pair of …* , which we often use with plural nouns: *a pair of trousers*, *a pair of boots*, etc. Also highlight that *clothes* is always plural and takes a plural verb (*All my clothes are dirty.*). When we want to use the singular, we can say *an item of clothing*.

> a tie **2**; a shirt **1**; a T-shirt **9**; a jumper **5**; a jacket **8**; a coat **13**; a skirt **6**; a dress **12**; trousers **4**; jeans **10**; shoes **14**; trainers **11**; boots **7**

b **CD2 54** **PRONUNCIATION** Play the recording. Students listen and practise. Alternatively, model the words yourself and ask students to repeat chorally and individually.

Highlight the pronunciation of *suit* /suːt/, *shirt* /ʃɜːt/, *jumper* /ˈdʒʌmpə/, *jacket* /ˈdʒækɪt/, *trousers* /ˈtraʊzəz/ and *jeans* /dʒiːnz/. Repeat the drill if necessary.

Note that the /dʒ/ sound in *jumper*, *jacket*, *jeans* etc. is practised in the *Help with Pronunciation* section for this unit on SB p53.

c Students do the activity in new pairs, as shown in the speech bubbles.

EXTRA IDEA

● If you don't think your class will know any of the words in **1a**, teach the vocabulary yourself first by using photos or examples from your or students' own clothes. You can then use the matching activity in **1a** for practice.

2 **CD2 55** **PRONUNCIATION** Focus students on the words for colours. Play the recording. Students listen and practise. Repeat the drill if necessary.

3 **a** Focus students on the photos. Allow students two minutes to memorise the people's names, their clothes and the colour of each item of clothing.

b Use the speech bubbles to teach *What colour … ?*. Point out that we say *What colour are (Monica's boots)?* for plural words, and *What colour is (Wayne's tie)?* for singular words. Also highlight the possessive *'s* in *Monica's*.

Put students into pairs, student A and student B. Ask student Bs to close their books. Student A in each pair asks his/her partner what colour the people's clothes are. After a minute or two, ask students to change roles.

4 **a** **CD2 56** Play the recording (SB p110). Students listen and put the people in the order they hear them. Check answers with the class. Ask students to give reasons for their answers.

> **1** Lisa **2** Brad **3** Wayne **4** Monica

b Pre-teach *wear* by saying an example sentence about yourself in the Present Simple, for example, *I usually wear jeans at the weekend*. Avoid using the Present Continuous (*I'm wearing a green shirt.*, etc.) as students don't study this tense until **face2face** Second edition Elementary.

Play the recording again. Students listen and write what the people never wear. Check answers with the class.

> **Lisa** never wears trainers.
> **Brad** never wears brown.
> **Wayne** never wears jeans.
> **Monica** never wears dresses.

5 **a** Check students remember *usually*, *sometimes* and *never*. Students do the exercise on their own.

b Students work in groups and take turns to tell each other about the things on their lists, as shown in the speech bubbles.
Ask a few students to tell the class one thing they usually, sometimes or never wear.

HELP WITH VOCABULARY *favourite*

6 **a** Teach *favourite* by telling students your favourite colour, singer, etc. Tell students that your favourite is the thing or person you like best.
Students do the exercise on their own. Check answers with the class.

> • **Answers** 1 My 2 This 3 These 4 What 5 Who
> • Highlight the word order in sentence 1 and teach the phrase *My favourite* (colour, singer, etc.) *is* … .
> • Use sentences 2 and 3 to show that we use *This is my favourite* … for singular nouns and *These are my favourite* … for plural nouns. Point out that we say *favourite* in sentence 3, not ~~favourites~~.
> • Use sentences 4 and 5 to teach the phrases *What's your favourite* … ? and *Who's your favourite* … ?. Check students understand that we use *What* to ask about a thing and *Who* to ask about a person.

b **CD2** 57 Play the recording (SB p111). Students listen and practise the sentences in **6a**. Check that students pronounce *favourite* /ˈfeɪvrət/ correctly in each sentence. Point out that *favourite* is two syllables, not three.

7 **a** Focus students on the blog and the photos. Students do the exercise on their own. You can set a time limit of one or two minutes to encourage students to read for gist.
Check answers with the class.

> 1 restaurant 2 clothes shop 3 café

b Students do the exercise on their own, then compare answers in pairs. Check answers with the class. You can also use Tyrone and Keira's blog entries to teach *delicious* /dɪˈlɪʃəs/.

> 1 Yes, they are. 2 (He always has their) apple pie and vanilla ice cream. 3 No, they aren't. 4 Every Saturday. 5 (She goes there for breakfast) every morning. 6 Yes, they are.

8 **a** Use the examples to remind students that we use *What's your favourite* … ? to ask about things and *Who's your favourite* … ? to ask about people. Students do the exercise on their own, using the words in the box or their own ideas.

b Students work in pairs and take turns to ask their questions. You can teach the answer *I don't have one.* before they begin.

c Finally, ask each student to tell the class two things about their partner.

WRITING

Students write a description of their favourite clothes shop, restaurant or café (or all three). At the beginning of the next class, students can swap papers and read each other's descriptions.

FURTHER PRACTICE

Ph **Class Activity** 6D Review snakes and ladders p147 (Instructions p121)
Extra Practice 6 SB p102
Self-study DVD-ROM Lesson 6D
Workbook Lesson 6D p32
Workbook Reading and Writing Portfolio 6 p62–p63
Ph **Progress Test** 6 p186

HELP WITH PRONUNCIATION
/tʃ/ and /dʒ/

1 Focus students on the phonemes /tʃ/ and /dʒ/, the pictures and the words.

CD2► 58 Play the recording. Students listen to the sounds and the words. Point out that *ch* in *cheese* is pronounced with a /tʃ/ sound and both *ge* and *j* in *orange juice* are pronounced with a /dʒ/ sound.

Play the recording again. Students listen and practise. If students are having problems, help them with the mouth position for each sound.

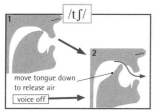
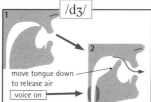

Point out that we make the /tʃ/ sound by placing the tongue on the top of the mouth behind the teeth, then moving the tongue down to release air. Highlight that this is an unvoiced sound (there is no vibration in the throat).

Also highlight that we use the same mouth position to make the /dʒ/ sound, but that this sound is voiced (there is vibration from the throat).

2 **CD2► 59** Focus students on the boxes. Play the recording. Students listen and notice how we say the pink and blue letters.

Play the recording again. Students listen and practise.

3 **a** Tell the class that many common English first names start with the /dʒ/ sound. Put students into pairs. Students work with their partner and try to say the names using a /dʒ/ sound.

b **CD2► 60** Play the recording. Students listen and check their pronunciation of the names.

Play the recording again. Students listen and practise. Finally, ask students to say the names around the class.

---

continue2learn

Focus students on the **continue2learn** section on SB p53. See p33 in this book for ideas on how to use this section in class.

Extra Practice 6 SB p102

See p34 for ideas on how to use this section in class.

6A
1 2 a shopping centre **3** a theatre **4** a station **5** a river **6** an airport **7** a building **8** a bus station **9** a museum
2 2 's **3** a lot of **4** are **5** some **6** a lot of **7** 's **8** an

6B
3 2 bus stop **3** bank **4** market **5** supermarket **6** post office **7** square **8** chemist's
4 2 isn't **3** 's **4** aren't **5** isn't **6** are **7** aren't
5a 2 Is; a **3** Are; any **4** Is; a **5** Are; any **6** Is; a **7** Are; any
5b 2 No, there isn't. **3** No, there aren't. **4** Yes, there is. **5** No, there aren't. **6** Yes, there is. **7** Yes, there are.

6C
6 2 Do you have **3** where's **4** show me **5** minutes away **6** When is **7** It's open **8** we book **9** per person
7 2 a passport **3** a wallet **4** money **5** a laptop (a computer) **6** a credit card **7** a bunch of keys **8** a guide book

6D
8

J	A	C	K	E	T	S	C
E	T	V	O	Q	R	K	O
A	S	U	I	T	A	I	A
N	Z	T	S	H	I	R	T
S	D	B	J	E	N	T	L
T	R	O	U	S	E	R	S
E	E	O	M	X	R	B	H
K	S	T	P	O	S	U	O
G	S	S	E	M	T	I	E
S	H	I	R	T	F	N	S

Progress Portfolio 6

See p34 for ideas on how to use this section in class.

7A ▶ **We're twins**
Student's Book p54–p55

Vocabulary things you like and don't like;
love, like, don't like, hate
Grammar object pronouns

QUICK REVIEW This activity reviews phrases with *favourite*. Students do the first part of the activity on their own. Tell students that they can write film and book titles in their own language. Put students into groups of three. Students take turns to say what their favourite things are, as shown in the examples, and make a note of any that are the same. At the end of the activity, ask each group to tell the class about any favourite things that are the same for more than one student.

Things you like and don't like

1 a Focus students on pictures 1–9. Students do the activity in pairs. Early finishers can check answers in Language Summary 7 **VOCABULARY 7.1** ▶ SB p126. Check answers with the class.

Point out that *visiting new places, flying, dancing, watching sport on TV* and *shopping for clothes* are all activities. You can also teach the corresponding verbs *visit, fly, dance* and *shop*. (Note that students learned the verb *watch* in lesson 4B.)

Check that students don't confuse *a soap opera* (a type of TV programme) with *opera* (a type of music). Highlight the preposition in *watching sport on TV*.

Also point out that we say *a film* in British English and *a movie* in American English (although this is now quite common in the UK too).

visiting new places 3; classical music 2; flying 9; dancing 8; watching sport on TV 5; animals 1; horror films 4; shopping for clothes 6

┌─ **EXTRA IDEA** ─

• If you have a strong class, you can teach more types of music (*rap, dance music, opera, folk music*, etc.) and types of film (*adventure films, musicals, comedies, sci-fi films*, etc.).

b **CD2** 61 **PRONUNCIATION** Play the recording. Students listen and practise. Highlight the pronunciation of *horror* /ˈhɒrə/ and *clothes* /kləʊðz/. Also check students stress the phrases correctly. Point out that the stress in *soap opera* is on the first word, not the second. Repeat the drill if necessary. Note that only the main stress is shown in the vocabulary boxes and Language Summaries.

2 Focus students on pictures A–D. Students do the exercise on their own before comparing answers in pairs. Check answers with the class. Model and drill the phrases if necessary.

A I love … **B** I like … **C** I don't like … **D** I hate …

HELP WITH VOCABULARY
love, like, don't like, hate

3 a Focus students on the example sentences. Point out the nouns in blue and the verb+*ing* forms in pink. Go through the following points with the class.

• Highlight that after *love, like, don't like* and *hate* we can use a noun or verb+*ing*.
• Also point out that we use the plural form of most nouns after *love, like, don't like* and *hate* (*animals, soap operas*, etc.) because we are talking about things in general.
• You can also highlight that we don't use *the* when we talk about things we like or don't like in general: *I love animals*. (= all animals), *I don't like sport*. (= all sport), etc.
• Students may ask why we don't say *I like classical musics*. We suggest you simply tell the class that some nouns don't have a plural form. This will probably be enough explanation without introducing the difference between countable and uncountable nouns, which may overload students. The difference between countable and uncountable nouns is taught in **face2face** Second edition Elementary. Note that all the words and phrases in **1a** are already in the correct form to be used with *love, like, don't like* and *hate*.

b Students do the exercise on their own. Check answers with the class.

visiting (new places); flying; dancing; watching (sport on TV); shopping (for clothes)

c Ask students to turn to **VOCABULARY 7.2** ▶ SB p126. Focus students on the **SPELLING OF VERB+*ING* FORMS** section. Give students time to read the information, or go through the bullet points with the class.

Check students understand that if a verb ends in -*e*, we drop the -*e* and add -*ing* (*dance* → *dancing*, *live* → *living*, etc.). Also check they understand that verbs ending in consonant + vowel + consonant double the final consonant (*shop* → *shopping*, *get* → *getting*, etc.).

Also point out that if a verb ends in -*y*, we don't double the final consonant (*play* → *playing*, etc.).

4 a Students do the exercise on their own.

b Students compare answers in pairs and discuss which sentences are true for them.

Check answers with the class. Ask each student to tell the class one sentence that is true for them.

2 having **3** going **4** getting up **5** sleeping **6** living

5 **a** Students do the exercise on their own, as shown in the examples. While they are working, monitor and check their sentences for accuracy.

b Students do the exercise in pairs, as shown in the speech bubbles.
Ask students to tell the class one or two of their (or their partner's) true sentences.

We're very different

6 **a** Pre-teach the words in the box using examples, pictures, translation, etc. Note that the aim of this box is to highlight which new words students need in order to understand the text they are about to read and listen to.
Note that in English we use *twins* to refer to two people who were born at the same time, whether they are identical twins or fraternal (non-identical) twins. Point out that *different* and *the same* are opposites. Model and drill the words with the class. Highlight that *different* /ˈdɪfrənt/ is two syllables, not three.

b Ask the class if they know any twins. If so, ask students to tell the class about them. If you know any twins, you can tell the class about them before asking students to do the same.

7 **a** Focus students on the photo of Adam and Hugo /ˈhjuːɡəʊ/, and the speech bubbles.
CD2 62 Play the recording. Students listen, read and find two things that Adam and Hugo both like.
Check answers with the class.

They both like watching TV.
They both like having a twin brother.

b Students do the exercise on their own before comparing answers in pairs.
Check answers with the class.

2 Adam 3 Hugo 4 Adam 5 Hugo
6 Hugo 7 Hugo; Adam

HELP WITH GRAMMAR Object pronouns

8 **a** ✍ Draw the table on the board and write in the example sentences. Alternatively, focus students on the table in the Student's Book. Go through the following points with the class.

- Use the example sentences to highlight the typical word order in positive sentences: subject + verb + object.
- Highlight *I* in pink in the first sentence and remind students that this is a subject pronoun.
- Highlight *them* in blue in the second sentence. Teach students this is called an object pronoun.
- Point out that subject pronouns go before the verb and object pronouns go after the verb in sentences. If possible, compare this structure to that of your students' own language(s).

- Drill *subject* /ˈsʌbdʒekt/ and *object* /ˈɒbdʒekt/ with the class, highlighting the /dʒ/ sound in both words.

b Focus students on the speech bubbles about Adam and Hugo and point out the object pronouns in blue. Students do the exercise on their own or in pairs.
✍ While they are working, draw the table from **7b** on the board. Check answers with the class.

- **Object pronouns** me, (you), him, her, it, us, them

9 **a** Students do the exercise on their own.

b **CD2** 63 Play the recording. Students listen and check their answers. Check answers with the class.
Highlight that we usually use *Do you like … ?* to ask for people's opinions, not *Do you love … ?* or *Do you hate … ?*.
You can point out that when we say that we like, love or hate famous people, we are usually referring to their music, acting, etc., not the people themselves. Also use question 3 to highlight that we use *it* to refer to a word/phrase with verb+*ing* (*shopping for clothes*, *dancing*, etc.).
Note that while *Yes, I do.* and *No, I don't.* are also correct answers to *Do you like … ?* questions, they are not as common as you might expect. This exercise therefore aims to provide students with a variety of more common ways to respond to these types of question.
PRONUNCIATION Play the recording again, pausing after each question and answer for students to repeat chorally and individually.

2 her 3 it 4 him 5 them 6 me

c Students do the exercise in pairs. Before they begin, remind students to give their own answers.

10 **a** Students do the exercise on their own, as shown in the example. They can refer to the speech bubbles on the photo if they wish.
✍ While they are working, write the following possible answers on the board: *Yes, he/she loves it/them.*, *No, he/she hates it/them.*, *Yes, he/she does.*, *No, he/she doesn't.* and *I don't remember.*

b Students work in pairs and ask their questions. You can ask students to close their books during the activity. Remind students to answer the questions with one of the short answer forms on the board before they begin.

┌ **EXTRA IDEA** ┐

- Students do **10a** in pairs. Ask students to make a note of the answers to their questions. Put two pairs together in groups of four and ask them to close their books. Each pair takes turns to ask their questions. The pair who answers more questions correctly wins.

Get ready … Get it right!

11 Put students into new pairs, student A and student B. If possible, ask students to work with someone they don't know very well. Student As turn to SB p86 and student Bs turn to SB p91. Check they are all looking at the correct exercise.

a Students do the exercise on their own, as shown in the example. Note that some of the pictures represent vocabulary from **1a**, while other pictures represent vocabulary taught in earlier lessons. While they are working, monitor and check their questions for accuracy.

If possible, avoid checking the questions with the class to prevent students hearing the questions they are about to be asked.

Student A 2 Do you like playing video games? **3** Do you like flying? **4** Do you like (playing) tennis? **5** Do you like rock music?/Do you like going to concerts? **6** Do you like eggs?

Student B b Do you like shopping for clothes? **c** Do you like cats? **d** Do you like watching sport on TV? **e** Do you like (listening to) classical music? **f** Do you like (black) coffee?

b Students do the exercise on their own. They are not allowed to talk to their partners during this stage of the activity.

c Students work with their partners. Student A in each pair asks his/her questions from **a** and puts a tick or a cross in column C of the table.

Remind students to use the correct short answers (*Yes, I love it/them. No, I hate it/them. Yes, I do. No, I don't.*). ✐ If necessary, write these short answers on the board before they begin.

After student As have asked their questions, they tell their partners how many of their guesses in column B of the table are correct.

d Students swap roles and repeat the activity, with student B in each pair asking his/her questions from **a**.

e Finally, ask each student to tell the class two things about his/her partner. Check students use the *he/she* forms *likes*, *doesn't like*, *loves* and *hates* in their sentences, as shown in the speech bubbles.

WRITING

Students choose one person they know well and write sentences comparing this person's likes and dislikes to their own, using language from the lesson (*I love watching football on TV, but my brother Marco hates it. Marco doesn't like eating out, but I love it.* etc.).

FURTHER PRACTICE

Ph **Class Activity** 7A I like dominoes p148 (Instructions p121)
Extra Practice 7A SB p103
Self-study DVD-ROM Lesson 7A
Workbook Lesson 7A p33

7B ▶ Can you drive?
Student's Book p56–p57

Vocabulary abilities
Grammar *can* for ability

QUICK REVIEW This activity reviews things you like and don't like. Students do the activity in pairs, as shown in the examples. At the end of the activity, ask each pair to tell the class one or two of the things they both like.

Abilities

1 **a** Focus students on pictures 1–10. Students do the exercise on their own or in pairs. Early finishers can check their answers in **VOCABULARY 7.3** ▶ SB p126. Check answers with the class.

Point out that we can say *ride a bike* or *ride a bicycle*. You can also teach *ride a motorbike/scooter*. Note that we say *play basketball* not *play basket*.

Also highlight that we say *play basketball, football, tennis,* etc. but *play the piano* and *play the guitar*. While the alternative form (*play piano, play guitar,* etc.) is also used in some situations, at this level we feel it is more helpful to give students a clear rule that will always result in correct sentences.

cook **10**; drive **3**; ride a bike **2**; play basketball **9**; play the piano **6**; sing **7**; play the guitar **8**; speak German **5**; ski **1**

EXTRA IDEA

● If you have a strong class, teach other sports that are played with a ball (*volleyball, baseball, rugby,* etc.) and other musical instruments (*the violin, the drums,* etc.).

b `CD2` **64** `PRONUNCIATION` Play the recording. Students listen and practise. Repeat the drill if necessary.

c Pre-teach *mime* by miming one of the activities from **1a**.

Put students into pairs. Students take turns to mime activities from **1a** for their partner to guess.

I can't swim!

2 Focus students on pictures A–D. Students do the exercise on their own before comparing answers in pairs.

Check answers with the class. Use picture C and sentence 1 to teach *Help!*.

1C 2A 3B 4D

HELP WITH GRAMMAR

can: positive and negative

3 ✎ Focus students on the tables in the Student's Book or draw them on the board. Go through the following points with the class.

- We use *can* or *can't* to talk about ability.
- Use the first table to highlight the word order in positive sentences: subject + *can* + verb + … .
- Use the second table to highlight the word order in negative sentences: subject + *can't* + verb + … .
- Point out that *can* and *can't* are the same for *I, you, he, she, it, we* and *they*.
- Highlight that we sometimes use *(very) well* with *can*: *She can swim **well**. They can ski **very** **well**.* (not ~~They can ski (very) good.~~)
- Point out that we say *She can play the piano.* not ~~She can to play the piano.~~
- Remind students that we also use *can* for offers (*Can I help you?*) and requests (*Can I have the bill, please?*, *Can you show me on this map?*).

HELP WITH LISTENING *can* or *can't*

This *Help with Listening* section focuses on how we say *can* and *can't* in sentences.

4 **a** `CD2` **65** Focus students on the four sentences and highlight the sentence stress. Play the recording. Students listen and notice how we say *can* /kən/ and *can't* /kɑːnt/.

Ask students if *can* is stressed (it isn't). Point out that *can* is usually pronounced in its weak form in positive sentences and that the vowel sound is a schwa /ə/.

Ask if *can't* is stressed (it is). Point out that *can't* is stressed because it is negative.

Play the recording again if necessary.

You can also teach students that *can't* is pronounced /kænt/ in American English.

b `CD2` **66** Play the recording (SB p111). Students listen and decide if they hear *can* or *can't*. Tell students to write their answers for each question as they listen.

Play the recording again, pausing after each sentence to check students' answers.

1 can 2 can't 3 can 4 can't 5 can't 6 can

5 `CD2` **66** `PRONUNCIATION` Play the recording again. Students listen and practise. Check that students pronounce *can* and *can't* correctly. Repeat the drill if necessary, pausing after each sentence for students to practise individually.

6 **a** Students do the exercise on their own, as shown in the examples. Students can use words and phrases from **1a** or their own ideas.

b Students do the exercise in pairs. Ask each student to tell the class one or two of their true sentences.

Help with the children

7 **a** Pre-teach *au pair* /əʊ ˈpeə/. Focus students on the photo. Explain that Mrs Taylor is going to interview Natalia because she wants an au pair to help her with her two children, Megan and Harry, who are in the photo by the window.

`CD2` **67** Play the recording (SB p111). Students listen to the interview. Ask students if Natalia gets the job (she does).

b Give students time to read prompts 1–10. Play the recording again. Students listen and tick the things Natalia can do and put a cross next to the things she can't do.

c Students compare answers in pairs. Check answers with the class.

2 ✓ 3 ✗ 4 ✓ 5 ✓ 6 ✗ 7 ✓ 8 ✗ 9 ✓ 10 ✓

> ⌐ EXTRA IDEA ┐
> - Ask students to look at Audio Script `CD2` **67** SB p111. Play the recording again. Students listen, read and underline all the examples of *can* and *can't* in the conversation. Students then compare answers in pairs.

HELP WITH GRAMMAR

can: yes / no questions and short answers

8 Students do the exercise on their own, then compare answers in pairs. Check answers with the class and go through the following points.

- Focus students on the first column of the table. Highlight the inverted word order of *yes/no* questions: *Can* + subject + verb + … .
- Point out that we don't use *do* or *does* in questions with *can*: *Can you cook?* not ~~Do you can cook?~~

- Focus students on the second column of the table. Check that students have completed the short answers correctly: *Yes, I **can**. / No, I **can't**. Yes, he **can**. / No, he **can't**. Yes, she **can**. / No, she **can't**. Yes, they **can**. / No, they **can't**.*
- Remind students that *can* and *can't* are the same for all subjects (*I, you, he, she,* etc.) in *yes/no* questions and short answers.
- Note that we also make *Wh-* questions with *can*: *How many languages can you speak?, Which instrument can you play?,* etc. However, these are less common than *yes/no* questions with *can* and are therefore taught in **face2face** Second edition Elementary.

9 Focus students on the examples. Highlight that we usually use the weak form of *can* /kən/ in *yes/no* questions and that we always use the strong form of *can* /kæn/ in short answers.

CD2▸68 PRONUNCIATION Play the recording. Students listen and practise the questions and short answers in **8**. Encourage them to copy the weak and strong forms of *can* and remind students that *can't* is always stressed. Repeat the drill if necessary.

Note that we can also use the strong form of *can* in *yes/no* questions: *Can /kæn/ you cook?*.

10 Put students into pairs, student A and student B. Student As turn to SB p90 and student Bs turn to SB p95. Check that they are all looking at the correct exercise.

a Focus students on the photos of Megan and Harry. Check students understand that they are Mrs Taylor's children.

Students do the exercise on their own, as shown in the example. Point out that all the pictures correspond to words and phrases in **1a**.

If necessary, check answers with the class. Note that all the answers are the same for student As and student Bs, apart from the person's name.

Student A/Student B
2 Can Megan/Harry play the piano?
3 Can Megan/Harry play the guitar?
4 Can Megan/Harry ride a bike?
5 Can Megan/Harry ski?
6 Can Megan/Harry swim?
7 Can Megan/Harry play tennis?
8 Can Megan/Harry play basketball?

b Students do the activity with their partners. Remind students to use the correct short answers (*Yes, he/she can.* and *No, he/she can't.*) when answering their partner's questions. Students are not allowed to look at their partner's book.

c Students compare tables with their partner and find out what both children can do.
Check answers with the class. (They can both ride a bike and swim.)

Get ready … Get it right!

11 Students work on their own and make a list of things they can do, using phrases from **1a** and their own ideas. Students should just write the things they can do (*play the guitar, swim,* etc.), not complete sentences, as shown in the example.
While students are working, monitor and help them with any new vocabulary they might need.

12 **a** Put students into new pairs. Students take turns to ask questions about the things on their list in **11**, as shown in the speech bubbles. Each pair must find out how many things on their lists they can both do. While they are working, monitor and correct any grammar or pronunciation mistakes you hear.

b Finally, ask each pair of students to tell the class some of the things they can both do, using *We can both … .*

┌─ **WRITING** ─────────────────────────────────┐
Students write a short description of each person in their family, saying what they can and can't do. Tell students that they should also include other information about each person (age, job, free time activities, etc.). At the beginning of the next class, students can swap papers and read about other students' families.
└──┘

┌─ **FURTHER PRACTICE** ────────────────────────┐
Ph **Class Activity** 7B What can the class do? p149 (Instructions p122)
Ph **Vocabulary Plus** 7 Parts of the body p173 (Instructions p165)
Extra Practice 7B SB p103
Self-study DVD-ROM Lesson 7B
Workbook Lesson 7B p34
└──┘

QUICK REVIEW This activity reviews vocabulary for abilities and *can*. Put students into pairs, if possible with someone that they don't know very well. Students do the activity in their pairs, as shown in the examples. At the end of the activity, ask a few students to tell the class one or two things they can do, but their partner can't do.

Where's the café?

1 **a** Ask students to close their books. Students work on their own and write down ten places in a town or city, as shown in the examples.

b Put students into groups of three or four. Students compare lists to find out if they have the same places.
✎ Ask one group to tell you their words and write them on the board. Ask other groups to tell you any other words they have and add them to the list on the board.
Check that students have remembered all the vocabulary in **VOCABULARY 6.1** and **VOCABULARY 6.2** SB p124. Drill the words chorally with the class if necessary.

HELP WITH VOCABULARY
Prepositions of place

2 Focus students on pictures a–f. Check students understand that the building with the cup and saucer symbol is a café and the building with a pound sign is a bank.
Students do the exercise on their own or in pairs. Check answers with the class.
Point out that we can say *in* or *on* with streets and roads (*The café is in/on King Street.*, etc.).
Use pictures e and f to highlight the difference between *next to* and *near*.
Also check students understand *left* and *right*, and highlight that we say *It's on the left/right.* not *It's on left/right.*

2f 3e 4d 5a 6b

3 **a** **CD3** 1 **PRONUNCIATION** Play the recording. Students listen and practise. Highlight the pronunciation of *opposite* /ˈɒpəzɪt/ and the weak form of *to* /tə/ in *next to*.

b Drill the sentences in the speech bubbles. Students then do the exercise in pairs.

It's over there

4 **a** Focus students on the map on SB p59. Students work in pairs and decide what places 1–12 are on the map. Check answers with the class.

1 a museum 2 a theatre 3 a café 4 a hotel
5 a supermarket 6 a chemist's 7 a bank
8 a park 9 a cinema 10 a post office
11 a restaurant 12 a station

b Students do the activity in the same pairs, as shown in the speech bubbles. Remind students to use the prepositions of place in **2** in their sentences. Ask students to say four or five sentences each. If necessary, demonstrate this activity with the whole class before they begin.

┌─ **EXTRA IDEA** ─────────────────────────
• If you have a low-level class, you can ask students to write down their sentences before they do **4b** in pairs.
└──

5 **a** Focus students on the photos of Rachel and Jack asking for directions. Tell students that they are at ✷ on the map. Then ask students to cover the conversations in **5b** or close their books.
VIDEO 7 **CD3** 2 Play the video or audio recording (SB p111). Students watch or listen and decide which places Rachel and Jack want to go to. Note that all the Real World videos can be found on the **Teacher's DVD** at the back of this book.
Check answers with the class.

Rachel wants to go to the museum and a café.
Jack wants to go to the post office and a bank.

b Students do the exercise in pairs. Tell students that they can refer to the map on SB p59 if necessary. Do not check students' answers at this stage.

c Play the video or audio recording again. Students watch or listen and check their answers. Check answers with the class.
You can use the conversations to teach the phrases *No problem.*, *Oh, yes. I can see it.* and *You're welcome.* Also highlight three different ways to say *thank you* in the conversations: *Thank you very much.*, *Thanks.* and *Thanks a lot.* Point out that we can't say *Thank you a lot.*

1 museum 2 museum 3 on 4 next to 5 café
6 on 7 next to 8 post office 9 near 10 can
11 bank 12 in 13 bank 14 left

REAL WORLD
Asking for and giving directions

6 Check students understand the headings ASKING FOR DIRECTIONS and GIVING DIRECTIONS by referring students to the conversations in **5b**.
Students do the exercise on their own before comparing answers in pairs. Check answers with the class.

- **Answers** 2 here 3 road 4 turn 5 to 6 on 7 over
- Point out the use of *the* and *a* in the questions *Where's the (museum)?* and *Is there a (bank) near here?*. This is because in the first question, we know there is only one museum in the town and we only want to know its location. In the second question we want to know if there is a bank near here or not (i.e. if a bank near here exists). However, at this level it is probably easier just to teach *Where's the … ?* and *Is there a … (near here)?* as fixed phrases.
- Check students understand the new phrases *go along, turn left/right* and *It's over there*.
- Point out that we can say *on the right/left* or *on your right/left* when giving directions.
- Note that native speakers say *go along, go up* or *go down* to mean the same thing when giving directions. If your students are studying in an English-speaking country, you can teach these alternatives.

7 **a** [CD3] 3 [PRONUNCIATION] Play the recording (SB p111). Students listen and practise. Check that students sound polite and copy the sentence stress correctly. Play the recording again, pausing after each sentence for students to repeat individually.

┌─ **EXTRA IDEA** ┐
- Ask students to turn to Audio Script [CD3] 3 SB p111. Students can then follow the stress on the sentences while they listen and practise.
└──────────────────────────────────────┘

b Students do the exercise in pairs. Make sure that all students take turns to be Rachel and Jack.

While students are working, check they are sounding polite and help them with any pronunciation problems they may have.

You can ask one or two pairs to role-play their conversations for the class. Students don't have to leave their seats.

8 **a** Students do the exercise on their own. Before they begin, remind them to refer to the map when choosing the correct words.

b [CD3] 4 Play the recording. Students listen and check their answers. Check answers with the class.

1 me 2 here 3 right 4 on 5 near 6 Where's 7 over 8 next to 9 near 10 along 11 right 12 hotel

c Students practise the conversations in **8a** in pairs, taking turns to ask for directions.

9 Put students into new pairs. Students take turns to ask for directions to places on the map. When students are listening to their partner's directions, they should follow the route and make sure the directions are correct.

Before they begin, remind students that they must start every conversation from ✣ on the map.

Finally, ask a few pairs to role-play one of their conversations for the class.

┌─ **FURTHER PRACTICE** ┐
[Ph] **Class Activity** 7C It's on the left p150–p151 (Instructions p122)
Self-study DVD-ROM Lesson 7C
Workbook Lesson 7C p36
└──────────────────────────────────────┘

7D **VOCABULARY AND SKILLS** ▷ **The internet**
Student's Book p60–p61

Vocabulary things people do online
Skills Reading: It's my internet!;
Listening: an internet questionnaire

QUICK REVIEW This activity reviews ways to ask for and give directions. Students do the first part of the activity on their own. Encourage them to write the names of places near the school (or near the building where the class is taking place), but not to write very famous places that all students know. Students complete the activity in pairs. ✍ Write this sentence on the board to help them when giving directions: *Go out of the school and turn left/right. Then … .* At the end of the activity, ask a few students to tell the class one new place they talked about.

1 **a** Check students understand *the internet*. Focus students on the vocabulary and highlight the example (*send emails*). Students do the exercise in pairs.

Check answers with the class. Go through the new vocabulary with the class and teach any words students don't know.

Point out that we can say *receive emails* or *get emails*, and that *receive* is more formal than *get*. Note that we always use *receive* in the phrase *send and receive emails*, but we usually use *get* in everyday conversation, for example, *I get about 50 emails every day.*, etc.

Point out that *online* = connected to the internet. Check students understand *a blog* (a website where people regularly write their own thoughts and experiences) and *an app* (a computer program that you can download onto your mobile phone or computer).

Teach students that you *download music/videos/apps onto your computer/laptop/phone*, etc.

Highlight the prepositions in *listen **to** the radio* and *chat **to** friends and family*.

Also teach students that we say *a TV programme* in British English and *a TV show* in American English (although this is now quite common in the UK too). Avoid asking students how they use the internet at this stage of the lesson, as students complete an internet questionnaire in **5a**.

buy/sell things online; **read**/write a blog; **watch** TV programmes/videos; **be** on Facebook/on Twitter; download videos/**music**/apps; book **hotels**/holidays/**flights**; listen to **the radio**/to music; **chat** to friends and family; search for **information**

b **CD3 5** **PRONUNCIATION** Play the recording. Students listen and practise the phrases in **1a**. Note that each phrase is said separately on the recording (*send emails*, *get emails*, etc.).

Highlight the pronunciation of *receive* /rɪˈsiːv/, *videos* /ˈvɪdɪəʊz/, *flights* /flaɪts/, *search* /sɜːtʃ/ and point out the silent *t* in *listen* /ˈlɪsən/.

You can ask students to work in pairs and test each other on the collocations. One student says a verb, for example *listen*, and his/her partner says a phrase with that verb, for example *listen to the radio*.

c Students do the activity in pairs, as shown in the speech bubbles. You can ask the person who is being tested to close their books.

2 Pre-teach *a website*. Focus students on the website logos. Check students remember how to say . (= dot) in website addresses. Highlight the phrase *You can …* in the speech bubble. Point out that we usually use *on* with websites (*I bought it on eBay.* etc.) but we can also use *at* when we say the whole website address (*You can book flights at cheapflights.co.uk.*). Students do the activity in pairs. Check students' ideas with the class.

Possible answers You can book flights or holidays at **Cheapflights.co.uk.** You can watch TV programmes at **itv.com.** You can buy and sell things on **amazon.com.** You can watch videos on **YouTube.** You can listen to the radio at **realradio.** You can read or write blogs on **Blogger.** You can buy and sell things on **eBay.** You can use **Google** to search for information and send or receive emails. You can buy concert or theatre tickets on **ticketmaster.**

> **EXTRA IDEA**
>
> • Students work in pairs and think of other things people use the internet for. ✎ Check answers with the class by eliciting students' ideas and writing correct phrases on the board. **Possible answers** send and receive photos; buy cinema/concert/theatre tickets; buy clothes; buy food; buy DVDs and CDs; book a restaurant; play computer games; read the news; bank online, etc.

3 **a** Focus students on the online article and the photos of Sunita, Brian and Millie. Tell students the article is about how these people use the internet. Students do the exercise on their own.

b Students compare answers in pairs. Check answers with the class.

2 Sunita **3** Brian **4** Millie **5** Brian **6** Sunita **7** Millie **8** Brian **9** Sunita, Millie

c Students do the exercise on their own, then work with another student and check if they have underlined the same phrases from **1a**. Check answers with the class.

SUNITA (I)'m on Facebook; chat (online) to my brother; download (a lot of) music, watch music videos; buy (a lot of) things online
BRIAN send and receive emails; (I)'m (not) on Facebook (or) Twitter; search for information; book hotels; buy things online
MILLIE write a blog; watch (a lot of) TV shows; buy (a lot of) things online

4 **a** Focus students on column A of the internet questionnaire. Students work on their own and choose the correct verbs. You can ask students to cover the phrases in **1a** before they begin. Check answers with the class.

1 watch **2** listen **3** be **4** chat **5** sell **6** book **7** read **8** download

b Focus students on the photo. Tell students that the interviewer is asking Sam about things he does online.
CD3 6 Play the recording (SB p111). Students listen and put a tick or a cross in column B of the questionnaire. Students compare answers in pairs. Check answers with the class.

1 ✗ **2** ✗ **3** ✓ **4** ✓ **5** ✓ **6** ✗ **7** ✗ **8** ✓

c Give students time to read questions 1–7. Play the recording again. Students listen and answer the questions. Students compare answers in pairs. Check answers with the class.

1 Yes, he does. **2** YouTube. **3** Yes, he is. **4** In Poland. **5** He buys DVDs. **6** He's married. **7** On the train.

5 **a** Put students into pairs. If possible, ask students to work with someone they don't know very well. Students take turns to interview their partner. Students put a tick or a cross for each of their partner's answers in column C on the questionnaire. Encourage students to give more information if possible when answering the questions.

b Students work in new pairs and take turns to tell each other about their partners in **5a**. Before they begin, remind students to use *he/she* forms of the verbs: *Gloria* **watches** *TV programmes online. She* **doesn't listen** *to the radio online.*, etc.

c Finally, ask students to tell the class two things about their first partner.

> **WRITING**
>
> Students write a description of how they use the internet, using phrases from **1a**. Encourage students to include interesting details (their favourite websites/blogs, etc.) in their descriptions.

> **FURTHER PRACTICE**
>
> **Extra Practice** 7 SB p103
> **Self-study DVD-ROM** Lesson 7D
> **Workbook** Lesson 7D p37
> **Workbook** Reading and Writing Portfolio 7 p64–p65
> **Ph Progress Test** 7 p187

HELP WITH PRONUNCIATION /s/ and /ʃ/

1 Focus students on the phonemes /s/ and /ʃ/, the pictures and the words.

CD3 7 Play the recording. Students listen to the sounds and the words. Point out that *s* in *suit* is pronounced with a /s/ sound and *sh* in *shirt* is pronounced with a /ʃ/ sound.

Play the recording again. Students listen and practise. If students are having problems, help them with the mouth position for each sound.

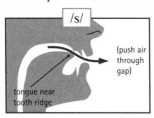
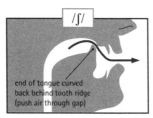

Point out that when we make the /s/ sound, the lips are relaxed, the tongue is near the back of the teeth, and there is some contact between the tongue and the teeth at the sides of the mouth. Highlight that /s/ is an unvoiced sound (there is no vibration in the throat).

Also point out that when we make the /ʃ/ sound, the lips are more rounded and pushed forward slightly. The end of the tongue is curved back behind the teeth and we push air through the gap. Highlight that /ʃ/ is also an unvoiced sound.

You can also tell students that /ssss/ is the sound a snake makes, and that /ʃʃʃʃ/ is the sound people make when they want someone to be quiet.

2 CD3 8 Focus students on the boxes. Play the recording. Students listen and notice how we say the pink and blue consonants.

Play the recording again. Students listen and practise.

3 a CD3 9 Play the recording. Students listen and read the poem. Highlight that the pink consonants are pronounced /s/ and the blue consonants are pronounced /ʃ/.

Play the recording again, pausing after each line for students to practise chorally and individually.

b Students work in pairs and take turns to say lines of the poem. Tell students to practise the poem at least three times. Finally, ask one or two students to say the poem for the class.

continue2learn

Focus students on the **continue2learn** section on SB p61. See p33 of this book for ideas on how to use this section in class.

Extra Practice 7 SB p103

See p34 for ideas on how to use this section in class.

7A
1 2 animals 3 horror films 4 dancing 5 flying 6 classical music 7 watching sport on TV 8 visiting new places 9 shopping for clothes
2 2 don't like 3 doesn't like 4 hates 5 likes 6 hate 7 loves 8 loves
3 2 She; us 3 he; me 4 I; her 5 We; them 6 him

7B
4 3 He can't **speak** Japanese. 4 ✓ 5 **Can you** play tennis? 6 Lydia can dance very **well**. 7 ✓ 8 ✓ 9 Paul can play **football well**.
5 2 She can play the guitar. 3 She can ride a bike. 4 He can swim. 5 She can drive (a car). 6 He can play the piano. 7 They can play basketball. 8 She can cook. 9 He can ski.

7C
6 2 Where's 3 along 4 right 5 left 6 opposite 7 welcome 8 near 9 along 10 left 11 right 12 next 13 where's 14 over 15 near 16 station

7D
7 2 receive 3 write 4 reading 5 search 6 book 7 watch 8 watching 9 download 10 listen 11 chat 12 buy

Progress Portfolio 7

See p34 for ideas on how to use this section in class.

I was there

Student's Book p62–p63

Vocabulary adjectives (2)
Grammar Past Simple of *be*:
positive and negative

QUICK REVIEW This activity reviews things people do online. Students do the first part of the activity on their own. Put students into groups of three or four. Students complete the activity in their groups. At the end of the activity, ask a few students to tell the class one thing they do online, using phrases from their lists.

Adjectives (2)

1 **a** Focus students on pictures a–h. Students do the exercise on their own or in pairs. Early finishers can check their answers in **VOCABULARY 8.1** SB p128. Check answers with the class.

Point out that we can use *short* or *long* for amount of time (*It's a short/long film.*, etc.) and for physical length (*It's a short/long dress.*, etc.).

Use the pictures in e to point out that the book (which is arrowed in each picture) is *interesting* or *boring*, not the person. Note that *bored* is taught in lesson 10C.

Point out that we use *old/young* for people or animals, and *old/new* for things, buildings, etc.

With a strong class you can teach the synonyms *sad* (= *unhappy*), *hard* (= *difficult*) and *wonderful* (= *fantastic*).

happy/unhappy **f**; interesting/boring **e**; full/empty **h**; difficult/easy **d**; right/wrong **c**; old/young **g**; terrible, awful/great, fantastic, amazing **b**

b **CD3▶10** **PRONUNCIATION** Play the recording. Students listen and practise. Alternatively, model and drill the adjectives yourself. Highlight the pronunciation of *awful* /ˈɔːfəl/ and *great* /greɪt/. Also point out that *interesting* /ˈɪntrəstɪŋ/ is three syllables, not four, with the stress on the first syllable. Repeat the drill if necessary.

Three amazing days

2 **a** Pre-teach the words in the box using pictures, board diagrams, translation, etc. Note that the aim of this box is to highlight which new words students need in order to understand the text they are about to read.

You can also teach *New Year's Day* and *Holland*. Model and drill all the words and phrases with the class.

b Focus students on the photos and speech bubbles at the bottom of SB p62–p63.
CD3▶11 Play the recording. Students listen, read and decide what the people's amazing days were.
Check answers with the class. If students ask you about the meaning of *was* or *were* at this stage, simply say they are the past of the verb *be*. Note that these verb forms are studied in **3**.

If necessary, teach students how to say the years in the texts (1966, 1999 and 2010). Note that years are practised in lesson 8B.

Melanie The Beatles' last concert in San Francisco in 1966 **Tania** New Year's Eve in Sydney in 1999 **Diego** the World Cup Final in Johannesburg in 2010

c Students read the texts in the speech bubbles again and choose the correct words in sentences 1–6.
Check answers with the class. You can also ask the class which of the three amazing days they think was the best.

1 the USA 2 half an hour 3 parents
4 fantastic 5 Holland 6 two

HELP WITH GRAMMAR
Past Simple of *be*: positive and negative

3 **a** Give students time to read the sentences. Ask students if the sentences are in the present or the past (the past). Check students understand that *was*, *were*, *wasn't* and *weren't* are all past forms of the verb *be*.

b Students do the exercise on their own before comparing answers in pairs.
✏ While they are working, draw the table from **3b** on the board. Check answers with the class.

- Focus students on the table on the board.
✏ Elicit which words go in each column and write them in the table (see the table in **GRAMMAR 8.1** SB p129).
- Point out that *wasn't* = *was not* and *weren't* = *were not*. Tell students that we usually use contracted forms when speaking and writing.
- Highlight that we use *was* or *wasn't* with *I*, *he*, *she* and *it*, and *were* or *weren't* with *you*, *we* and *they*.
- Also point out that the past of *there is/there are* is *there was/there were*. Elicit the negative forms (*there wasn't* and *there weren't*).

⌐ **EXTRA IDEA** ¬

- Students read the texts in the speech bubbles again and underline all the examples of *was*, *were*, *wasn't* or *weren't*. Students then compare answers in pairs.

4 **CD3▶12** **PRONUNCIATION** Play the recording (SB p111). Students listen and practise. Use the examples to highlight how we say *was* /wəz/ and *were* /wə/ in positive sentences. Point out that *was* and *were* are not usually stressed, but that *wasn't* and *weren't* are always stressed because they are negative words.
Play the recording again, pausing after each sentence for students to repeat individually.

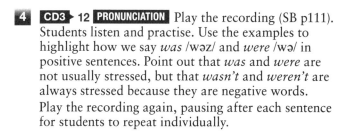

Alternatively, ask students to turn to Audio Script **CD3▸ 12** SB p111, which has the stress marked on the sentences. Play the recording again. Students listen, read and practise.

5 **a** Students do the exercise on their own.

b Put students into pairs. Students compare answers and decide who says each sentence, Melanie, Tania or Diego. Check answers with the class.

> **1** was (Diego) **2** weren't (Melanie) **3** were (Tania)
> **4** was (Melanie) **5** were (Tania) **6** was (Diego)
> **7** weren't (Diego) **8** were, wasn't (Tania)
> **9** wasn't, was (Melanie)

Get ready … Get it right!

6 Put students into groups of three. Ask all students to turn to SB p96. Check they are all looking at the correct exercise.

a Ask students to think about their lives when they were ten. Go through the words and phrases in the box. Check students remember *favourite* and point out the phrase *good at* (*sports*, *languages*, etc.).

Students work on their own and write six sentences about their lives when they were ten, using *was*, *were* and prompts from the box or their own ideas. While students are working, check their sentences for accuracy and help them with any new vocabulary they need.

> **EXTRA IDEA**
>
> • 🖊 Introduce this activity by writing sentences about your own life when you were ten on the board as examples.

b Students work in their groups and take turns to say their sentences, as shown in the speech bubbles. Students decide if any of the other students' sentences are true for them. While they are working, monitor and correct any mistakes you hear.

c Finally, ask a few students to tell the class two interesting things they found out about other students in their group.

> **WRITING**
>
> Students write eight or ten sentences about their lives when they were fifteen (or another age in the past, depending on the age of your students). Students can use the prompts in the box on SB p96 or their own ideas.

> **FURTHER PRACTICE**
>
> **Ph** **Class Activity** 8A Opposite adjectives p152 (Instructions p123)
> **Extra Practice** 8A SB p104
> **Self-study DVD-ROM** Lesson 8A
> **Workbook** Lesson 7B p38

8B ▸ Happy anniversary!
Student's Book p64–p65

Vocabulary years and past time phrases
Grammar Past Simple of *be*: questions and short answers; *was born / were born*

QUICK REVIEW This activity reviews adjectives from lessons 3A and 8A. Students work on their own and write six adjectives and their opposites. Put students into pairs to complete the activity, as shown in the examples.

Years and past time phrases

1 **a** Students do the exercise in pairs. Check answers with the class.
Point out that for the years 2000–2009, we usually say *two thousand, two thousand and one*, etc. For the years 2010–2099, we usually say *twenty ten, twenty eleven*, etc.
Also highlight that we use *in* with years: *in 1980, in 2009*, etc.

> **2e 3a 4f 5d 6b**

b **CD3▸ 13** **PRONUNCIATION** Play the recording. Students listen and practise.
Check students stress the years correctly. Repeat the drill if necessary.

c Students do the exercise with their partners from **1a**. Check answers with the class.

> 2012 twenty twelve 1977 nineteen seventy-seven
> 2018 twenty eighteen 1815 eighteen fifteen
> 1990 nineteen ninety 2003 two thousand and three

2 **a** Focus students on pictures A–D of Joe. Students do the exercise on their own. Check answers with the class. Point out that we use *last* with days (*last Monday*, etc.) and months (*last June*, etc.), and that we also say *last night, last week, last weekend, last month, last year*, etc.
Also highlight that we say *yesterday morning, yesterday afternoon* and *yesterday evening*, but *last night*, not ~~yesterday night~~.

Check students understand *now*, and point out that *ago* means 'before now'. Check students' understanding by asking them what time it was three hours ago, what day it was four days ago, etc. Use the example sentences to highlight that we usually put past time phrases (*last week*, *four hours ago*, *yesterday afternoon*, etc.) at the end of the sentence (or clause).

2D 3C 4B

b CD3 14 **PRONUNCIATION** Play the recording. Students listen and practise sentences 1–4. Point out that we don't usually pronounce the *t* in *last week* /lɑːs 'wiːk/, etc. and that the stress on *yesterday* is on the first syllable, not the last.

3 Students do the exercise on their own before comparing answers in pairs. Check answers with the class.

2 last 3 in 4 yesterday 5 last 6 ago

┌─ **EXTRA IDEA** ┐
- Students tick the sentences in **3** that are true for them. Put students in pairs to compare sentences, then ask a few students to tell the class one sentence that is true for them.
└────────────────┘

An Indian wedding

4 **a** Pre-teach the words in the box using pictures, definitions, translation, etc. Note that the aim of this box is to highlight which new words students need in order to understand the conversation they are about to listen to.
Drill the words and phrases with the class. You can also teach the phrase *Happy anniversary!* (the title of the lesson).

b Focus students on the photo of an Indian wedding on SB p64. Ask students who is *the bride* (the woman in pink sitting down) and who is *the groom* (the man in white sitting next to her).
Note that the photos on SB p64 show other aspects of a traditional Indian wedding, such as a woman's hennaed hands, bangles and sweets.

c Tell the class they are going to listen to Sunil, the groom in the photo, talk to a friend about his wedding. Give students time to read sentences 1–5.
CD3 15 Play the recording (SB p111). Students listen and choose the correct words. Students compare answers in pairs. Check answers with the class.

1 Sunday 2 five 3 India 4 were 5 was

d Give students time to read questions 1–6. Play the recording again. Students listen and answer the questions. Students compare answers in pairs. Check answers with the class. Note that Mumbai used to be called Bombay.

1 In Mumbai.
2 Sunil was 28 and Pria was 24.
3 There were 250 people there.
4 She was in the USA.
5 Yes, they were.
6 Three days.

┌─ **EXTRA IDEA** ┐
- If you have a strong class, put students in pairs and ask them to try and guess the answers to questions 1–6 in **4d** before playing the recording. Then play CD3 15 again for students to check their answers.
└────────────────┘

HELP WITH GRAMMAR
Past Simple of *be*: questions and short answers; *was born / were born*

5 **a–b** Students do the exercises on their own.
✎ While they are working, draw the table from **5a** on the board. Check answers with the class and highlight the following points.

- Focus students on the table on the board.
  ✎ Elicit which words in questions 1 and 2 from **5b** go in each column and complete the table (see the table in **GRAMMAR 8.2** SB p129).
- Use the questions sentences to highlight the word order:
  question word + *was/were* + subject + … ?
- Remind students that we use *was* or *wasn't* with *I*, *he*, *she* and *it*, and *were* or *weren't* with *you*, *we* and *they*.
- Use question 1 to highlight that we sometimes use a noun after *How many … ?*: *How many people were at the wedding?*, etc.
- You can compare the questions in the table to questions with *be* in the present: *Where are you from?*, *What's your name?*, etc.

c Students do the exercise on their own, then compare answers in pairs.
Check answers with the class.

- **Answers** *Was I/he/she/it at the wedding?*
  Were you/we/they at the wedding?
  Yes, I/he/she/it **was.**
  No, I/he/she/it **wasn't.**
  Yes, you/we/they **were.**
  No, you/we/they **weren't.**
- Use the questions in the first column of the table to highlight the word order in *yes/no* questions with *was* and *were*:
  Was/Were + subject + … ?
- Point out that we use contractions in the negative short answers (*No, I wasn't.*, *No, you weren't.*, etc.).
- Check students understand that the short answers to *Was I at the wedding?* are *Yes, you were./No, you weren't.*

- Also highlight that the short answers to *Were you at the wedding?* are *Yes, I was./No, I wasn't.* if *you* in the question is singular, and *Yes, we were./No, we weren't.* if *you* in the question is plural.
- Point out that we can also make questions with *Was there ... ?* and *Were there ... ? (Was there a party? Were there a lot of people at the wedding?*, etc.).

d Students do the exercise on their own. Check answers with the class.

- **Answers 1 A** Where **was** Pria born?
  B She **was** born in London.
  2 A When **were** you born?
  B I **was** born in 1991.
- Point out that we say *I was born (in 1991).* not *I borned (in 1991).*, etc.
- Point out that we often answer these questions with short forms, for example, *In the UK.* and *In 1987.*, not complete sentences.

6 **CD3** 16 **PRONUNCIATION** Play the recording (SB p111). Students listen and practise. Point out that we don't stress *was* and *were* in questions, but that these words are stressed in short answers.

Play the recording again, pausing after each sentence for students to practise individually. You can ask students to turn to Audio Script **CD3** 16 SB p111 and follow the stress as they listen and practise.

7 **a** Check students understand the phrase *the same age*. Students do the exercise on their own. Check answers with the class.

1 were 2 Were 3 was 4 Were 5 was 6 was

b Students ask and answer the questions in pairs. Check answers with the class.

1 Sunil and Pria. 2 No, they weren't. 3 Five years ago. 4 Yes, they were. 5 Sunil's sister. 6 (She was born) in London.

8 **a** Students do the exercise on their own, as shown in the example. Early finishers can compare answers in pairs. Check answers with the class.

2 Where were you yesterday evening?
3 Were you on holiday three months ago?
4 Where were you on New Year's Eve 1999?
5 Were you at work last Monday?
6 Where were you born?

b Students work in pairs and take turns to ask and answer the questions. Alternatively, students can move around the room and talk to as many people as possible.

Ask students to tell the class any interesting things they found out about their partner or classmates.

9 **a** Students do the exercise on their own. Tell students **not** to write when and where the people were born.

b Put students into pairs. Students swap papers and ask each other about the people on their partner's paper, as shown in the speech bubbles.

Ask a few students to tell the class about someone on their (or their partner's) list.

Get ready ... Get it right!

10 Put students into new pairs, student A and student B. Student As turn to SB p88 and student Bs turn to SB p93. Check they are all looking at the correct exercise.

a Pre-teach *went* and tell students this is the Past Simple of *go*. Students do the exercise on their own. Note that student As prepare questions about a wedding and student Bs prepare questions about a party.

Check answers with the class. Only check the words they need to fill in the gaps, so that students don't hear the questions they are about to be asked. Note that these answers are the same for student As and student Bs.

Student A/Student B 2 was/Was 3 were/Were 4 were 5 Was/was 6 Were 7 Was 8 Was

b Students work with their partners. Student A in each pair asks his/her questions from **a** about the last wedding that student B went to. Tell student As to make brief notes on their partner's answers, but not to write complete sentences for each answer.

c Students swap roles so that student B in each pair asks his/her questions from **a** about the last party that student A went to. Again, tell student Bs to make brief notes on their partner's answers.

d Put students into pairs with someone from the same group. Students take turns to talk about the last wedding or party their first partner went to.

Finally, ask students to tell the class about any interesting weddings or parties they or their partners went to.

FURTHER PRACTICE

Ph **Class Activity** 8B Were you or weren't you? p153 (Instructions p123)
Ph **Vocabulary Plus** 8 Places with *at, in, on* p174 (Instructions p165)
Extra Practice 8B SB p104
Self-study DVD-ROM Lesson 8B
Workbook Lesson 8B p39

8C REAL WORLD ► Birthdays

Student's Book p66–p67

Vocabulary months and dates
Real World talking about days and dates; making suggestions

Months and dates

1 **a** Focus students on the months in the box. Point out that months always start with a capital letter. Highlight that we use *in* with months: *in May*, etc.
CD3► 17 **PRONUNCIATION** Play the recording. Students listen and practise. Alternatively, model and drill the months yourself.

Months that students often find hard to pronounce are *January* /'dʒænjʊəri/, *February* /'februəri/, *June* /dʒuːn/, *July* /dʒʊ'laɪ/ and *August* /'ɔːɡəst/. Also check that students stress the months correctly.

> **EXTRA IDEA**
>
> • Teach students these abbreviations for months: *Jan, Feb, Mar, Apr, Aug, Sept, Oct, Nov, Dec*. Students will often see these abbreviations on calendars, timetables, etc. Point out that *May, June* and *July* are not usually abbreviated.

b Students do the activity in pairs, as shown in the examples.

2 **a** Focus students on the dates in the box. Point out the letters in pink and highlight the relationship between the last two letters of each word (*first, second, third*, etc.) and the way we write dates (*1ˢᵗ, 2ⁿᵈ, 3ʳᵈ*, etc.). Note that we can also write dates with normal lower-case letters (*1st, 2nd, 3rd*, etc.).
Highlight the irregular spelling of these *th* words: *fifth, ninth, twelfth, twentieth* and *thirtieth*.
Point out the hyphen in *twenty-first* and tell students that we also write *twenty-second, twenty-third*, etc.
CD3► 18 **PRONUNCIATION** Play the recording. Students listen and practise the dates. Note that students often have difficulty with the 'consonant clusters' at the end of these words (*sixth, twelfth*, etc.).
If necessary, play the recording again, pausing after each word so that students can practise individually.

b Students do the exercise in pairs.

c **CD3► 19** Play the recording. Students listen and check they said the words correctly. Point out that we usually stress the final syllable in the *-teenth* words (*thirteenth, fourteenth*, etc.).
PRONUNCIATION Play the recording again. Students listen and practise.

REAL WORLD
Talking about days and dates

3 Go through the questions and answers with the class and highlight the following points.

- **1** Highlight the question and point out that we can answer with *It's Monday.* or just *Monday.*
- **2** Highlight the question and point out that we say *the* in dates: *(It's) March the seventh.*
- Point out that we can write *March 7ᵗʰ* or *7ᵗʰ March*.
- Teach students that we can also say dates in another way: *the seventh of March*, etc. However, at this level we feel students only need to know one way to say dates. The alternative form is introduced and practised in **face2face** Second edition Elementary.
- Also note that dates are often said without *the* in American English: *It's March seventh.*
- **3** Point out that *When's* = *When is* in the question *When's your birthday?*.
- Also highlight that we use *on* with dates: *(It's on) June the second.* Remind students that we also use *on* with days (*on Monday*, etc.).
- Highlight the difference between these questions: **A** *When's your birthday?* **B** *July 12ᵗʰ*. (every year); **A** *When were you born?* **B** *July 12ᵗʰ 1989*. (one specific day in the past)
- You can also point out that dates are written differently in the UK and in the USA. In the UK, *5/6/15* = *5ᵗʰ June 2015* (day/month/year), whereas in the USA, *5/6/15* = *6ᵗʰ May 2015* (month/day/year).

4 **CD3► 20** **PRONUNCIATION** Play the recording. Students listen and practise. Repeat the drill if necessary.

5 **CD3► 21** Give students time to read the dates in 1–4. Play the recording (SB p111). Students listen and circle the dates they hear. Play the recording again if necessary.
Students compare answers in pairs. Check answers with the class.

1 June 22ⁿᵈ 2 March 30ᵗʰ
3 October 3ʳᵈ 4 April 1ˢᵗ

6 **a** Focus students on the examples to remind them how we write dates. Students work on their own and write five dates.

b Students do the activity in pairs. At the end of the activity, tell students to swap papers so they can check that their partners have written down the dates correctly.

c Students move around the room and ask each other when their birthdays are, as shown in the speech bubbles. Students must find out if any other students have birthdays in the same month as them. If students can't move around the room, they should ask as many students as they can sitting near them. At the end of the activity, ask students to tell the class who has a birthday in the same month as them.

Happy birthday!

7 **a** Pre-teach the words and phrases in the box using examples, definitions, translation, etc. Note that the aim of this box is to highlight which new words students need in order to understand the conversation they are about to watch or listen to.

Tell students that we *give someone a present* (not ~~*present someone*~~). Ask students what kind of presents people give each other (*a birthday present*, *a wedding present*, *an anniversary present*, etc.). Remind students of the phrase *Happy birthday!*.

Check students understand the difference between *a driving test* and *a driving lesson*. You can also teach students that you can *pass* or *fail a driving test*. Note that in this context *go to a club* means 'go to a place to listen to music and dance'.

Model and drill the new words and phrases with the class.

b Focus students on the photo of Karen and Danny on SB p67. Ask students where they are (in a café). Note that Danny was one of the customers in Café Pronto in lesson 3C.

VIDEO 8 **CD3** 22 Play the video or audio recording (SB p112). Students watch or listen and find out what Karen and Danny decide to do this evening. Check the answer with the class.

Note that all the Real World videos can be found on the **Teacher's DVD** at the back of this book.

> Karen and Danny decide to go to the cinema / see a (Johnny Depp) film.

c Focus students on sentences 1–6. Students work in pairs and try to choose the correct words or phrases, based on what they remember from the video or audio recording.

If you feel this is too difficult for your students, give students time to read sentences 1–7, then play the video or audio recording again. Students choose the correct words or phrases as they listen.

d Play the video or audio recording again. Students watch or listen and check their answers. Students can compare their answers in pairs.

Check answers with the class. Ask students if any pair got all the answers right.

> 2 Karen; 11.30 3 yesterday 4 Mexican; Danny's
> 5 Danny; every week 6 cinema; half past seven

REAL WORLD Making suggestions

8 Focus students on the flow chart. Students do the exercise on their own, then compare answers in pairs. Check answers with the class.

- **Answers** 2 we 3 idea 4 don't 5 meet 6 time
  7 seven
- Point out that we use *Let's …* , *Why don't we … ?* and *Shall we … ?* to make suggestions.
- Also highlight that we use *What / Where / What time shall we … ?* to ask for suggestions.
- Use the example sentences in the flow chart to highlight that *Let's …* , *Why don't we … ?* and *Shall we … ?* are followed by a verb: *Let's go to the cinema.* etc.

9 **CD3** 23 **PRONUNCIATION** Play the recording (SB p112). Students listen and practise the sentences in 10. Point out that *shall* is pronounced /ʃəl/ in the questions. You can also ask students to turn to Audio Script **CD3** 23 SB p112, where the stress is marked. Play the recording again. Students listen, read and practise the stress as shown in the Student's Book.

10 **a** Focus students on George and Jessica's sentences and highlight the examples. Students do the exercise on their own. Early finishers can compare answers in pairs.

b **CD3** 24 Play the recording (SB p112). Students listen and check their answers.
Check answers with the class.

> 3c 4i 5e 6f 7d 8h 9b

c Students practise the conversation in pairs. While they are working, help them with any pronunciation problems and make sure they sound polite and interested when asking and answering questions.

11 **a** Students do the activity in new pairs. Remind students to use phrases from **8** in their conversations. While they are working, monitor and check their conversations for accuracy.

b Students practise their conversation until they can remember it.

c Put two pairs together so that they are working in groups of four. Each pair takes turns to role-play their conversation. The other pair writes down what they decide to do.

d Ask one pair in each group to role-play the conversation for the class. Students don't have to leave their seats.
Finally, students can decide which conversation they liked best.

> **FURTHER PRACTICE**
> **Extra Practice** 8C SB p104
> **Self-study DVD-ROM** Lesson 8C
> **Workbook** Lesson 8C p41

Life's a party!
Student's Book p68–p69

QUICK REVIEW This activity reviews ways of making suggestions. Check students understand *tomorrow evening*. Students do the exercise in pairs, as shown in the examples. If students are having problems remembering what language to use, ask them to look at the flow chart in **REAL WORLD 8.2** SB p129.

1 **a** Students do the exercise on their own before comparing answers in pairs. Check answers with the class.
Point out that we don't use a plural -s with *hundred*, *thousand* or *million*. We say *three hundred* not ~~three hundreds~~, etc. Also point out that we use *and* after *hundred*, but not after *thousand*. We say *a hundred and fifty*, but *sixteen thousand, two hundred* not ~~sixteen thousand and two hundred~~.
Highlight that we can say *a hundred* or *one hundred*, *a thousand* or *one thousand* and *a million* or *one million*. Point out that using *a* with these numbers is more common.

390 = three hundred and ninety 1,000 = a thousand 16,200 = sixteen thousand, two hundred 750,000 = seven hundred and fifty thousand 1,000,000 = a million 50,000,000 = fifty million

b **CD3** 25 **PRONUNCIATION** Play the recording. Students listen and practise the numbers. Highlight the pronunciation of *hundred* /ˈhʌndrəd/ and *thousand* /ˈθaʊzənd/. Repeat the drill if necessary.

2 **a** **CD3** 26 Play the recording (SB p112). Students listen and write the numbers.

b Students compare answers in pairs by saying the numbers to each other. ✎ Check answers with the class and write them on the board.

a 365 b 999 c 17,000 d 62,400 e 250,000 f 1,200,000 g 18,000,000 (18 million)

3 **a** Students do the exercise on their own.

b Students do the exercise in new pairs, then swap papers to check that their partners have written down the numbers correctly.

4 **a** Pre-teach the words in the box using examples, mime, pictures, translation, etc. Check students understand that *samba* is a type of music (from Brazil) and also a type of dance. Drill the new words with the class.

b Focus students on the *Fantastic Festivals* article. Students read the article and try to fill in the gaps with the numbers in the box.

c **CD3** 27 Play the recording. Students listen and check their answers. Check answers with the class.

a 30,000 b 125,000 c 150,000 d 1,500 e 177,500 f 5 million g 70 million

5 Students read the article again and answer the questions. Students compare answers in pairs. Check answers with the class.

1 It's on the last Wednesday in August every year in Buñol, Spain. **2** They throw tomatoes at each other. **3** They throw oranges at each other (for three days). **4** It's every/in July. **5** They eat garlic bread, garlic chicken, garlic chocolate and garlic ice cream. **6** It was in June 1970. **7** People dance in the street to samba bands (all day and all night). **8** 41 days.

6 Students do the exercise in pairs. Encourage students to give reasons for their choices if possible. Ask a few students to share their ideas with the class.

7 **a** Ask students to close their books. Tell students that they are going to listen to two friends, Ella and Owen, talking about festivals.
CD3 28 Play the recording (SB p112). Students listen and write down the two festivals that Ella and Owen talk about. Check answers with the class (Glastonbury Festival and Carnival in Brazil).

b Give students time to read sentences 1–8, then play the recording again. Students listen and choose the correct answers. Ask students to compare answers in pairs. Check answers with the class.

1 four **2** things you can do **3** the people you meet **4** February **5** loves **6** difficult **7** can't **8** new friends

HELP WITH LISTENING Linking (2)
This *Help with Listening* section reviews consonant–vowel linking in sentences.

8 **a** **CD3** 29 Focus students on the sentences, then play the recording. Students listen and decide why we link the words in pink and blue. Check the answer with the class (because the words in pink end in a consonant sound and the words in blue start with a vowel sound).

EXTRA IDEA

- Play **CD3** 29 again and ask students to repeat the sentences chorally and individually. Check they are copying the consonant–vowel linking correctly.

b Ask students to look at Audio Script **CD3** 28 SB p112. Play this recording again. Note that this is the recording of the whole conversation, not the four sentences in **8a**. Students listen, read and notice the linking as shown in the Student's Book.

9 **a** Students do the activity in groups of three or four. If possible, put students into groups with people from different countries, towns/cities or regions.

> **EXTRA IDEA** ⟩
>
> • Before doing **9a**, give students a few minutes to gather their ideas and make notes about the festivals they want to talk about. While they are working, monitor and help students with any vocabulary they might need.

b Finally, ask each group to tell the class about one festival they talked about.

> **WRITING** ⟩
>
> Students write a description of a festival (or festivals) in their town, city or country, which they discussed in **9a**.

> **FURTHER PRACTICE** ⟩
>
> **Ph** **Class Activity** 8D Numbers, years and dates p154 (Instructions p123)
> **Extra Practice** 8 SB p104
> **Self-study DVD-ROM** Lesson 8D
> **Workbook** Lesson 8D p42
> **Workbook** Reading and Writing Portfolio 8 p66–p67
> **Ph** **Progress Test** 8 p188

HELP WITH PRONUNCIATION /ɔː/ and /ɜː/

Focus students on the phonemes /ɔː/ and /ɜː/, the pictures and the words.

CD3 30 Play the recording. Students listen to the sounds and the words.

Point out that *or* in *forty* is pronounced with an /ɔː/ sound and *ur* in *burger* is pronounced with an /ɜː/ sound. Note that in British English we don't usually pronounce the letter *r* after a vowel sound.

Play the recording again. Students listen and practise. If students are having problems producing the sounds, help them with the mouth position for each sound.

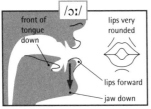
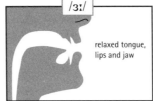

Point out that when we make the /ɔː/ sound, the lips are very rounded and pushed forward, the front of the tongue is down and the jaw is also down. Also point out that /ɔː/ is a long sound.

Highlight that when we make the /ɜː/ sound, the mouth is slightly open and the lips, tongue and jaw are in a relaxed position. Highlight that /ɜː/ is also a long sound. Note that this is the same mouth position that we use for the schwa /ə/, which is a short sound.

---

2 **CD3** 31 Focus students on the boxes. Play the recording. Students listen and notice how we say the pink and blue letters.
Play the recording again. Students listen and practise.

3 **a** **CD3** 32 Play the recording. Students listen and read the sentences.
Play the recording again. Students listen and practise.

b Students practise the sentences in pairs.
Finally, ask each student to say one of the sentences for the class.

continue2learn

Focus students on the **continue2learn** section on SB p69. See p33 of this book for ideas on how to use this section in class.

Extra Practice 8 SB p104

See p34 for ideas on how to use this section in class.

8A
1 2 young 3 empty 4 easy 5 wrong 6 great
  7 fantastic 8 short 9 terrible 10 long 11 right
  ↓ interesting
2 2 weren't; were 3 wasn't; was 4 were 5 wasn't
  6 weren't; were 7 were, wasn't

8B
3a b last c yesterday d ago e in f ago g in h last
3b 1a 2c 3b 4h 5f 6d 7e 8g
4 2 Where was your son born? 3 Where were you on your last birthday? 4 Who was your first English teacher? 5 When was your first English class? 6 Where were you three years ago?
5 2 Was; No, she wasn't. 3 Was; Yes, it was.
  4 Were; No, they weren't. 5 Was; Yes, he was.
  6 Were; No, I wasn't. / No, we weren't.

8C
6 2 Why 3 think 4 let's 5 good 6 Where 7 meet
  8 shall 9 past
7 1st first; 5th fifth; 9th ninth; 2nd second;
  3rd third; 10th tenth; 15th fifteenth;
  12th twelfth; 19th nineteenth; 20th twentieth;
  26th twenty-sixth; 30th thirtieth;
  31st thirty-first

8D
8 b 1,000,000 c 673 d 4,500 e 947 f 750,000
  g 50,000,000 h 99,990

Progress Portfolio 8

See p34 for ideas on how to use this section in class.

QUICK REVIEW This activity reviews dates and *was born*. Students do the first part of the activity on their own. Go through the example conversation with the class. Check students remember the question *When was he/she born?* and how to say months, dates and years (*On June the second, nineteen ninety-four*, etc.). Students complete the activity in pairs.

Transport

1 **a** Students work on their own and tick the words they know. Students then turn to Language Summary 9 **VOCABULARY 9.1** SB p130 to check their ideas. Check the words with the class.

Highlight that we can say *a taxi* or *a cab*. Also remind students that *a bike = a bicycle*.

You can also teach *a scooter*, *a ferry* and *a tram* if they are relevant to your students.

b **CD3 ▶ 33** **PRONUNCIATION** Play the recording. Students listen and practise.

c Focus students on sentences 1–4. Students underline the verbs in the sentences. Check answers with the class (*go, come, travel, walk*).

Use the sentences to highlight the difference between *come* (travel from another place to where you are now) and *go* (travel to another place away from where you are now). Check students understand *walk*.

Point out that we say *by car*, *by bus*, etc. Note that we say *on foot* not *by foot*. However, this phrase is rarely used nowadays and we are more likely to use the verb *walk* (*I usually walk to school*., etc.).

Also teach students that *go by plane = fly*, *go by car = drive* and *go by bike = cycle*.

Model and drill sentences 1–4 with the class. Highlight the difference in pronunciation between the vowel sounds in *walk* /wɔːk/ and *work* /wɜːk/ in sentence 4, which students studied in the *Help with Pronunciation* section in unit 8.

2 **a** Students do the exercise on their own, as shown in the example.

b Students do the exercise in pairs. Ask each pair to tell the class any sentences that are the same for both students.

Bangkok to Brighton

3 **a** Pre-teach the words in the box using pictures, examples, translation, etc. Note that the aim of this box is to highlight which new words students need to understand the article they are about to read.

Note that *a tuk-tuk* is a small motorised taxi that is commonly used in Asian countries, as shown in the photo.

Drill the words, highlighting the pronunciation of *tuk-tuk* /ˈtʊk tʊk/ and *journey* /ˈdʒɜːni/.

b Focus students on the newspaper article and ask them to cover the text. Students look at the photo, the book cover and the map and discuss what they think the article is about. This can be done in pairs or with the whole class.

c Students read the article to find out if their ideas in **3b** are correct. Check the answer with the class. (The article is about two women who travelled from Thailand to the UK by tuk-tuk.)

Check students know that Bangkok is the capital of Thailand and that Brighton /ˈbraɪtən/ is a city in the south of England.

Tell students not to worry about the pink and blue words in the text at this stage. If students ask about them, simply say that they are all verbs in the past.

4 Check students remember *miles*. Students do the exercise on their own. Point out that students should write dates, places and numbers in the table, not complete sentences, as shown in the examples.

Students compare their answers in pairs by saying the dates, places and numbers to each other. Check answers with the class. You can also ask students if they would like to do the same journey.

b May 28th 2006 **c** Bangkok, Thailand **d** Brighton, England **e** 12,500 **f** 12 **g** 98 **h** £50,000

HELP WITH GRAMMAR Past Simple: positive (regular and irregular verbs)

5 **a–c** Focus students on the Past Simple forms in blue and pink in the article. Point out the words in blue are Past Simple forms of regular verbs and the words in pink are Past Simple forms of irregular verbs. Students do the exercises on their own or in pairs, then check their answers in **GRAMMAR 9.1** SB p131. Check answers with the class, highlighting the following points.

- **a** To make the Past Simple of regular verbs, we usually add *-ed* to the verb: *wanted*, *started*, etc.
- For regular verbs that end in *-e* (*like*, *arrive*, etc.), we add *-d* to the verb: *liked*, *arrived*, etc.
- Check students understand the meaning of the new verbs *want*, *visit* and *arrive*.
- Point out that the Past Simple of *travel* is *travelled* and the Past Simple of *study* is *studied*. This is because *travel* ends in consonant + vowel + consonant and *study* ends in consonant + *-y*. However, at this level we suggest that you don't overburden students with spelling rules, as they are not asked to use any other Past Simple forms of this type in **face2face** Second edition Starter.

- **Answers b** 2 came 3 got 4 gave 5 went 6 had 7 left 8 met 9 told 10 wrote
- Check students understand the meaning of the new verbs *give*, *leave*, *meet* and *tell*.
- Point out that there are no spelling rules for irregular verbs.
- Also highlight that the Past Simple of both regular and irregular verbs is the same for all subjects (*I, you, he, she, it, we, they*).
- Remind students that the Past Simple of *be* is *was* or *were*.
- Highlight the lists of regular verbs and irregular verbs in **GRAMMAR 9.1** ▶ SB p131. Encourage students to learn the irregular Past Simple forms at home.

EXTRA IDEA

- If your students are finding the lesson difficult, go through **5a** and **5b** with the whole class, highlighting the points above. You can then point out the lists of regular and irregular verbs in **GRAMMAR 9.1** ▶ SB p131.

6 **a** Point out that verbs 1–12 are all regular verbs. Students do the exercise on their own before comparing answers in pairs.

✍ Check answers with the class by writing them on the board so students can check their spelling. Include the answer to question 1 (*visited*). Leave the words on the board to help you check **6b**.

1 visited 2 watched
3 played 4 hated
5 walked 6 worked
7 lived 8 wanted
9 loved 10 talked
11 started 12 finished

b **CD3** 34 **PRONUNCIATION** Play the recording (SB p112). Students listen and practise. Note that students should repeat both the verb and its Past Simple form together (*visit, visited*, etc.), not separately.

✍ Ask students which Past Simple forms end in /ɪd/ and underline them on the board (*visited, hated, wanted, started*).

Point out that the *-ed* ending in these words is said as an extra syllable because the verbs end in *-t* (*visit*, etc.). This is also true of verbs that end in *-d* (*needed* /ˈniːdɪd/, *ended* /ˈendɪd/, etc.), but this has not been highlighted in this lesson as students haven't met any of these verbs yet.

Also note that students often have difficulty pronouncing the 'consonant clusters' at the end of regular Past Simple forms (*watched* /wɒtʃt/, *worked* /wɜːkt/, *finished* /ˈfɪnɪʃt/, etc.), and often mistakenly say these *-ed* endings as extra syllables.

Play the recording again if necessary, pausing after each pair of words for students to repeat chorally and individually.

c **CD3** 35 **PRONUNCIATION** Focus students on the Past Simple forms in **5b**, then play the recording (SB p112). Students listen and practise. Alternatively, drill the Past Simple forms yourself.

You can highlight the /ɔː/ sound in *bought* /bɔːt/, which students studied in the *Help with Pronunciation* section in unit 8.

EXTRA IDEA

- Students work in pairs and take turns to test each other on the regular and irregular Past Simple forms from the lesson. One student says a verb, for example *buy*, and his/her partner says the Past Simple form, for example *bought*.

HELP WITH LISTENING
Present Simple or Past Simple

This *Help with Listening* section helps students to hear the difference between Present Simple and Past Simple verb forms.

7 **a** Focus students on sentences 1–3. Point out that the verbs in blue are in the Present Simple and the verbs in pink are in the Past Simple.

CD3 36 Play the recording. Students listen and notice the different pronunciation of these verb forms.

Play the recording again if necessary, asking students if they can hear the final consonant sound of the Past Simple forms.

b **CD3** 37 Play the recording (SB p112). Students listen and decide which they hear first, the Present Simple or the Past Simple, as shown in the example. Play the recording again if necessary. Check answers with the class.

2 Present Simple (live)
3 Past Simple (arrived)
4 Present Simple (talk)
5 Present Simple (want)
6 Past Simple (played)

Around the world by bike

8 **a** Focus students on the photo of Mark Beaumont. Teach the phrase *travel around the world*. Ask how Mark travelled around the world (by bike).
Students do the exercise on their own.

b Students compare answers in pairs. Check answers with the class. Also point out the regular verb *cycle* /ˈsaɪkəl/ in the example. You can also ask students which Past Simple forms are regular and which are irregular.

2 had 3 left 4 started 5 travelled
6 visited 7 met 8 wrote 9 got
10 finished 11 went 12 told
13 was 14 raised

Get ready ... Get it right!

9 Put students into groups of three or four. Ask all students to turn to SB p96. Check they are looking at the correct exercise.

a Students do the exercise on their own. Remind students to put the verbs in brackets in the Past Simple, as shown in the example. If necessary, go through the prompts with the class before they begin.

b Students practise saying their sentences on their own until they can remember them.

c Students work in their groups and take turns to tell each other about the last time they visited a different town or city, using the sentences they have memorised. Encourage students to include more information if possible.

Students may ask each other questions about the places they visited, but don't worry if these are inaccurate at this point. Note that Past Simple questions are taught in lesson 9B.

d Finally, ask each student to tell the class two things about the place they visited.

EXTRA IDEA

● Introduce the activity by telling the class about the last time you visited a town or city before asking them to turn to SB p96.

WRITING

Students write a description of a time when they visited a different town or city. You can ask them to write about the place they discussed in **9**, adding more details if possible, or to describe a different occasion.

FURTHER PRACTICE

Ph **Class Activity** 9A My past p155 (Instructions p124)
Extra Practice 9A SB p105
Self-study DVD-ROM Lesson 9A
Workbook Lesson 9A p43

9B ▶ My last holiday
Student's Book p72–p73

Vocabulary holiday activities
Grammar Past Simple: negative, questions and short answers

QUICK REVIEW This activity reviews the Past Simple of regular and irregular verbs. Students do the first part of the activity on their own. Demonstrate the second part of the activity by asking students to tell you one or two of their verbs and then saying sentences with the correct Past Simple form, as shown in the example. Students complete the activity in pairs.

Holiday activities

1 **a** Students work in pairs and tick the phrases they know, then do the exercise in **VOCABULARY 9.2▶** SB p130. They can then compare answers in pairs. Check answers with the class.

Point out that we say *go on holiday* in British English and *go on vacation* in American English.

Check students understand *go sightseeing* (visit the famous buildings in a town, city or country) and *travel around* (travel from place to place).

Highlight the different words and phrases that follow the verb go: go **on** holiday, go **to** the beach, go sightsee**ing**, go swimming, go **for** a walk.

Also tell students we can *rent a car* or *hire a car*.

2g 3k 4d 5i 6a 7c 8f 9b 10j 11h

b **CD3▶ 38** **PRONUNCIATION** Play the recording. Students listen and practise. Highlight the pronunciation of *beach* /biːtʃ/ and *sightseeing* /ˈsaɪtsiːɪŋ/. Repeat the drill if necessary.

Note that only the main stress is shown in the vocabulary boxes and Language Summaries.

c Students do the exercise with their partners from **1a**.

Elicit the Past Simple forms of the verbs in **1a** and write them on the board. Point out that *take* is irregular. Drill these words with the class, highlighting the extra syllable in *rented* /ˈrentɪd/.

(go → went take → took)
stay → stayed rent → rented
travel → travelled have → had

2 **a** Check students remember *always*, *usually* and *sometimes*. Students do the exercise on their own, as shown in the examples.

b Students do the exercise in pairs.

Ask students to tell the class which of their sentences are also true for their partner (*Nico and I sometimes go to the beach.*, etc.).

Favourite places

3 **a** Pre-teach the words in the box using photos, definitions, translation, etc. Note that the aim of this box is to highlight which new words students need in order to understand the texts they are about to read and listen to.

Model and drill the new words with the class, highlighting the pronunciation of *palace* /ˈpælɪs/ and *scenery* /ˈsiːnəri/.

b Focus students on the photos of the people and the texts on SB p72, and the photos on SB p73.

CD3▶ 39 Play the recording. Students read and listen, then match the people to the photos on SB p73 and decide which countries the places are in. Check answers with the class.

> **Heidi** Red Square (in Moscow, Russia)
> **Charlie** the Alhambra (in Granada, Spain)
> **John and Diane** Cappadocia (in Turkey)

c Students do the exercise on their own before comparing answers in pairs.

Check answers with the class. Ask students which of the three places they would like to visit.

> 2 Heidi 3 Charlie 4 Heidi 5 John ... Diane
> 6 Heidi ... Charlie 7 Charlie, John ... Diane

HELP WITH GRAMMAR
Past Simple: negative

4 **a–b** Students do the exercises on their own or in pairs. ✐ While students are working, draw the table from **4a** on the board. Check answers with the class.

- Focus students on the table on the board. Elicit which words in sentences 1 and 2 in **4b** go in each column and complete the table (see the table in **GRAMMAR 9.2▶** SB p131).
- Highlight the word order in Past Simple negatives: subject + *didn't* + verb + ...
- Point out that *didn't* is the contracted form of *did not* and that we usually use this form when speaking and writing.
- Also point out that we use *didn't* with all subjects (*I, you, he, she, it, we, they*) and with all verbs except *be*.
- Highlight that we use the verb in negative sentences, not its Past Simple form: *I didn't stay in a hotel.* not *I didn't stayed in a hotel.*, etc.
- Remind students that the Past Simple negative of *be* is *wasn't* or *weren't*, not *didn't be*.

5 **CD3▶ 40** **PRONUNCIATION** Play the recording. Students listen and practise the sentences in **4**. Check that students copy the sentence stress correctly. Also point out that *didn't* is always stressed because it has a negative meaning.

6 **a** Focus students on the example. Point out that we use the verb *go* in the negative sentence (*didn't go*), but its Past Simple form in the positive sentence (*went*). Students do the exercise on their own.

b Students compare answers in pairs. Check answers with the class.

> **1b** She didn't go sightseeing in the afternoons. She went sightseeing in the mornings.
> **2a** Charlie didn't go to Spain two years ago. He went to Spain last year. **b** He didn't stay with friends in Valencia. He stayed in a hotel.
> **3a** John and Diane didn't rent bikes. They rented a car. **b** They didn't stay in a big hotel in Cappadocia. They stayed in a small hotel.

7 Ask students to cover the texts on SB p72. Students answer the questions on their own before comparing answers in pairs. Check answers with the class. Highlight the position of *with* in question 2 and tell students that it is common in English to end a sentence with a preposition: *Who do you live with?*, *Where are you from?*, etc.

> **1** (She went to) Moscow/Russia. **2** (She stayed with) some friends. **3** (He went to the beach) every afternoon. **4** No, he didn't. **5** No, they didn't. **6** (They took) about 500 photos.

HELP WITH GRAMMAR Past Simple: questions and short answers

8 **a–c** Students do the exercises on their own or in pairs. ✐ While they are working, draw the table from **8a** on the board. Check answers with the class.

- **a–b** Focus students on the *Wh-* questions table on the board. Elicit which words in sentences 1 and 2 go in each column and complete the table (see the table in **GRAMMAR 9.3▶** SB p131).
- Highlight the word order in *Wh-* questions: question word + *did* + subject + verb + ...
- Point out that the auxiliary *did* has no meaning, but is used to make the Past Simple questions.
- Use sentence 2 to highlight that we often use a noun after *How many ... ?*: *How many photos did they take?*
- Point out that we use *did* with all subjects (*I, you, he, she, it, we, they*) and with all verbs except *be*.
- Highlight that we use the verb in questions, not its Past Simple form: *Where did Heidi go?* not *Where did Heidi went?*.
- Remind students that we don't use *did* in questions with *was* and *were*: *Where were you?* not *Where did you be?*, etc.

- **c Answers** Did he go swimming? Yes, he **did**. No, he **didn't**. Did they visit Turkey last year? Yes, they **did**. No, they **didn't**.

- Use the table to highlight the word order in Past Simple *yes/no* questions:
  Did + subject + verb + … .
- Point out that, as with other forms of the Past Simple, the form of *yes/no* questions and short answers is the same for all subjects (*I*, *you*, *he*, *she*, *it*, *we*, *they*).

EXTRA IDEA

- Ask students to turn to **GRAMMAR 9.3** SB p131. Focus students on the final **TIP**. Use the table below the **TIP** to highlight the difference between negative and question forms in the Present Simple and Past Simple. Point out that only the auxiliary in pink changes (*don't/doesn't* → *didn't*, *do/does* → *did*).

9 **CD3** 41 **PRONUNCIATION** Play the recording. Students listen and practise. Check that students copy the sentence stress correctly. If necessary, play the recording again, pausing after each sentence for students to repeat individually.

10 Put students into pairs, student A and student B. Student As turn to SB p90 and student Bs turn to SB p95. Check they are all looking at the correct exercise.

a Focus students on the photos of Heidi and Charlie and ask students where they went on holiday last year (Russia and Spain). Check students understand the phrase *buy presents*.
Students do the exercise on their own.
If necessary, check the questions with the whole class. Note that the questions are the same for student As and student Bs, apart from *he/she* and *his/her*.

Student A/Student B 2 Did she/he visit any museums? 3 What did she/he do in the evenings? 4 How did she/he travel around? 5 Did she/he buy any presents?

b Students work with their partners. Student A in each pair asks his/her questions from **a** about Heidi. Before they begin, tell student Bs that the answers are in column C of their table and remind them to use the Past Simple form of the verbs in brackets in their answers. Student As should write the answers in column B of their table.

c Students swap roles so that student B in each pair asks his/her questions from **a** about Charlie. Students can then compare tables and check their partner's answers. Check answers with the class if necessary.

Student A 1 She went for a walk. 2 Yes, she did. 3 She had dinner with her friends. 4 She went by bus and taxi. 5 No, she didn't.
Student B 1 He went sightseeing. 2 No, he didn't. 3 He had dinner in his hotel. 4 He rented a car. 5 Yes, he did.

Get ready … Get it right!

11 **a** Focus students on the example. Check students understand that *When did you last go on holiday?* asks about your most recent holiday (the one nearest to now).
Students do the exercise on their own. Check the questions with the class. Drill the questions if necessary.

Where did you go?
What did you do there?
Who did you go with?
Where did you stay?
How did you travel around?
Did you have a good time?

b Ask students to think about their last holiday and answer the questions in **11a** for themselves. Students can make brief notes if necessary or just answer the questions in their heads. Tell students not to write complete sentences. Note that this stage will help prepare students with ideas to talk about in **12a**.

12 **a** Put students into pairs, student A and student B. If possible, ask students to work with someone they don't know very well. Student A in each pair asks his or her partner all the questions from **11a**. Students then swap roles so that student B asks all his or her questions. Encourage students to give more information if possible.

b Finally, ask a few students to tell the class about their partner's holiday.

EXTRA IDEA

- Use the photocopiable **Class Activity** 9B What did you do on holiday? p156–p157 (Instructions p124) as an alternative way to finish the lesson. This might be appropriate if you have a young class, or your students are unlikely to have been on holiday.

WRITING

Students write about their last holiday, as discussed in **12**. Alternatively, ask students to imagine they went on their perfect holiday last month. Students write a short description of their holiday.

FURTHER PRACTICE

Ph **Class Activity** 9B What did you do on holiday? p156–p157 (Instructions p124)
Extra Practice 9B SB p105
Self-study DVD-ROM Lesson 9B
Workbook Lesson 9B p44

A weekend away
Student's Book p74–p75

Vocabulary at the station
Real World buying train tickets; asking about last weekend

QUICK REVIEW This activity reviews holiday activities and the Past Simple. Students do the first part of the activity on their own before comparing lists in pairs. Students then talk about their favourite holiday with their partner. At the end of the activity, you can ask a few students to tell the class about their (or their partner's) favourite holiday.

At the station

1 a Focus students on the photos. Students do the exercise in pairs. Check answers with the class. Point out that *a single* = a single ticket and *a return* = a return ticket. However, we rarely say *ticket* with these words.

a single 5; a return 6; a ticket office 2;
a ticket machine 3; a platform 4

b CD3▶42 PRONUNCIATION Play the recording. Students listen and practise.

2 Focus students on the photo of Sally at the ticket office, and point out that she was the teacher in the language school in lesson 1C.
VIDEO▶9.1 CD3▶43 Play the video or audio recording (SB p112). Students watch or listen and write down where Sally wants to go and how much her ticket is. Check answers with the class.
Note that all the Real World videos can be found on the **Teacher's DVD** at the back of this book.

Sally wants to go to **London**.
Her ticket is **£46.70**.

REAL WORLD Buying train tickets

3 Focus students on the flow chart and give them time to read the conversation.
VIDEO▶ 9.1 CD3▶ 43 Play the video or audio recording again. Students listen and fill in the gaps in the conversation. Students compare answers in pairs. Check answers with the class.

Go through the sentences in the flow chart with the class and check students understand them. Point out the new phrases *come back*, *the next train* and *Which platform?*.

a London b £46.70 c 10.23 d platform
e 3 f London g 11.56

4 CD3▶ 44 PRONUNCIATION Play the recording. Students listen and practise. Check that students copy the sentence stress and polite intonation correctly. Play the recording again if necessary, pausing after each sentence or question for students to repeat individually.

5 a Students do the exercise in pairs, taking turns to be the customer. Ask students to practise a few times in each role and encourage them to memorise the conversation.

b Ask students to close their books. Students practise the conversation in pairs.
You can ask one or two pairs to role-play the conversation for the class.

┌─ EXTRA IDEA ─┐

• ✍ Write answers a–e in **5a** on the board so that students don't have to remember the place, price, train times and platform number when they practise the conversation with their books closed.

6 a Ask students to cover the conversation in **3**. Students do the exercise on their own.

b CD3▶ 45 Play the recording. Students listen and check their answers. Check answers with the class.

1 to 2 That's 3 your 4 next 5 at
6 Which 7 does 8 At 9 a lot

7 Put students into new pairs, student A and student B. Student As turn to SB p90 and student Bs turn to SB p95. Check they are all looking at the correct exercise.

a Tell student As that they are customers and student Bs that they are ticket sellers. Give students a few moments to read the information in the table. Point out that student As must buy two different pairs of tickets. Tell the class that the time is now 9 a.m.
Students work with their partners. Student As buy two returns to Bath and fill in the gaps in the first row of the table. Remind students to use language from **3** in their conversations.
Student As then buy two singles to Bristol and fill in the gaps in the second row of the table.

b Students swap roles so that student Bs are customers and student As are ticket sellers. Give students time to read the information in the second table. Tell students that Leeds is a city in the north of England.
Students work with their partners. Student Bs buy two returns to Leeds and fill in the gaps in the first row of the table.
Student Bs then buy two singles to Manchester and fill in the gaps in the second row of the table.
At the end of the activity, ask students to compare tables and check the information is correct. You can also ask one or two pairs to role-play a conversation for the class.

Last weekend

8 **a** Focus students on the photo of Rob and Sally. Tell the class that it's now Monday morning and Sally is talking to another teacher, Rob, about her trip to London.

Focus students on photos A–D and check students know that they are all famous places in London. Teach the pronunciation of *Leicester* /ˈlestə/ *Square*. If necessary, tell the class that the West End is in the centre of London and is very popular with tourists because there are a lot of theatres, cinemas, restaurants and cafés. Also check your students know the famous musical *Les Misérables*.

VIDEO 9.2 **CD3** 46 Play the video or audio recording (SB p112). Students watch or listen and put photos A–D in the order that Sally and Rob talk about them.

Check answers with the class.

1B 2C 3D 4A

b Students work in pairs and try to choose the correct words or phrases, based on what they can remember from the conversation. Do not check answers at this stage.

c Play the video or audio recording again. Students watch or listen and check their answers. Check answers with the class.

2 Saturday 3 enjoyed 4 Her brother
5 some friends 6 Turkish

> **EXTRA IDEA**
>
> • If you feel this 'How much can you remember?' approach is too challenging for your class, give students time to read sentences 1–6, then play **VIDEO** 9.2 **CD3** 46 again. Students watch or listen and choose the correct answers.

REAL WORLD Asking about last weekend

9 Students do the exercise on their own or in pairs. Check answers and go through the following points with the class.

- **Answers** 2 What 3 Where 4 do 5 good
  6 did 7 you
- Check students remember that questions 1–7 are all in the Past Simple. Point out that we ask these questions to find out what someone did last weekend.
- Highlight the word order in the questions: (question word) + *did* + *you* + verb + … ?
- Ask students what the short answers are for Past Simple *yes/no* questions (*Yes, I did.*/ *No, I didn't.*). Point out that when answering question 1, we would usually say *Yes, I did, thanks.* not just *Yes, I did.*

- Point out that in question 2, we can also say *What did you do **last** weekend?* if we are asking the question later in the week.
- You can teach *Nothing special.* as a possible answer to question 2.
- With a strong class, you can also teach students *How was your weekend?* as an alternative to question 1. Note that we only ask this question on Mondays, not on other days in the week.

10 **CD3** 47 **PRONUNCIATION** Play the recording (SB p113). Students listen and practise. Check students copy the sentence stress correctly.

Play the recording again, pausing after each sentence for students to repeat individually. Alternatively, ask students to turn to Audio Script **CD3** 47 SB p113, which has the stress marked on the sentences. Play the recording again. Students listen, read and practise the sentences.

11 **a** Students work on their own and make notes about things they did last weekend, as in the examples. Encourage students to write at least six things. While they are working, monitor and help students with any new vocabulary they need.

b Students do the exercise in pairs, as shown in the speech bubbles. Before they begin, remind students to use questions from **9** and point out that they can ask their own questions as well. Also encourage students to give more information if possible when answering the questions.

While they are working, monitor and help students with any communication problems.

c Finally, ask a few students to tell the class one thing their partner did at the weekend.

> **EXTRA IDEA**
>
> • Begin the activity in **11a** by inviting students to ask you about what you did last weekend.

> **WRITING**
>
> Students write a description of what they did last weekend, based on the notes they made in **11a**.

> **FURTHER PRACTICE**
>
> **Ph** Vocabulary Plus 9 Irregular verbs p175 (Instructions p166)
> Extra Practice 9C SB p105
> Self-study DVD-ROM Lesson 9C
> Workbook Lesson 9C p46

VOCABULARY
9D AND SKILLS — Who, what, when?
Student's Book p76–p77

Vocabulary question words
Skills Reading: a quiz;
Listening: How many did
I get right?

QUICK REVIEW This activity reviews Past Simple *yes/no* questions. Students do the activity in pairs. At the end of the activity, ask each pair to tell the class one thing that they both did yesterday.

1 a Pre-teach the vocabulary in the box using definitions, examples or pictures from the quiz.
Point out that we say *the Earth* and *the moon*, and that *Earth* is often spelt with a capital letter. Also check students understand that we *earn* money by doing a job.
Model and drill the words, highlighting the /ɜː/ sound in *Earth* /ɜːθ/ and *earn* /ɜːn/.

b Students do the quiz in pairs. Set a time limit of five minutes. Do not check answers at this stage.

2 Tell the class they are going to listen to two people doing the quiz. Check students understand that they must listen and tick the **correct** answers in the quiz, **not** the answers that Mark gives on the recording.
CD3 48 Play the recording. Students listen and tick the correct answers to the quiz questions.
Ask students to compare answers in pairs and to work out how many answers they got right. Check answers with the class. Find out if any pairs got all the answers right.

1a 2c 3b 4c 5b 6a 7c 8c

HELP WITH LISTENING
Sentence stress (3)

This *Help with Listening* section reviews sentence stress in the context of an informal conversation.

3 a Focus students on the beginning of Jackie and Mark's conversation.
CD3 48 Play the beginning of the recording again. Students listen and notice the sentence stress.
Remind students that we stress the important words (the words that carry the meaning).
You can use the sentences to highlight what types of word are stressed (names, verbs, nouns, question words, etc.) and what types of word are not usually stressed (auxiliaries, pronouns, prepositions, articles, etc.).

b Ask students to turn to Audio Script **CD3** 48 SB p113, which has all the sentence stress marked. Play the whole recording again. Students listen, read and follow the sentence stress. Students should also find out how many questions Mark got right.
Check the answer with the class.

Mark got three questions right – questions 4, 5 and 8.

HELP WITH VOCABULARY
Question words

4 Focus students on the words in pink in the quiz. Students do the exercise on their own, then compare answers in pairs. Check answers with the class.

- **Answers What** = a thing **When** = a time **Where** = a place **Why** = a reason **How old** = age **How many** = a number **How much** = an amount of money
- Point out that we also use *What time … ?* to ask about a time:
  A *What time do you go to bed?*
  B *At half past eleven.*
- Highlight that we usually answer *Why … ?* questions with *Because … :*
  A *Why are you tired?*
  B *Because I got up at 5 a.m.*
- Use question 7 to remind students that we often use a noun after *How many … ?*: *How many countries are there in Africa?*.
- Note that the difference between *What* and *Which* is dealt with in **face2face** Second edition Elementary. We suggest you don't focus on the difference here.

5 a Pre-teach *spend (money)* **on** *something* (food, clothes, CDs, etc.).
Students do the exercise on their own. Check answers with the class.

2 What 3 How old 4 How many
5 Who 6 Why 7 Where 8 When
9 How many 10 How much

b Focus students on the speech bubbles and check students remember that *When did you last (go to the cinema)?* asks about the most recent time they did this (the time nearest to now).
Students do the exercise in pairs. Encourage students to ask more questions if possible. While they are working, monitor and help with any communication problems.
You can ask a few students to tell the class anything interesting they found out about their partner.

6 a Students do the exercise on their own. Before they begin, point out that these questions can be in the Present Simple or the Past Simple. While they are working, monitor and check their questions for accuracy.

b Put students into new pairs. If possible, ask students to work with someone they don't know very well. Students take turns to ask their questions, again asking more questions if possible.

c Finally, ask students to tell the class two things they found out about their partner.

HELP WITH PRONUNCIATION /l/ and /r/

1 Focus students on the phonemes /l/ and /r/, the pictures and the words.

CD3▶ 49 Play the recording. Students listen to the sounds and the words. Point out that *l* in *leave* is pronounced with a /l/ sound and *rr* in *arrive* is pronounced with a /r/ sound.
Play the recording again. Students listen and practise. If students are having problems, help them with the mouth position for each sound.

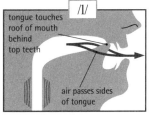
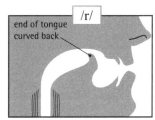

Point out that we make the /l/ sound by touching the roof of the mouth behind the top teeth with the tongue, so that the air passes either side of the tongue. Also highlight that /l/ is a voiced sound (there is vibration in the throat).
We make the /r/ sound by pointing the tip of the tongue upwards and backwards, but the tongue does not touch the roof of the mouth. There is some contact between the sides of the tongue and the teeth. Point out that /r/ is also a voiced sound (there is vibration in the throat).

2 **CD3▶ 50** Focus students on the boxes. Play the recording. Students listen and notice how we say the pink and blue consonants.
Play the recording again. Students listen and practise.

3 **a** Tell the class that sometimes we don't say the letter *r* in standard British English, particularly after certain vowel sounds like /ə/ and /ɔː/, or at the end of a word.
Highlight that we always pronounce *rr* (double *r*).
Also point out that in standard American English the letter *r* is always pronounced.
Focus students on the examples in the box. Point out that we say the *r* in *friend*, but not the *r* in *first*.
Students do the exercise on their own or in pairs.

✍ While they are working, write the words on the board so that you can check their answers.

b **CD3▶ 51** Play the recording. Students listen and check their answers. **✍** Check answers with the class by eliciting students' answers and putting ticks or crosses next to the words on the board.
Play the recording again. Students listen and practise. Students can then practise saying the words in pairs.

friend ✓ first ✗ doctor ✗ green ✓ morning ✗
radio ✓ sport ✗ park ✗ right ✓ theatre ✗
fruit ✓ start ✗ tomorrow ✓ great ✓ terrible ✓

continue2learn

Focus students on the **continue2learn** section on SB p77. See p33 of this book for ideas on how to use this section in class.

Extra Practice 9 SB p105

See p34 for ideas on how to use this section in class.

9A
1 2 a plane 3 a bike / a bicycle 4 a car 5 a boat
6 a bus 7 a motorbike 8 a train
2a leave → left; watch → watched; have → had;
write → wrote; start → started; buy → bought;
meet → met; play → played; go → went.
Watch, *start* and *play* are regular verbs.
2b 2 left 3 started 4 had 5 bought 6 met
7 watched 8 played 9 wrote 10 went

9B
3 rent a car; stay in a hotel; take photos; go
swimming; go for a walk; go to the beach;
stay with friends; go sightseeing; travel around
4 2 She didn't tell me her surname. 3 I wasn't at
school yesterday. 4 He didn't come home last
night. 5 We weren't in Poland in 2012.
6 They didn't like the food.
5 2 Did 3 did 4 was 5 Was 6 wasn't 7 were 8 did
9 didn't 10 Were 11 weren't 12 were 13 did

9C
6 2 come 3 back 4 That's 5 ticket 6 next
7 There's 8 platform 9 Platform 10 arrive

9D
7 2 Who is your favourite actor? 3 How
many children do you have? 4 Where were
you born? 5 How old is your car? 6 How
much was your jacket? 7 What did you buy
yesterday? 8 Why are you tired?

Progress Portfolio 9

See p33 for ideas on how to use this section in class.

QUICK REVIEW This activity reviews question words and question forms. ✍ Write these question words on the board: *Who, What, When, Where, Why, How old, How many, How much*. Students do the first part of the activity in pairs. Students can write questions in the Present Simple or the Past Simple. Students complete the activity in groups of four, as shown in the examples.

Future plans

1 **a** Focus students on the diagram and highlight the example *start*. Point out that we can say *start school*, *start university* or *start a new job*.

Students do the exercise in pairs before checking in Language Summary 10 **VOCABULARY 10.1** ▶ SB p132. Check answers with the class.

Point out that in this lesson, *start/leave school or university* are used to mean 'start or finish our education at that place', rather than the time that people begin classes or leave the building as part of their daily routine. Also highlight that we say *start school*, etc. not *start the school*, etc.

Point out the difference between *start a new job* and *look for a new job*.

Also highlight that we say **do** *a (computer) course/ an exam*, not *make a (computer) course/an exam*. Elicit other types of course people do, for example, *do an English course, do a film course, do a business course*, etc. Note that we can also say **take** *an exam*.

Check that students understand the difference between *get engaged* and *get married*.

Establish that *move house* means 'go and live in a different house or flat', and that we say *move house* not *move a house* or *move flat*.

Point out that we also say *look for a house/a flat* not *look for house/flat*.

Highlight that we can also say *move to* + city or country: *move to London, move to the USA*, etc.

> **leave** school or university/your job
> **do** a (computer) course/an exam
> **move** house/to another city or country
> **get** engaged/married
> **look for** a house or a flat/a (new) job

b **CD3**▶ 52 **PRONUNCIATION** Play the recording. Students listen and practise. Note that each phrase is said separately on the recording (*start school*, *start university*, etc.). Highlight the pronunciation of *university* /juːnɪˈvɜːsəti/, *course* /kɔːs/ and *engaged* /ɪnˈɡeɪdʒd/. Repeat the drill if necessary, pausing after each phrase for students to repeat individually.

c Students do the activity in new pairs, as shown in the speech bubbles. Remind students that we can sometimes use more than one verb with some nouns (*start school, leave school*, etc.).

A world language

2 **a** Focus students on the photos of the four people and the texts. Tell the class that these people all study English in different parts of the world.

CD3▶ 53 Play the recording. Students listen, read and decide where each person studies English. Students compare answers in pairs. Check answers with the class.

If students ask you the meaning of *'m/'re/is going to* in the texts, you can simply say that these sentences are about the future and that students are going to study *be going to* later in the lesson.

Isabella studies English at university. **Kamil** studies English at school. **Ali** studies English at a language school in London. **Colette** studies English online.

b Students do the exercise on their own.

c Students compare answers in pairs. Check answers with the class.

2 Kamil 3 Ali 4 Colette 5 Kamil 6 Ali 7 Isabella

> **EXTRA IDEA**
>
> ● Put students into pairs, student A and student B. Student As read the texts about Isabella and Kamil and circle all the phrases from **1a** they can find. Student Bs do the same for the texts about Ali and Colette. Students then compare answers with their partners.

HELP WITH GRAMMAR
be going to: positive and negative

3 **a–c** Students do the exercises on their own or in pairs. Early finishers can check in **GRAMMAR 10.1** ▶ SB p133. ✍ While students are working, draw the tables from **3b** on the board. Check answers with the class.

● **a** We use *be going to* + verb to talk about **future plans**.
● Use the sentences in **2b** to help students understand what we mean by 'a future plan'. While there are various different ways to express the future in English, we feel that *be going to* is the most useful for Starter students and is likely to be correct in the majority of situations, particularly when talking about future plans.
● **b–c** Focus students on the tables on the board. ✍ Elicit which sentences in **3c** go in each table and write the words in each sentence in the appropriate columns (see **GRAMMAR 10.1** ▶ SB p133).
● Focus students on the **POSITIVE** table. Ask students when the people decided to do these things, 'now' or 'before now' (before now).

- Highlight the word order in positive and negative sentences with *be going to*:
  subject + *be* (+ *not*) + *going to* + verb + ...
- Point out that *be* changes according to the subject and whether the sentence is positive or negative:
  (+) *I'm, you're, he's, she's, it's, we're, they're*
  (–) *I'm not, you aren't, he/she/it isn't, we aren't, they aren't.*
- Point out that we can also use the alternative negative forms *you're not, he's not,* etc.
- Also highlight that with the verb *go* we usually say *I'm going to the cinema.* not *I'm going to go to the cinema.*, but that both sentences are correct.

4 Focus students on the example drill. Highlight the sentence stress and the weak form of *to* /tə/.
CD3▶ 54 PRONUNCIATION Play the recording (SB p113). Students listen and practise. Check students copy the sentence stress and the weak form of *to* correctly. Play the recording again, pausing after each sentence for students to practise individually.

5 a Students do the exercise on their own.

b Students compare answers in pairs and decide which sentences are negative. Check answers with the class if necessary.

Isabella ... he's going to be a doctor.; We're going to get married ... ; we aren't going to live in São Paulo ... (negative); we're going to move to Rio.
Kamil I'm going to leave school ... ; ... I'm not going to start university ... (negative); ... I'm going to do a computer course ... ; ... I'm going to look for a job ...
Ali ... my sister is going to visit me ... ; ... we're going to travel around the UK. She isn't going to stay here for very long ... (negative); ... I'm going to start a new job ...
Colette ... I'm going to do an exam ... ; they're going to move to Paris ... ; ... Oliver's going to leave his job ... ; ... we're going to move to Sydney!

6 a Students do the exercise on their own. Remind students to use contracted forms of *be* ('m, 's, 're) in positive sentences.

b Students compare answers in pairs, then match the sentences to the people in the photos. Check answers with the class.

1b 's going to stay (Ali) **2a** 're not / aren't going to look for **2b** 're going to buy (Colette) **3a** 's going to leave **3b** 're not / aren't going to have (Isabella) **4a** 'm going to do **4b** 'm not going to look for (Kamil)

Future time phrases

7 a Students do the exercise on their own before comparing answers in pairs. Check answers with the class.

Point out that we say *tonight* not ~~*this night*~~, and that we can say *tomorrow morning, tomorrow afternoon, tomorrow evening* and *tomorrow night*.
Highlight that we use *next* in these phrases: *next weekend, next week, next month, next year*.
Point out that we also use *in* with months (*in December*, etc.) and years (*in 2025*, etc.) to refer to the future. We can also use *next* with months (*next June*, etc.) and days (*next Monday*, etc.).
Highlight that we can also use *on* with days to refer to the future (*on Monday*, etc.).
Tell students that it is very common to use a future time phrase in sentences or questions with *be going to*.

in June next year **5**; next month **4**; in 2025 **6**; tomorrow morning **2**; next week **3**

b Students do the activity on their own, as shown in the example. While students are working, monitor and check their sentences for accuracy.

c Students work in pairs and take turns to tell each other their sentences. Encourage students to give more information if possible.
Ask each student to tell the class one of their sentences.

Get ready ... Get it right!

8 Students do the exercise on their own. Tell students to write phrases, as in the examples, not complete sentences with *be going to*. Students should write six things in total, one for each time phrase (*after class, tomorrow evening, next Sunday*, etc.).

9 a Put students into groups of three or four. Students take turns to talk about their plans, using their phrases from **8**. Students make a note of any plans that are the same for more than one student in the group.
Students may try to ask questions with *be going to* at this stage, but don't worry if these are inaccurate at this point. Note that questions with *be going to* are taught in lesson 10B.

b Finally, ask students to tell the class about their group's plans, as in the speech bubble.

WRITING

Students write about their future plans, and those of their family and friends. Encourage students to give more information about each person or plan if possible.

FURTHER PRACTICE

Extra Practice 10A SB p106
Self-study DVD-ROM Lesson 10A
Workbook Lesson 10A p48

QUICK REVIEW This activity reviews vocabulary for future plans and *be going to*. ✍ Write these verbs on the board: *start*, *leave*, *do*, *move*, *get*, *look for*. Students do the first part of the activity on their own. Put students into pairs to compare phrases. Students complete the activity in pairs, as shown in the example. Remind students to use *be going to* in their sentences. At the end of the activity, you can ask one or two students to tell the class about some of their future plans.

Phrases with *have*, *watch*, *go*, *go to*

1 a Focus students on the coloured boxes and highlight the verbs *have*, *watch*, *go* and *go to*. Students do the exercise in pairs, then check their answers in **VOCABULARY 10.3** ▶ SB p132. Check answers with the class.

Point out the difference between *have a party* (it's your party) and *go to a party* (it's another person's party). Also point out that we don't say *make a party*.
Highlight *the* in these phrases: *watch the news*, *go to the cinema* and *go to the gym*.

You can also tell the class that we say *the news* to refer to what is happening in the world and also for a type of TV or radio programme. Also point out that *the news* takes a singular verb: *The news is on at 10.00.* not *The news are on at 10.00.*

Establish that we usually use *go* with verb+*ing* forms: *go shopping*, *go swimming*, *go running*, etc. You can also point out the double letters in these verb+*ing* forms. Note that this is because the verbs *shop*, *swim* and *run* end in consonant + vowel + consonant (see **VOCABULARY 7.2** ▶ SB p126).

have coffee with friends, a party
watch TV, the news, sport on TV
go shopping, swimming, running
go to the cinema, the gym, a party

b **CD3** ▶ **55** **PRONUNCIATION** Play the recording. Students listen and practise. Repeat the drill if necessary, pausing after each phrase for students to repeat individually.

c Students do the exercise with their partners from **1a**, as shown in the examples.
✍ While students are working, draw a table with four columns on the board. Write *have*, *watch*, *go* and *go to* at the top of the columns.
Elicit students' ideas and write correct phrases in the appropriate column on the board for other students to copy. Leave the phrases on the board to help students with **2a**.

Possible answers
have breakfast, lunch, children, a brother, a sister, a car, a computer, a laptop, etc.
watch a DVD, a video, a TV programme, a soap opera, a horror film, football, tennis, etc.
go sightseeing, home, on holiday, for a walk, skiing, dancing, out with friends, etc.
go to a concert, the theatre, a museum, the beach, work, school, university, bed, etc.

┌─ **EXTRA IDEA** ─┐
- Write the phrases (but not the verbs) from the **Possible answers** box above in random order on a handout. Give each student a copy of the handout. Students work in pairs and decide which verb goes with each word or phrase. ✍ Check answers on the board as in **1c**.

2 a Students do the exercise on their own. Students can use phrases from **1a** or those on the board.

b Students do the exercise in pairs. Ask each student to tell the class one of their true sentences.

Future plans

3 a Focus students on the photo on SB p81. Ask students where Rosie, Andy and Jason are (in a pub). **CD3** ▶ **56** Play the recording (SB p113). Students listen and decide what Rosie, Andy and Jason are going to do on Friday.
Check the answer with the class. (They're going to have dinner together in a restaurant.)

b Check students know where *South Africa* is. Give students time to read questions 1–6.
Play the recording again. Students listen and answer the questions. Students compare answers in pairs. Check answers with the class.

1 Next month. **2** He's going to work for a travel company (in Cape Town). **3** Yes, she is. **4** They're going to live in Rosie and her husband's flat. **5** No, they aren't. **6** He's going to (go to) the cinema.

HELP WITH GRAMMAR
be going to: questions and short answers

4 a–c Students do the exercises on their own or in pairs. Early finishers can check their answers in **GRAMMAR 10.2** ▶ SB p133.
✍ While students are working, draw the table from **4a** on the board. Check answers with the class.

- **a–b** Focus students on the table on the board. Elicit which words in questions 1 and 2 in **4b** go in each column and complete the table (see the table in **GRAMMAR 10.2** SB p133).
- Highlight the word order in *Wh-* questions with *be going to*: question word + *be* + subject + *going to* + verb + … .
- **c Answers** **Are** you going to see a film? Yes, I **am**. / No, I'm not.; **Is** she going to look for a job? Yes, she **is**. / No, she **isn't**.; **Are** you going to sell your flat? Yes, we **are**. / No, we **aren't**.; **Are** they going to have a party? Yes, they **are**. / No, they **aren't**.
- Use the questions in the first column to highlight that the word order in *yes/no* questions with *be going to* is the same as for *Wh-* questions, but without the question word.
- Highlight that we only use a form of the verb *be* in the short answers, not *going to*.
- Also point out that the short answers are the same as for *yes/no* questions with the verb *be* (*Are you British?*, *Is she a doctor?*, etc.).
- Remind students that we can also say the short answers *No, he's not.*, *No, she's not.*, *No, we're not.* and *No, they're not.*

> **EXTRA IDEA**
>
> - Ask students to look at Audio Script **CD3** 56 SB p113. Play the recording again. Students listen, read and underline all the questions and sentences with *be going to*. Students can then compare answers in pairs.

5 **a** Students do the exercise on their own.

b **CD3** 57 Play the recording (SB p113). Students listen and check their answers. Check answers with the class.

PRONUNCIATION Focus students on the example drill. Highlight the sentence stress and the weak form of *to* /tə/. Play the recording again. Students listen and practise.

Alternatively, ask students to turn to Audio Script **CD3** 57 SB p113, where the stress in the questions is marked. Play the recording again. Students listen, read and copy the sentence stress as shown in the Student's Book.

2 What are you going to do after class?
3 When are you going to do your homework?
4 What time are you going to get up tomorrow?
5 Where are you going to have dinner tomorrow evening?
6 Where are you going to go on holiday next year?

c Students do the activity in pairs. Before they begin, remind students to make notes on their partner's answers as they will need them when they talk to a different student in **5d**.

d Put students into new pairs. Students take turns to talk about their partner in **5c**.

Ask students to tell the class two things they found out about their first partner.

Get ready … Get it right!

6 Focus students on the prompts. Students do the exercise on their own.

If necessary, check and drill the questions with the class. Also remind students that for questions with *go*, we can say *Are you going to go shopping on Saturday?* or *Are you going shopping on Saturday?*, etc. and that both forms of the question are correct. Also point out the alternative questions *Are you going to **have a party next weekend?** and *Are you going to **go to a party next weekend?***

Are you going to watch TV tonight?
Are you going to (go to) the cinema this week?
Are you going to have coffee with friends after class?
Are you going (to go) swimming or running next weekend?
Are you going to (go to) the gym next week?
Are you going to have/go to a party next weekend?
Are you going to have dinner with friends on Saturday evening?

7 **a** Students move around the room and ask their questions from **6**, or ask as many people as they can sitting near them. When they find a student who answers *yes*, they write the person's name next to the question. Students then ask one more question, as shown in the speech bubbles. Students should try and find a different person who answers *yes* for each question.

b Finally, ask a few students to tell the class about one student's plans.

> **EXTRA IDEA**
>
> - When students have finished **7a**, put them into pairs. Students take turns to tell each other about other students' plans.

FURTHER PRACTICE

Ph **Class Activity** 10B Guess your partner's future p160 (Instructions p125)
Ph **Vocabulary Plus** 10 Weather p176 (Instructions p166)
Extra Practice 10B SB p106
Self-study DVD-ROM Lesson 10B
Workbook Lesson 10B p49

10C ▶ **REAL WORLD** ▶ Good luck!
Student's Book p82–p83

Vocabulary adjectives (3): feelings
Real World saying goodbye and good luck

QUICK REVIEW This activity reviews phrases with *have, watch, go, go to*. Students do the first part of the activity in pairs. You can set a time limit of two or three minutes. Then put students into groups of four with another pair. Students compare lists and find out who has more phrases. If necessary, check students' ideas by asking one pair to tell the class their phrases and eliciting other possible phrases from the rest of the class.

How do you feel?

1 **a** Focus students on pictures 1–8. Students do the exercise in pairs, then check their answers in **VOCABULARY 10.4** ▶ SB p132.

Check answers with the class, using the situations in the pictures to clarify meaning if necessary.

Point out that the opposite of *happy* is *sad* or *unhappy*.

Use the **TIP** to highlight that we can use the verbs *be* or *feel* with these adjectives: *I'm excited.* = *I feel excited.*, etc.

Depending on your students' first language, you may want to point out that *excited* is a positive adjective, and that we feel excited before something good or interesting happens (a holiday, a party, a concert, etc.). We feel *nervous* /ˈnɜːvəs/ before something we are worried about or don't want to do (an exam, speaking in public, a driving test, etc.).

You can also point out that the woman in picture 5 is *bored* because the man is *boring* (which students learned in lesson 8A). However, we suggest that you don't focus on the difference between *-ed* and *-ing* adjectives too much at this level.

With a strong class you can also teach *thirsty* /ˈθɜːsti/ and *frightened* /ˈfraɪtənd/. Note that *frightened* is a synonym of *scared*.

> tired 7; happy 1; sad 2; bored 5;
> scared 8; hungry 6; angry 4

b **CD3** **58** **PRONUNCIATION** Play the recording. Students listen and practise. Alternatively, model and drill the words yourself.

Highlight the difference in pronunciation between *hungry* /ˈhʌŋgri/ and *angry* /ˈæŋgri/. Also point out that *scared* /skeəd/ is one syllable, not two. Repeat the drill if necessary.

c Focus students on the speech bubbles and highlight the use of *Who's ... ?* in the question. Students do the activity in new pairs.

2 **a** Check students remember *always, usually, sometimes* and *never*. Drill these words with the class if necessary. Students do the exercise on their own.

b Students work in pairs and take turns to say their sentences to each other. You can also ask students to tick any sentences that are the same.

Ask a few students to tell the class one or two things they found out about their partner.

See you soon!

3 **a** Focus students on photos A–C. Ask students where the people are. You can also ask students what they know about the people in the photos.

> **A** **Sally** is at a station and she is talking to her brother **Chris**, who is standing in the street somewhere in London. Sally is the teacher from lesson 1C, and in lesson 9C she bought a train ticket to London to go and visit Chris for the weekend.
> **B** **Danny** and **Karen** are in a café called Café Pronto. In lesson 8C, Karen gave Danny a present for his birthday and they decided to go to the cinema that evening to see a Johnny Depp film.
> **C** **Dorota** and **Khalid** are in a language school. They were two of the students in Sally's class in lesson 1C.

b Ask students to close their books to avoid them reading the conversations in **4a** at this stage of the lesson.

VIDEO **10** **CD3** **59** Play the video or audio recording. Students watch or listen and find out when the people are going to see each other again.

Note that all the Real World videos can be found on the **Teacher's DVD** at the back of this book.

4 **a** Students work in pairs and try to choose the correct words or phrases, based on what they can remember from the conversations. Do not check answers at this stage.

b **VIDEO** **10** **CD3** **59** Play the video or audio recording again. Students watch or listen and check their answers to **4a**. Check answers with the class.

> 2 journey 3 London 4 two 5 ten 6 this 7 day
> 8 driving test 9 course 10 September 11 job

REAL WORLD
Saying goodbye and good luck

5 **a** Students do the exercise on their own, then compare answers in pairs.

Check answers with the class.

- **Answers** 2 lot 3 September 4 see 5 job 6 much
- Highlight the new phrase *Good luck* and the preposition in *Good luck **with** your new job.*
- Check students understand that *Thanks a lot.* and *Thanks very much.* mean the same.

b Students do the exercise in pairs, as shown in the example. Early finishers can check answers in REAL WORLD 10.1 ▶ SB p133.
Check answers with the class.

- **Answers** **Have a good** holiday/day/weekend/birthday/time.
  See you in two hours/this evening/on Monday/soon/later.
  Good luck with your driving test/exam/new school/English test.
- Check students remember *journey* and remind them that *a journey* is in one direction only. You can compare this to *a trip*, which is when you travel to a place and come back again. You can also teach the phrase *Have a good trip!*.
- Tell students we can also say *Good luck in your (exam, new job,* etc.*)*.

6 CD3▶ 60 PRONUNCIATION Play the recording (SB p113). Students listen and practise the sentences in **4**. Highlight the /ɜː/ sounds in *journey* /ˈdʒɜːni/ and *birthday* /ˈbɜːθdeɪ/, which students studied in the *Help with Pronunciation* section in unit 8. Also encourage students to copy the interested intonation on the recording. Repeat the drill if necessary.
You can ask students to turn to Audio Script CD3▶ 60 SB p113, where the stress is marked on all phrases. Play the recording again. Students listen, read and copy the stress.

7 **a** Students do the exercise on their own.

b CD3▶ 61 Play the recording (SB p113). Students listen and check their answers.
Check answers with the class.

A
ALAN   What are you going to do after work?
JANE   I'm going to have dinner with friends.
ALAN   Oh, nice. Have a good time.
JANE   Thanks a lot. And good luck with your exam.
ALAN   Thanks very much. See you tomorrow.
JANE   Yes, see you. Bye!

B
RYAN   I'm going to go on holiday next week.
LILY   Really? Where are you going?
RYAN   To Edinburgh, in Scotland.
LILY   Well, have a good holiday.
RYAN   Thanks. Oh, and good luck with your new job.
LILY   Thanks a lot.

c Students practise the conversations in pairs. While students are working, monitor and check they are saying the phrases with correct stress and that they sound cheerful and interested.

┌─ EXTRA IDEA ┐

- Before doing **7c**, play CD3▶ 61 again, pausing after each sentence for students to repeat chorally and individually. Students can then practise the conversations in pairs.

8 **a** Students do the exercise on their own. Ask students not to write anything at this stage.

b Ask students to move around the room and talk about their plans with other students. Remind students to use *I'm going to …* to talk about their plans, and to respond to other people's plans with phrases from **5** (*Have a good time.*, etc.). Encourage students to have natural conversations and ask questions or give more information as necessary. Alternatively, students can do the activity in groups. Finally, ask students to tell the class about any interesting or exciting plans they talked about.

┌─ EXTRA IDEAS ┐

- Introduce or conclude the activity in **8** by talking about your own future plans.
- As a non-personalised alternative to the speaking activity in **8**, use **Class Activity** 10C After the course p161 (Instructions p126).

FURTHER PRACTICE

Ph **Class Activity** 10C After the course p161 (Instructions p126)
Extra Practice 10 SB p106
Self-study DVD-ROM Lesson 10C
Workbook Lesson 10C p51
Workbook Reading and Writing Portfolio 10 p70–p71
Ph **Progress Test** 10 p190–p191 (note that this is a two-page test with a listening section)

HELP WITH PRONUNCIATION
Vowel sounds: review

1 Focus students on the table and highlight the phonemes and the words at the top of each column. Tell students that they have studied all these sounds earlier in the course.

CD3▶ 62 Play the recording. Students listen to the sounds and the words. Remind students that *a* in *bag* is pronounced with an /æ/ sound, *o* and *er* in *computer* are pronounced with an /ə/ sound, etc. Play the recording again. Students listen and practise.

2 a Focus students on the words in the box. Tell students to write words with pink letters in the first and third columns of the table, under the words with letters in pink (*bag, six, coffee, forty*) and words with blue letters in the second and fourth columns of the table, under the words with letters in blue (*computer, nineteen, umbrella, burger*).

Students do the exercise in pairs. Encourage students to say the words out loud to each other when deciding which section of the table they go in.

b CD3▶ 63 Play the recording. Students listen and check their answers.

Play the recording again. Students listen and practise all the words in the table.

/æ/ b<u>a</u>g	/ə/ <u>compute</u>r	/ɪ/ s<u>i</u>x	/iː/ nin<u>e</u>teen
h<u>a</u>ve <u>a</u>ngry fant<u>a</u>stic	br<u>ea</u>kf<u>a</u>st <u>a</u>mazing cin<u>e</u>ma	d<u>i</u>fferent m<u>a</u>rket t<u>i</u>cket	k<u>ey</u>s j<u>ea</u>ns b<u>ea</u>ch

/ɒ/ c<u>o</u>ffee	/ʌ/ <u>u</u>mbrella	/ɔː/ f<u>o</u>rty	/ɜː/ b<u>u</u>rger
l<u>o</u>ng h<u>o</u>liday bec<u>au</u>se	c<u>ou</u>ntry h<u>u</u>ngry m<u>o</u>ney	b<u>o</u>red w<u>a</u>lk b<u>ou</u>ght	g<u>i</u>rl w<u>o</u>rk univ<u>e</u>rsity

> **EXTRA IDEA**
>
> • ✍ Before doing **2b**, draw the table in **1** on the board, then ask students where they think each word goes in the table. If students disagree where a particular word should go, write it in more than one section of the table without saying which is correct. Then play **CD3▶ 63** and ask students to check the answers on the board. You can pause the recording after each section of the table, tick the correct words and cross out any incorrect words.

3 a CD3▶ 64 Focus students on sentences 1–6. Play the recording. Students listen and read the sentences. Play the recording again, pausing after each sentence for students to practice chorally and individually. Encourage students to say the sentences with natural speed and rhythm.

b Students do the exercise in pairs. Encourage students to say each sentence at least three times. Finally, ask each student to say one sentence for the class.

continue2learn

Focus students on the **continue2learn** section on SB p84. See p33 of this book for ideas on how to use this section in class.

Extra Practice 10 SB p106

See p34 for ideas on how to use this section in class.

10A
1 2 ~~married~~ 3 ~~a flat~~ 4 ~~a job~~ 5 ~~school~~ 6 ~~a new job~~
2 2 's / is going to play 3 'm going to stay 4 aren't going to eat out 5 're going to study 6 isn't going to get up 7 'm not going to see 8 they're going to have
3 2 next 3 in 4 tomorrow 5 next 6 tomorrow 7 on 8 on 9 tomorrow 10 next 11 next 12 in

10B
4 2 go to the gym 3 watch the news 4 go swimming 5 have dinner with friends 6 go running 7 have a party 8 go to a party 9 watch sport on TV
5 2 When are they going to move house? 3 Who is he going to stay with? 4 Why are you going to leave your job? 5 Where's / Where is she going (to go) on holiday?
6 1 Yes, I am. 2 Is; No, she isn't. / No, she's not. 3 Are; Yes, they are. 4 Is; No, he isn't. / No, he's not. 5 Am; Yes, you are.

10C
7

H	A	P	P	Y	J	O	S
B	Q	A	N	G	R	Y	A
O	E	X	C	I	T	E	D
R	I	K	G	V	I	S	F
E	H	U	N	G	R	Y	M
D	E	A	J	L	E	N	B
S	C	A	R	E	D	U	C

8 2 good 3 lot 4 See 5 in 6 you 7 luck 8 with 9 much

Progress Portfolio 10

See p34 for ideas on how to use this section in class.

End of Course Review

The aim of this activity is to review language that students have learned throughout the course in a fun, student-centred way. The activity takes about 25–40 minutes.

Pre-teach *a counter, throw a dice, land on a square* and *move forward/back.*

Give students time to read the rules on SB p84 and answer any questions they may have. Alternatively, go through the instructions section by section with the class. If possible, demonstrate how to play the game to the whole class while you go through the instructions. If you have a monolingual class, you can give the instructions in the students' own language.

To check students have understood, ask what happens when a student lands on a Grammar or Vocabulary square for the first time (he/she answers question 1 only). Ask what happens when a second student lands on the same square (he/she answers question 2). Also check what happens when a third student lands on the square (he/she can stay there without answering a question).

Put students into groups of four and give a dice and counters to each group (or students can make their own counters).

Ask a student with a watch in each group to be the time-keeper for the group. He/She should time students when they land on a **Talk about** square and have to talk about a topic for 15 seconds.

Students take turns to throw the dice and move around the board.

If a student thinks another student's answer to a question on a **Grammar** or **Vocabulary** square is wrong, he/she can check in the Language Summaries in the Student's Book, or ask you to adjudicate.

While students are working, monitor and help with any problems.

The first student to get to **FINISH** is the winner.

Students can continue playing until three students have finished.

If one group finishes early, ask them to look at all the squares they didn't land on and answer the questions.

1 1 See **VOCABULARY 1.2** SB p114.
   2 See **VOCABULARY 2.1** SB p116.
3 1 men, chairs, sandwiches, people
   2 women, watches, parents, children
4 1 I'm going to the cinema on Sunday.
   2 He **doesn't** like classical music.
6 1 What does he do in the evenings?
   2 What did you do on Sunday?
8 1 I didn't **go** out, I stayed at home.
   2 Karen always **gets** up early in the week.
10 1 was, wasn't 2 was, weren't
12 1 She **doesn't like** watching TV.
   2 We **didn't go** out last night.
13 1 See **VOCABULARY 2.2** SB p116.
   2 See **VOCABULARY 6.1** and **VOCABULARY 6.2** SB p124.
14 1 'm, 's 2 's, 're
15 1 some 2 shopping
17 1 cold, expensive, beautiful, unfriendly
   2 short, interesting, empty, difficult
18 1 Yes, they are. No, they aren't./No, they're not.
   2 Yes, she does. No, she doesn't.
20 1 Are there any shops near your flat?
   2 What are you going to do tomorrow?
21 1 go to the cinema, go running, play football
   2 play tennis, go to concerts, go on holiday
23 1 at the weekend, at night, in the evening
   2 on Friday, at midday, in the morning
25 1 half past seven/seven thirty, five to four/three fifty-five, eight o'clock/eight, (a) quarter past two/two fifteen
   2 (a) quarter to seven/six forty-five, twenty past eleven/eleven twenty, twenty-five to five/four thirty-five, half past twelve/twelve thirty
27 1 See **VOCABULARY 7.5** SB p127.
   2 See **VOCABULARY 4.2** SB p120 and **VOCABULARY 10.3** SB p132.
29 1 have a party, do a course, get married
   2 get engaged, do an exam, have coffee with friends
30 1 bought, travelled, got, met
   2 told, came, visited, left
32 1 See **VOCABULARY 3.4** SB p118, **VOCABULARY 3.5** SB p118 and **VOCABULARY 5.3** SB p122.
   2 See **VOCABULARY 9.2** SB p130.
34 1 Where did you go last Saturday?
   2 What does your sister do?
35 1 on, to 2 along (up, down), turn
36 1 my, She 2 He, them
38 1 Yes, there is. No, there isn't.
   2 Yes, he did. No, he didn't.

Photocopiable Materials

Class Activities

Instructions

There are 29 Class Activities worksheets (p127–p161). These worksheets give extra communicative speaking practice of the key language taught in the Student's Book. Each activity matches a lesson in the Student's Book, for example, *1B Where's he from?* matches lesson 1B, etc. There are three activities for units 1–9 and two activities for unit 10.

The Class Activities can be used as extra practice when you have finished the relevant lesson or as review activities in the next class or later in the course.

Many of the activities involve students working in pairs or groups. When you have an odd number of students, you can:

- ask two students to share a role card or worksheet.
- give extra cards to stronger students.
- vary the size of the groups.

At this level it is usually advisable to demonstrate the activity to the whole class before students begin working in pairs or groups.

1B Where's he from? p127

Language

countries; *What's his / her name?*; *Where's he / she from?*

Activity type, when to use and time

Memory game. Use any time after lesson 1B.
10–20 minutes.

Preparation

Photocopy one worksheet for each pair of students. Cut into separate worksheets.

Procedure

- ✍ Write *What's his name?*, *Where's he from?*, *What's her name?*, *Where's she from?* and *I don't know.* on the board. Check students remember the questions by asking the names and countries of students in the class. Teach and drill *I don't know.*
- Put students into pairs. Give a copy of worksheet A to each pair. Tell students that they have two minutes to remember the names and countries of all the people in the picture. Students are not allowed to make notes.
- Collect the worksheets from each pair (or ask students to turn over their worksheets). Give a copy of worksheet B to each pair.
- Students work in the same pairs. They take turns to point at a person on the worksheet and ask their partner the person's name and country, using the questions on the board. Demonstrate this activity before they begin by holding up a copy of worksheet B, pointing to a person on the worksheet and asking the class to tell you the person's name and country.

- Students continue working in pairs until they have asked about all the people on the worksheet. If they are finding it hard to remember the information, collect in worksheet B and redistribute worksheet A. Allow the class one minute to look at worksheet A again, then collect them in and redistribute worksheet B.
- If you want to give your class more practice, put students into new pairs and ask them to repeat the second stage of the activity with their new partner.
- Finally, check the name and country of each person on worksheet B with the whole class.

1C Real names p128

Language

first names and surnames; the alphabet; *How do you spell that?*

Activity type, when to use and time

Information gap. Use any time after lesson 1C.
15–20 minutes.

Preparation

Photocopy one worksheet for each pair of students. Cut into separate worksheets.

Procedure

- Pre-teach *real name*, for example by showing the class a photo of the singer Sting, or writing his name on the board, and asking the class if they think this is his real name. (His real name is Gordon Sumner.)
- Put students into pairs, A and B. Give each student a copy of the appropriate worksheet. Students are not allowed to look at their partner's worksheet.
- If you have a monolingual class, you can discuss where the people are from and what they do (see answer key).
- ✍ Write *Number 1. What's his real name?*, *Number 2. What's her real name?*, *His / Her first name is … *, *His / Her surname is … *, *How do you spell that?* and *Can you repeat that, please?* on the board. Drill these sentences with the class if necessary.
- Students take turns to ask their partner the real names of four people on their worksheets, using the questions on the board. Student A asks about people 1, 3, 5 and 7. Student B asks about people 2, 4, 6 and 8. Students must spell difficult names to each other. They are not allowed to copy them from their partner's worksheet.
- Students compare worksheets and check spelling.

Eminem is an American hip hop artist and record producer. **Natalie Portman** is an American actress. **Fatboy Slim** is a British DJ and record producer. **Lady Gaga** is an American singer-songwriter. **Katy Perry** is an American singer and actress. **Bono** is the singer of the Irish rock band U2 and a well-known anti-poverty campaigner. **Pink** is an American singer-songwriter. **Jay-Z** is an American hip hop artist and successful businessman.

1D Pictures and words p129

Language

people; things; plurals

Activity type, when to use and time

Pelmanism. Use any time after lesson 1D. 10–20 minutes.

Preparation

Photocopy one worksheet for each group of three students. Cut into sets. Shuffle each set.

Procedure

- Put students into groups of three. Give each group a set of cards. Ask them to spread the cards out **face-down** on the table in front of them, with the small cards on the left and the big cards on the right.
- Students take turns to turn over one small card and one big card. If a student thinks that the two cards match, he/she must say and spell the plural form of the word. If the two cards match and plural form is correct, the student keeps the pair of cards and has another turn. If the two cards don't match, the student puts both cards back on the table face-down **in exactly the same place**.
- If a student thinks that another student's cards don't match or that the plural is not correct, he/she can challenge him/her. If students can't agree, they can ask you to adjudicate. If the cards don't match or the plural form is incorrect, the student puts the cards back and the turn passes to the next student.
- Demonstrate the activity to the whole class before asking students to work in their groups.
- The activity continues until all the cards are matched up. The student who collects the most cards is the winner.
- If a group finishes early, students can take turns to test each other on the words by holding up a small card and asking the other students to say the word and its plural form.

2B New identities p130

Language

be (singular): *Wh-* questions; jobs; countries

Activity type, when to use and time

Mingle role play. Use any time after lesson 2B. 15–25 minutes.

Preparation

Photocopy one worksheet for every ten students in the class. Cut into separate role cards.

Procedure

- Give each student a role card. If you have more than ten students in the class, give out duplicate role cards. If you are using more than one set of cards, try to give the first role card A to a female student and the second role card A to a male student, etc. Students are not allowed to look at each other's cards.

- Tell students that the information on their role card is their new identity. Point out that the names with a ♂ sign are for male students and those with a ♀ sign are for female students.
- Students look at the pictures on their cards and complete the words for the country and the job. If necessary, monitor and check that students have written the correct words (see answer key). Give students a few moments to memorise their new name, job and country.
- Students move around the room and introduce themselves to each other. Before they begin, tell students that they must try to remember other people's names, jobs and countries, but they are not allowed to write anything down. If students are not able to leave their seats, they should ask as many students as they can sitting near them.
- Encourage students to use the following language during this stage of the activity: *Hello / Hi, my name's (David)., What's your name?, Nice to meet you., You too., Where are you from?, I'm from (the UK)., What's your job?, I'm a (taxi driver).* ✍ If necessary, write this language on the board before students begin the activity.
- When students have finished, put them into pairs. Students take turns to ask their partner about the other students in the room. Encourage students to use these questions and answers when working in pairs: *What's his / her name?, Where's he / she from?, What's his / her job?, He's / She's a (teacher)., I don't know.* ✍ If necessary, write this language on the board during the mingle stage of the activity.
- Finally, ask each student to tell the class about another student's new identity.

Bob/Carol the UK, a taxi driver
Nick/Sally the USA, a doctor
Pat/Susan Australia, a sales assistant
Adem/Deniz Turkey, a manager
Diego/Lara Spain, a teacher
Paulo/Paula Brazil, a musician
Max/Erica Germany, a police officer
Dario/Carla Mexico, a singer
Viktor/Anna Russia, an actor/actress
Marco/Maria Italy, a waiter/a waitress

2C The City Gym p131

Language

personal information questions

Activity type, when to use and time

Information gap.
Procedure A: use in place of exercise **9a** in lesson 2C.
Procedure B: use any time after lesson 2C.
10–20 minutes.

Preparation

Procedures A and B: photocopy one worksheet for each pair of students. Cut into separate worksheets.

Procedure A

This procedure is suitable for classes where the students know each other well or classes where you feel it is inappropriate for students to reveal their personal details to each other.

- After the class has done exercise **8** in lesson 2C (SB p19), put students into pairs, A and B. Give each student a copy of the appropriate worksheet. Students are not allowed to look at each other's worksheets.
- Tell students that they now live in London and that their new personal information is on form 1 on their worksheets. Note that Sam and Alex are names for men and women in English, so both worksheets can be used by male and female students.
- Students take turns to interview each other, using the personal information questions with *your* from exercise **7** in lesson 2C. Students answer the questions using the information on their form, not their real personal details. The interviewers can fill in form 2 either on the worksheet or in the Student's Book. Before students begin, remind them of the questions *How do you spell that?* and *Can you repeat that, please?*.
- When students have finished, they compare forms and check their spelling.

Procedure B

This procedure provides practice of personal information questions with *his* and *her*.

- ✍ Draw a blank **The City Gym – New Member Form** on the board and elicit the following questions: *What's his / her first name?*, *What's his / her surname?*, *What's his / her nationality?*, *What's his / her address?*, *What's his / her mobile number?*, *What's his / her email address?*. Drill these questions with the class.
- Put students into pairs, A and B. Give each student a copy of the appropriate worksheet. Students are not allowed to look at each other's worksheets.
- Tell the class that Sam (form 1 on worksheet A) is a man and Alex (form 1 on worksheet B) is a woman. Student A in each pair asks his/her partner about Alex and writes the personal information on form 2 on his/her worksheet, using the questions on the board.
- When he/she has finished, Student B asks his/her partner about Sam and writes the personal information on form 2 on his/her worksheet.
- Before students begin, remind them of the questions *How do you spell that?* and *Can you repeat that, please?*.
- When students have finished, they compare forms and check their spelling.

2D ▸ Hear a number, say a number p132

Language
numbers 0–100

Activity type, when to use and time
Hear/Say activity. Use any time after lesson 2D.
10–15 minutes.

Preparation
Photocopy one worksheet for every three students.
Cut into separate worksheets.

Procedure

- Put students into groups of three, A, B and C. Give each student a copy of the appropriate worksheet. If you have extra students, have one or two groups of four and ask two students to share one worksheet.
- Explain that students must listen to the numbers that the other two students in the group say. If the number is in the HEAR column on their worksheet, they must say the number next to it in the SAY column.
- Students do the activity in their groups. Student A in each group starts by saying *forty-one*. Student B hears *forty-one* and says *fifteen*. Student C hears *fifteen* and says *fifty*, etc. The activity continues until the students reach FINISH. Students should cross out numbers on their worksheets when they hear or say them.
- Demonstrate this activity by doing the first five numbers with the whole class before asking students to work in their groups.

3A ▸ Where are they? p133

Language
be (plural): questions and short answers; adjectives (1)

Activity type, when to use and time
Information gap. Use any time after lesson 3A.
15–25 minutes.

Preparation
Photocopy one worksheet for each pair of students.
Cut into separate worksheets.

Procedure

- Put students into pairs, A and B. Give each student a copy of the appropriate worksheet. Students are not allowed to look at their partner's worksheets.
- Focus students on the prompts in the first column on their worksheets. ✍ Elicit the following questions about Tom and Alice and write them on the board: *Where are Tom and Alice from?*, *How old are they?*, *What are their jobs?*, *Are they married?*, *Where are they now?*, *Are they in a new hotel?*, *Are the rooms very big?*, *Are the restaurants cheap?*. Drill the questions with the class.
- Students work with their partners and take turns to ask questions about the four couples. Student A starts by asking all the questions about Tom and Alice, then Student B asks all the questions about Paco and Ana. Encourage students to use correct short answers (*Yes, they are.* and *No, they aren't.*) when answering *yes / no* questions. Students write the answers on their worksheets. Before they begin, remind students of the questions *How do you spell that?* and *Can you repeat that, please?*.
- When students have finished, they compare answers with their partner and check their spelling.

3B ▶ Barry and Wendy's family p134–p135

Language
family; possessive *'s*; jobs; *How old … ?*

Activity type, when to use and time
Information gap. Use any time after lesson 3B.
15–25 minutes.

Preparation
Photocopy one student A worksheet and one student B worksheet for each pair of students.

Procedure
- Pre-teach *a writer* and *a footballer*.
- Put students into pairs, A and B. Give each student a copy of the appropriate worksheet. Students are not allowed to look at each other's worksheets.
- Tell students that their worksheet has some names, jobs and ages of ten people in the same family. Students must ask their partner questions to complete the information about each person in the family.
- ✎ Elicit the questions for 1–7 from the whole class and write them on the board: 1 *What's Barry's job?*, 2 *How old is he?*, 3 *What's his wife's name?*, 4 *What's Wendy's / her job?*, 5 *How old is she?*, 6 *What's their daughter's name?*, 7 *What's her husband's name?*. Drill these questions with the class.
- Students work with their partners and take turns to ask questions about the people on their worksheet **in number order**. Students write the information on their worksheets. Before they begin, remind students of the questions *How do you spell that?* and *Can you repeat that, please?*.
- When students have finished, they compare answers and check their spelling.
- As a follow-up activity, ask students to write three true sentences and three false sentences about the family, for example, *Barry is Wendy's husband.* (true) and *Amanda is Caroline's grandmother.* (false). When they are ready, tell students to turn over their worksheets. Students can then work in pairs, swap sentences, and decide which are true.

3D ▶ From start to finish p136

Language
Review of lessons 1A–3D

Activity type, when to use and time
Board game. Use any time after lesson 3D.
20–30 minutes.

Preparation
Photocopy one board for each group of three or four students. You also need a dice for each group and a counter for each student (or students can make their own counters).

Procedure
- Put the class into groups of three or four. Give each group a copy of the board, a dice and counters.
- Check students understand these squares on the board: START, FINISH, THROW AGAIN, MOVE FORWARD TWO / THREE SQUARES, MOVE BACK TWO / THREE SQUARES.
- Students take turns to throw the dice and move around the board. When a student lands on a square, he/she must answer the question correctly in order to stay on the square. If a student can't answer the question correctly, he/she must move back to his/her previous square.
- If a student thinks another student's answer is wrong, they can check in the Language Summaries in the Student's Book, or ask you to adjudicate. If the answer is wrong, the student must move back to his/her previous square.
- If a student lands on a square where the question has already been answered, he/she must answer the question again to show that he/she has been listening!
- The game ends when one student reaches the FINISH square. If some groups finish early, they can go through the squares in number order and take turns to answer the questions again.

1 five, fourteen, forty, sixty-three, ninety-nine 2 Brazilian, Spanish, American 4 **I'm not** from the UK. He **isn't** Russian. / **He's not** Russian. They **aren't** students. / **They're not** students. 5 **What's** your name? **Where's** he from? **How** old are they? 6 See **VOCABULARY 2.2** SB p116. 8 women, girls, babies, children 9 Yes, I am., Yes, he is., Yes, they are. 10 an apple, a book, a pen, an umbrella 11 A Ben, **this** is Carol. B Hello, Carol. Nice to **meet** you. C You too. 12 See SB p26. 13 See **VOCABULARY 3.3** SB p118. 15 three pounds seventy-five, fifty p / pence, sixty-four dollars, eight euros fifty, ninety-nine cents 16 China, Germany, Russia 17 It's an old car. Their dog is very nice. 18 cold, big, expensive 20 Where **are** you from? What's your job? **Are** you married? 21 See **VOCABULARY 1.3** SB p114. 22 No, she isn't. / No, she's not., No, I'm not., No, they aren't. / No, they're not. 24 unfriendly, old, beautiful 25 See **VOCABULARY 3.4** and **VOCABULARY 3.5** SB p118. 26 thirteen, twenty-seven, fifty-four, seventy-six, a / one hundred 27 Is she **your** sister? This is **our** cat. Are **they** actors? 29 things, people, watches, men 30 Italian, Turkish, Mexican 31 She **isn't** German. / **She's not** German. We **aren't** from Egypt. / **We're not** from Egypt. You **aren't** a teacher. / **You're not** a teacher. 32 oh two oh, seven six double nine, three oh double seven; oh one six double seven, three double two oh nine eight; c dot page at webmail dot com 33 **How** do you spell that? **Can** you repeat that, please? What does bag **mean**?

4B ▶ Find two people p137

Language

free time activities; Present Simple (*I*, *you*, *we*, *they*): yes / *no* questions and short answers

Activity type, when to use and time

'Find someone who' activity. Use any time after lesson 4B. 15–25 minutes.

Preparation

Photocopy one worksheet for each student.

Procedure

- Give a copy of the worksheet to each student. Students work on their own and choose the correct verb for each phrase in the first column. Students can compare answers in pairs before you check answers with the whole class (see answer key).
- Elicit questions with *Do you … ?* for prompts 1–12. Drill these questions if necessary.
- Tell students that they must find two people in the class who answer *yes* to each question and write their names in the second and third columns on their worksheets. Demonstrate this stage of the activity by asking individual students question 1 and writing the names of two students who answer *yes* on a copy of the worksheet.
- Students move around the room and ask each other questions 1–12. When they find a student who answers *yes* to a question, they should write his/her name in the second or third column on the worksheet. Encourage students to talk to as many people as possible. If students are not able to leave their seats, they should ask as many students as they can sitting near them.
- When they have finished, ask students to tick all the questions for which two students have answered *yes*.
- Put students into pairs. Students take turns to make sentences about each pair of students on their worksheets, for example, *Marco and Carolina watch TV a lot.*, *Yi Ling and Henri go to rock concerts.*, etc. Students should not make sentences about any prompt for which only one student has answered *yes*, as these would require the third person singular of the Present Simple.
- Finally, ask students to tell the class two things they have found out about their class.

1 watch 2 go to 3 play 4 go 5 eat 6 go 7 play
8 go to 9 work 10 live 11 have 12 like

4C ▶ Shopping bingo p138

Language

things to buy; food and drink (2)

Activity type, when to use and time

Bingo game. Use any time after lesson 4C. 10–15 minutes.

Preparation

Photocopy one worksheet for every four students. Cut into separate bingo cards.

Procedure

- Give one bingo card to each student in random order. Try to avoid giving the same bingo card to two students sitting next to each other.
- Give students a few minutes to check they know the words for all the pictures on their cards. Students can check in **VOCABULARY 3.5** ▶ SB p118 and **VOCABULARY 4.3** ▶ SB p120. Students are not allowed to write the words on their cards.
- Read out these things to the whole class **in this order**: *a magazine, cheese, a map, orange juice, coffee, fruit, a birthday card, milk, batteries, tissues, tea, chewing gum, eggs, a box of chocolates, vegetables, sweets, sugar, a postcard, bread, a newspaper, fish, meat* (student C card is completed), *rice* (student B card is completed), *pasta* (student A and student D cards are completed).
- When students hear the word for a picture on their card, they put a cross through it.
- When a student has crossed out all the pictures on his/her card, he/she shouts *Bingo!*. The first student to shout *Bingo!* wins the game.
- If necessary, check students understand how to play the game before you begin. Note that students must cross out **all** the pictures on the card, not just one line or one column.
- If you want to play the game again, distribute new cards and read out the words in random order.

4D ▶ Time dominoes p139

Language

telling the time

Activity type, when to use and time

Dominoes. Use any time after lesson 4D. 15–20 minutes.

Preparation

Photocopy one set of dominoes for each pair of students. Cut into sets and shuffle each set.

Procedure

- Put students into pairs. Give one set of dominoes to each pair. Students share out the dominoes equally. Students are not allowed to look at their partner's dominoes. If you have an extra student, have one group of three and ask them to share one set of dominoes between them.
- One student puts a domino on the table. His/Her partner puts another domino at either end of the first domino so that the times on the two dominoes match. Students must say the time aloud when they match the dominoes. Students then continue taking turns to put dominoes at either end of the domino chain.
- If a student thinks that a pair of dominoes don't match, he/she can challenge his/her partner. If the match is incorrect, the student must take back his/her domino

and the turn passes to his/her partner. If students can't agree, they should ask you to adjudicate.

- If a student can't put down a domino, the turn passes to his/her partner. The game continues until one student has put down all his/her dominoes, or until neither student can make a correct match. The student who finishes first, or who has fewer dominoes remaining, is the winner.
- If some pairs finish early, students can test each other on the times shown on the digital clocks on each domino.

5A ▶ My partner's life p140

Language
Present Simple (he, she, it): positive and negative; daily routines; free time activities

Activity type, when to use and time
Personalised information gap. Use any time after lesson 5A. 15–25 minutes.

Preparation
Photocopy one worksheet for each pair of students. Cut into separate worksheets.

Procedure
- Pre-teach *in the week* and *at the weekend*. Highlight the prepositions in these phrases.
- Put students into pairs, A and B. If possible, put students with someone they don't know very well. Give each student a copy of the appropriate worksheet. Students write their partner's name at the top of their worksheet. Students are not allowed to look at their partner's worksheet.
- ✍ Write sentence 1 from student A's worksheet on the board and elicit the two possible ways to complete the sentence by using the positive or negative Present Simple form of the verb in brackets (*gets up* or *doesn't get up*).
- Students work on their own and make sentences they think are true about their partner by putting the verb in brackets into the correct positive or negative form of the Present Simple. Students are not allowed to speak to their partner at this stage of the activity.
- ✍ Focus students on the sentence on the board and elicit the corresponding *yes / no* question: *Do you get up before 7 o'clock in the week?*. Remind students of the short answers *Yes, I do.* and *No, I don't.*
- Students work on their own and prepare *yes / no* questions with *Do you … ?* for each sentence on their worksheet.
- Students work with their partner and take turns to ask and answer questions. Students put a tick in the second column of their worksheet if their sentence is correct and a cross if their sentence is incorrect. The student with the most ticks wins.
- Finally, students can work in new pairs and tell their new partner about the person they have just talked to.

5B ▶ A writer's week p141–p142

Language
time phrases with *on*, *in*, *at*; Present Simple (he, she, it): Wh- questions

Activity type, when to use and time
Information gap. Use any time after lesson 5B. 15–25 minutes.

Preparation
Photocopy one student A worksheet and one student B worksheet for each pair of students.

Procedure
- Pre-teach *a writer*, *at home*, *a bookshop* and *quiet*.
- Put students into two groups, A and B. Give each student a copy of the appropriate worksheet.
- Focus students on the article on their worksheets. Ask students to look at the heading and the photo and say what the man's name and job is. (Oliver Richardson. He's a writer.)
- Students read the article on their own and choose *on*, *in* or *at* in time phrases 1–8. Tell the class not to worry about the gaps in the article at this stage. Check the answers with the class (see answer key).
- Students work in pairs with another student **from the same group**. They read the article about Oliver again and complete the questions at the bottom of their worksheets, as in the example. If necessary, check answers with the class (see answer key).
- Put students into pairs, with one student from group A and one student from group B in each pair. Students are not allowed to look at each other's worksheets. Students take turns to ask their questions and fill in the gaps in the article. Tell student A to ask the first question.
- When students have finished, they look at their partner's worksheet and check their answers.
- Students who finish early can test each other on Oliver's week by swapping worksheets, covering the article and asking the questions again.

Prepositions
2 in **3** at **4** In **5** at **6** at **7** On **8** in

Student A
2 What time **does** he **get** up in the **week**?
3 When **does** Ingrid **go** to **work**?
4 What time **does** Oliver **start work**?
5 Where **does** he **have lunch**?
6 What **does** he **do** on Saturday **morning**?

Student B
b When **does** he **have breakfast**?
c Where **does** Ingrid **work**?
d What time **does** Oliver **have lunch**?
e What **does** he **do** in the **evening**?
f What **does** he **do** on Saturday **afternoon**?

5D ▶ Always, sometimes, never p143

Language

frequency adverbs and phrases with *every*; Present Simple

Activity type, when to use and time

Personalised guessing game. Use any time after lesson 5D. 15–25 minutes.

Preparation

Photocopy one worksheet for each student.

Procedure

- Pre-teach *something* and *a TV programme*.
- Give a copy of the worksheet to each student. Tell students to read the prompts in box A and then write eight people, things, places and times in the empty boxes. Point out that students only need to write words or phrases for eight of the twelve prompts. Students should write single words or short phrases, for example, *play tennis*, *my sister Juliana*, *cheese*, etc., not complete sentences. They can write their words or phrases in any box they want, but **not** in the same order as the prompts. 🖉 Demonstrate this before students begin by drawing the boxes on the board and writing in your own answers in random order.
- When students have finished, put them into pairs and ask them to swap worksheets.
- Students work on their own and write eight sentences beginning with *You …* about their partner at the bottom of their partner's worksheet, based on the people, things, places and times that he/she has written in the boxes. For example, if a student has written *play tennis*, his/her partner could write: *You never play tennis at the weekend.* or *You sometimes play tennis at the weekend.* Students are not allowed to talk to their partners during this stage of the activity. 🖉 You can demonstrate this stage of the activity before students begin by eliciting sentences about you for the ideas in the boxes on the board.
- Students work in their pairs and take turns to say their sentences about their partner. Their partner says if the sentences are true or false. Students tick their true sentences. The student with more true sentences is the winner.
- Finally, ask each student to tell the class one or two true things they have found out about their partner.

6B ▶ London Road p144–p145

Language

there is / there are; places in a town or city (1) and (2); *a, some, a lot of, any*

Activity type, when to use and time

Spot the difference. Use any time after lesson 6B. 15–25 minutes.

Preparation

Photocopy one student A worksheet and one student B worksheet for each pair of students.

Procedure

- Put students into pairs, A and B. Give each student a copy of the appropriate worksheet.
- Tell the class that there are ten differences between the pictures. Students must work together to find the ten differences by asking questions or saying sentences with *there is / there are*. Students are not allowed to look at each other's worksheets.
- 🖉 If necessary, write these prompts on the board before giving out the worksheets: *There's a (café) in my picture.*, *There are two people at the bus stop.*, *There are some (cars).*, *Is there a (bank) in your picture?*, *Yes, there is.*, *No, there isn't.*, *Are there any (children)?*, *Yes, there are.*, *No, there aren't.* Model and drill the sentences with the class.
- Students work with their partners and take turns to ask questions or say sentences about their picture. When students find a difference, they mark it on their picture.
- When students have finished, they compare worksheets and check their differences.
- Finally, ask each pair to tell the class one difference they have found.

> **1 A** There's a chemist's. **B** There's a post office. **2 A** There isn't a cashpoint / an ATM. **B** There's a cashpoint / an ATM. **3 A** There are a lot of / some people in the café. **B** There aren't any people in the café. **4 A** There's a theatre. **B** There's a museum. **5 A** There's a cat. **B** There isn't a cat. **6 A** There are two women at the bus stop. **B** There are two men at the bus stop. **7 A** There are some / four children (near the bank). **B** There aren't any children. **8 A** There's a dog. **B** There are two dogs. **9 A** There are three cars. **B** There are four cars. **10 A** There's a bus. **B** There isn't a bus.

6C ▶ What's in your bag? p146

Language

things in your bag (1) and (2)

Activity type, when to use and time

Bingo game. Use any time after lesson 6C. 10–15 minutes.

Preparation

Photocopy one worksheet for every four students.
Cut into separate bingo cards.

Procedure

- Give one bingo card to each student in random order. Try to avoid giving the same bingo card to two students sitting next to each other. Tell students that each card shows what they have in their bags.
- Give students a few minutes to check they know the words for all the things in the bag on their cards. Students can check in **VOCABULARY 1.4** ▶ SB p114, **VOCABULARY 1.7** ▶ SB p114 and **VOCABULARY 6.3** ▶ SB p124. Students are not allowed to write the words on their cards.

- Read out these things to the whole class **in this order:** *a bag, a purse, a pen, keys, a credit card, a passport, a dictionary, money, a pencil, a camera, a guide book, a wallet, a notebook, a laptop, a map, an ID card, an umbrella* (student D card is completed), *an apple* (student A card is completed), *a sandwich* (student C card is completed), *a watch* (student B card is completed).
- When students hear the word for something on their bingo card, they put a cross through it on their card.
- When a student has crossed out all the things on his/her bingo card, he/she shouts *Bingo!*. The first student to shout *Bingo!* wins the game.
- If you want to play the game again, distribute new cards and read out the words in random order.

6D ▶ Review snakes and ladders p147

Language
Review of lessons 4A–6D

Activity type, when to use and time
Board game. Use any time after lesson 6D. 20–30 minutes.

Preparation
Photocopy one board for each group of three students. You also need a dice for each group and a counter for each student (or students can make their own counters).

Procedure
- Put the students into groups of three. If you have extra students, have one or two groups of four. Give each group a copy of the snakes and ladders board, a dice and counters.
- Students take turns to throw the dice and move around the board. When a student lands on a square, he/she must answer the question correctly in order to stay on the square. If a student can't answer the question correctly, he/she must move back to his/her previous square.
- If a student lands on the bottom of a ladder, he/she must answer the question correctly before he/she is allowed to go up it. He/She does not have to answer the question at the top of the ladder. If he/she lands on the head of a snake, he/she must always go down the snake to its tail. He/She does not have to answer the question at the snake's tail.
- If a student thinks another student's answer is wrong, they can check in the Language Summaries in the Student's Book, or ask you to adjudicate. If the answer is wrong, the student must move back to his/her previous square.
- The first student to reach the FINISH square is the winner.
- If some groups finish early, they can go through the squares in number order and answer the questions in their groups.

1 See VOCABULARY 6.5 ▶ SB p124. **2** in the week, at night, on Monday **3** See VOCABULARY 4.2 ▶ SB p120. **4** half past six / six thirty, quarter to eight / seven forty-five, quarter past three / three fifteen, nine o'clock / nine **5** always, usually, sometimes, not usually, never **6** Monday, Tuesday, Wednesday, Thursday, Friday, Saturday, Sunday **7** Does he like coffee? What music do you like? **8** I don't like football. He doesn't have a car. **9** I never have lunch. He works every day. **10** have breakfast, leave home, go to bed **11** 1 minute = 60 **seconds**, 1 day = 24 **hours**, 1 year = **12 months** **14** studies, watches, leaves, goes **15** See VOCABULARY 6.1 ▶ and VOCABULARY 6.2 ▶ SB p124. **16** Yes, there are. / No, there aren't. Yes, there is. / No, there isn't. **18** Can you show me on this map? **20** Yes, I do. / No, I don't. Yes, she does. / No, she doesn't. **22** I live here. She likes it. **23** See VOCABULARY 6.4 ▶ SB p124. **24** Are there **any** cafés? There are **some** shops. **26** study languages, have a car, live in a flat **27** See SB p42. **28** in the morning, at midnight, on Sunday morning **29** does, finishes, likes, has **30** Where does your son live? Do you have a car? **31** ten past four, five to one, twenty to three, twenty past eleven **33** There isn't a market. There aren't any restaurants.

7A ▶ I like dominoes p148

Language
things you like and don't like; object pronouns

Activity type, when to use and time
Dominoes. Use any time after lesson 7A. 15–20 minutes.

Preparation
Photocopy one set of dominoes for each pair of students. Cut into sets and shuffle each set.

Procedure
- Put students into pairs. Give one set of dominoes to each pair. Students share out the dominoes equally. Students are not allowed to look at their partner's dominoes. If you have an extra student, have one group of three and ask them to share one set of dominoes between them.
- Students work with their partners. One student puts a domino on the table. His/Her partner puts another domino at either end of the first domino so that the question and the short answer on the two dominoes match. Students must say the question and answer aloud when they match the dominoes. Students then continue taking turns to put dominoes at either end of the domino chain.
- If a student thinks that a pair of dominoes don't match, he/she can challenge his/her partner. If the match is incorrect, the student must take back his/her domino and the turn passes to his/her partner. If students can't agree, they should ask you to adjudicate.

- If a student can't put down a domino, the turn passes to his/her partner. The game continues until one student has put down all his/her dominoes, or until neither student can make a correct match. The student who finishes first, or who has fewer dominoes remaining, is the winner.
- If a pair finishes early, students can take turns to ask each other the questions with *you* on the dominoes and answer for themselves.

7B ▶ What can the class do? p149

Language

can for ability; abilities

Activity type, when to use and time

Class survey. Use any time after lesson 7B.
10–15 minutes.

Preparation

Procedure A: photocopy one worksheet for every twelve students in the class. Cut into separate cards.

Procedure B: photocopy one worksheet for every four students in the class. Cut into separate cards. Keep each set of cards separate.

Procedure A

This procedure is suitable for smaller classes and for classes where students can move around the room.

- Pre-teach *a motorbike*, *a musical instrument*, *metres*, *chess*, *backgammon*, *golf*, *a horse* and *run* by using photos, board illustrations, mime, examples or translation.
- Give one card to each student. If you have more than twelve students in the class, give out duplicate cards. Tell the class that they must find out the number of students who can do the activity on the card by talking to every person in the class.
- Students work on their own and make a question with *you* to ask other students. Tell students that they make this question with *Can you …* + the phrase in **bold** on their card. For example, a student with card A should ask *Can you play a musical instrument?*, etc.
- Students move around the room and ask their questions. Students should talk to all the students in the class if possible. Before they begin, tell students to keep a record of how many people say *yes* and *no* to their question on the back of their cards or in their notebooks.
- When they have finished, students complete the sentence on their card by writing a number in the gap. Finally, ask each student to tell the class the result of their survey by reading the sentence from their card. For example, a student with card A might say: *Four students in the class can play a musical instrument.*

Procedure B

This procedure is suitable for larger classes and for classes where students can't move around the room.

- Pre-teach the new vocabulary as in procedure A.
- Put students into groups of four. If you have extra students, have one or two groups of five.

- Give each group a set of 12 cards. Ask students to share the cards equally between them.
- Give students time to prepare their questions with *Can you … ?* as in procedure A.
- Students take turns to ask the other people in the group their questions. Before they begin, tell students to keep a record of how many people say *yes* and *no* to each question on the back of their cards or in their notebooks.
- When they have finished, ask each student to tell the class one or two things they have found out about their group. For example, a student with card A might say: *Four students in our group can play a musical instrument.*

7C ▶ It's on the left p150–p151

Language

asking for and giving directions; prepositions of place

Activity type, when to use and time

Information gap. Use any time after lesson 7C.
15–25 minutes.

Preparation

Photocopy one student A worksheet and one student B worksheet for each pair of students.

Procedure

- Put students into pairs, A and B. Give each student a copy of the appropriate worksheet. Students are not allowed to look at each other's worksheets.
- Tell the students that they are at ❖ on the map. Students must ask their partner for directions to places 1–5 at the top of their worksheets. Also explain that the places shaded in grey (the park, the shopping centre, the station and the supermarket) are on both maps.
- ✍ Before they begin, elicit the questions they need to ask for the first place on each worksheet and write them on the board, underlining *the* and *a*: *Excuse me. Where's the cinema?* and *Excuse me. Is there a bank near here?*. Point out that students should use *Where's the … ?* for places with *the* on their worksheets, and *Is there a … near here?* for places with *a* on their worksheets.
- ✍ If necessary, write the following prompts on the board to help students during the activity: *Go along this road and turn left / right.*, *That's (New Street).*, *The … is on the left / right, next to … , The … is on the left / right, opposite … , It's over there, near the … .*
- Students work with their partner and take turns to ask directions to the places at the top of their worksheets. Student A asks the first question. Encourage students to refer to the places shaded in grey on both maps if possible. Also remind them to thank their partner each time he/she gives directions.
- When a student thinks he/she has identified the correct location, he/she should write the place on the map. Students are not allowed to look at each other's worksheets at this stage of the activity.
- When students have finished, they compare worksheets and see if they have identified the places correctly.

8A ▶ Opposite adjectives p152

Language
adjectives (1) and (2)

Activity type, when to use and time
Pelmanism. Use any time after lesson 8A. 10–20 minutes.

Preparation
Photocopy one worksheet for each group of three students. Cut into sets. Shuffle each set.

Procedure
- Put students into groups of three. Give each group a set of cards. Ask them to spread the cards out **face-down** on the table in front of them, with the small cards on the left and the big cards on the right.
- Students take turns to turn over one small card and one big card. If a student thinks that the adjectives on the two cards are opposites, he/she says a sentence for each adjective. If the student is correct, he/she keeps the pair of cards and has another turn. If the two words are not opposites, the student puts both cards back on the table face-down **in exactly the same place.**
- If a student thinks that another student's cards aren't a pair of opposite adjectives or one of his/her sentences is incorrect, he/she can challenge him/her. If students can't agree, they can ask you to adjudicate. If the cards aren't a pair of opposite adjectives or one of the sentences is incorrect, the student puts the cards back and the turn passes to the next student.
- The activity continues until all the opposite adjectives are matched up. The student who collects the most cards wins.
- If a group finishes early, students can test each other on the adjectives by taking turns to hold up a card and asking the other students to say the opposite adjective.

8B ▶ Were you or weren't you? p153

Language
past time phrases; Past Simple of *be*; *was born / were born*

Activity type, when to use and time
'Find someone who' activity. Use any time after lesson 8B. 15–25 minutes.

Preparation
Photocopy one worksheet for each student.

Procedure
- Teach students how we say *the 1990s (the nineteen nineties)*. Also check students remember *a bus, a train* and *different*.
- Give a copy of the worksheet to each student. Students work on their own and choose the correct word for each time phrase in the first column. Students can compare answers in pairs before you check answers with the whole class (see answer key).
- Elicit questions with *Were you … ?* for prompts 1–12. Drill these questions if necessary.

- Tell students that they must find one person in the class who answers *yes* to each question and write his/her name in the second column on their worksheets. Demonstrate this stage of the activity by asking individual students question 1 and writing the name of a student who answers *yes* on a copy of the worksheet.
- Students move around the room and ask questions 1–12. When they find a student who answers *yes* to a question, they should write his/her name in the second column on the worksheet. Encourage students to talk to as many people as possible. If students are not able to leave their seats, they should ask as many students as they can sitting near them.
- When they have finished, put students into pairs. Students take turns to tell their partners what they have found out about the class.
- Finally, ask students to tell the class two things they have found out about their class.

1 yesterday **2** last **3** in **4** ago **5** last **6** yesterday
7 ago **8** in **9** last **10** ago **11** yesterday **12** ago

8D ▶ Numbers, years and dates p154

Language
big numbers; years; months and dates

Activity type, when to use and time
Hear/Say activity. Use any time after lesson 8D. 10–15 minutes.

Preparation
Photocopy one worksheet for every three students. Cut into separate worksheets.

Procedure
- Put the students into groups of three, A, B and C. Give each student a copy of the appropriate worksheet. If you have extra students, have one or two groups of four and ask two students to share one worksheet.
- Explain that students must listen to the big numbers, years and dates that the other two students in the group say. If the number, year or date is in the HEAR column on their worksheet, they must say the number, year or date next to it in the SAY column.
- Students do the activity in their groups. Student A in each group starts by saying *three hundred and sixty-five.* Student C hears *three hundred and sixty-five* and says *April the first.* Student B hears *April the first* and says *nineteen eighty*, etc. The activity continues until the students reach FINISH. Students should cross out the numbers, years or dates on their worksheets when they hear or say them.
- Demonstrate this activity by doing the first five numbers, years or dates together with the whole class before asking students to work in their groups.

9A ▶ My past p155

Language

Past Simple: positive (regular and irregular verbs)

Activity type, when to use and time

Personalised guessing game. Use any time after lesson 9A. 15–25 minutes.

Preparation

Photocopy one worksheet for each student.

Procedure

- Give a copy of the worksheet to each student. Tell students to read the prompts in the box and then write eight people, things, places and times in the circles. Point out that students only need to write words or phrases for eight of the twelve prompts. Students should write single words or short phrases, for example, *Madrid, my friend Antonio, a new suit,* etc., not complete sentences. They can write their words or phrases in any circle they want, but **not** in the same order as the prompts. ✏ Demonstrate this before students begin by drawing the circles on the board and writing in your own ideas in random order.
- When students have finished, put them into pairs and ask them to swap worksheets.
- Students work on their own and write eight sentences beginning with *I think you …* about their partner at the bottom of their partner's worksheet, based on the people, things, places and times that he/she has written in the circles. For example, if a student has written *Madrid,* his/her partner could write: *I think you lived in Madrid when you were ten., I think you went to Madrid last year.* or *I think you visited Madrid last month.* Students are not allowed to talk to their partners during this stage of the activity. ✏ You can demonstrate this stage of the activity by eliciting sentences about you for the ideas in the circles on the board.
- Students work in their pairs and take turns to say their sentences about their partner. Their partner says if the sentences are true or false. Students tick their true sentences. The student with more true sentences wins.
- Finally, ask each student to tell the class one or two true things they have found out about their partner.

9B ▶ What did you do on holiday? p156–p157

Language

Past Simple: questions and short answers; holiday activities

Activity type, when to use and time

'Find someone who' activity with role cards. Use any time after lesson 9B. 20–30 minutes.

Preparation

Photocopy one worksheet for each student and one set of role cards for every ten students in the class. Cut the role cards into separate cards. Shuffle the cards.

Procedure

- Pre-teach *the American President, a dolphin, an elephant, kilometres, a footballer, a football team* and *Africa.* Check students remember *a tuk-tuk* and *cycle* (verb). Also check students know where *Dubai, Cape Town, Cairo* and *New Zealand* are. Drill the new vocabulary with the class.
- Give each student a copy of the worksheet. Tell the class that they all went on holiday last year and that sentences 1–10 on the worksheet give information about the students' holidays. Focus students on sentences 1 and 2. ✏ Elicit the correct *yes/no* questions for each sentence and write them on the board (see answer key).
- Students work on their own or in pairs and write questions for sentences 3–10. ✏ While students are working, write these prompts on the board:
  - **A** *Where did you go on holiday last year?*
  - **B** *I went to … .*
  - **A** *Did you … ?*
  - **B** *Yes, I did. / No, I didn't.*
- Check questions 3–10 with the class (see answer key). Drill the questions with the class if necessary.
- Give each student a role card. If you have more than ten students in the class, distribute extra role cards. If you have fewer than ten students in the class, don't give out the extra role cards. Give students a few minutes to read their role cards and ask any questions. Students are not allowed to look at each other's role cards.
- Tell the class they must find out which student in the class did the things on the worksheet. ✏ Focus students on the prompts on the board and drill the question *Where did you go on holiday last year?* with the class. Point out that students must ask where each person went on holiday before they ask any of the *Did you … ?* questions on their worksheet.
- Students then move around the room and ask each other questions about where they went and what they did on their last holiday. When students find someone who did one of the things on the worksheet, they write his/her name in the second column. Encourage students to continue talking about their holidays for as long as possible, using the information on the cards and their own ideas. The aim of the activity is to find one person who did each of the things on the worksheet.
- When students have finished, they can compare answers and discuss what else they have found out about each person's holiday.
- Finally, you can ask each student to tell the class about one person's holiday.

1 Did you meet the American President? 2 Did you buy a tuk-tuk? 3 Did you stay in a seven-star hotel? 4 Did you go swimming with dolphins? 5 Did you cycle 13,000 kilometres? 6 Did you play football with some famous footballers? 7 Did you travel around on an elephant? 8 Did you take 15,000 photos? 9 Did you stay with Daniel Craig? 10 Did you walk 4,000 miles?

9D ▶ Money, money, money p158–p159

Language
Review of lessons 7A–9D

Activity type, when to use and time
Board game. Use any time after lesson 9D.
20–30 minutes.

Preparation
Photocopy one board, one set of Vocabulary cards and one set of Grammar cards for each group of four students. Cut the Vocabulary cards and Grammar cards into sets. Shuffle each set. Each group also needs a dice and counters (or students can make their own counters).

Procedure
- Put students into groups of four. Give each group a copy of the board, a set of Vocabulary cards and a set of Grammar cards, dice and counters. Students place the cards face-down in two separate piles in the middle of the board.
- Tell students that they can go round the board as many times as they like, and that they collect £1,000 every time they pass the START square. Students will need a pen and paper to keep a record of how much money they have during the game. Tell students that they all start the game with £2,000.
- Check students understand what to do if they land on the *Throw again!*, *Miss a turn!* or *Double your money!* squares.
- Students take turns to throw the dice and move around the board. When a student lands on a square that says Vocabulary card or Grammar card, he/she turns over the top card of the appropriate pile and reads out the question to the group. He/She must then answer the question himself/herself. If he/she answers the question correctly, he/she wins the amount of money on the square. He/She then puts the card at the bottom of the appropriate pile.
- Students always stay on the square they landed on, whether they win money or not.
- Students don't have to leave the game if they have a negative amount of money. They should keep playing to try and win more money.
- If a student thinks that another student's answer is wrong, they can ask you to adjudicate.
- The game can continue as long as you wish. Alternatively, students can continue playing until they have answered all the Grammar and Vocabulary cards. The student with the most money when the game finishes is the winner.
- If one or two groups finish early, ask them to shuffle the Grammar and Vocabulary cards, then place them in one pile in the middle of the board. Students then take turns to pick up a card and read out the question to the student on their right.

Vocabulary cards 1 visiting new places, shopping for clothes, watching sport on TV **2** nineteen eighty-seven, nineteen ninety-eight, two thousand and nine, twenty twelve (two thousand and twelve) **3** short, right, easy, interesting **4** What, Who, Where, When / What time **5 How much** was your car? **How many** people were there? **6 take** photos, **rent** a car, **stay** in a hotel **7** See VOCABULARY 8.3 ▶ SB p128. **8** ride a bike, play the guitar, speak German **9** unhappy, terrible / awful, empty, old **10 go to** the beach, **go** sightseeing, **go for** a walk **11** eight hundred and fifty thousand, seven million, fifteen thousand, four hundred and fifty **12** Students' own answers **13** April the first, May the second, June the third, July the fourth **14** chat to friends, book a holiday, download music **15** See VOCABULARY 9.1 ▶ SB p130. **16** It's **in** New Road. It's **on** the right. It's **near** the café.

Grammar cards 1 had, travelled, went, left **2** Yes, I can. (Yes, we can.) / No, I can't. (No, we can't.) Yes, he was. / No, he wasn't. **3** Where did you go on holiday last year? **4** Where **were** you? Where **did** you go? **5** We **weren't** late for class. I **didn't watch** TV last night. **6 They** know **us**. **She** loves **him**. **7** came, got, wrote, told **8** Yes, he did. / No, he didn't. Yes, she can. / No, she can't. **9** What did your children do yesterday afternoon? **10** What **did** he say? What **was** his name? **11** Students' own answers **12** I **was born** in 1987. Where **was** Jo born? **13** Yes, I did. / No, I didn't. Yes, they were. / No, they weren't. **14** bought, met, gave, took **15** I **wasn't** at home at 2 p.m. He **didn't go** to the beach. **16** I bought a computer four months ago.

10B ▶ Guess your partner's future p160

Language
be going to: *yes* / *no* questions and short answers; phrases with *have*, *watch*, *go*, *go to*

Activity type, when to use and time
Personalised information gap. Use any time after lesson 10B. 15–25 minutes.

Preparation
Photocopy one worksheet for each pair of students. Cut into separate worksheets.

Procedure
- Put students into pairs, A and B. If possible, put students with someone they don't know very well. Give each student a copy of the appropriate worksheet. Students are not allowed to look at their partner's worksheet.

- ✏️ Write sentence 1 from student A's worksheet on the board and elicit the correct verb (*have*). Highlight the collocation *have a party*.
- Students work on their own and choose the correct verb in each sentence on their worksheets. Tell students to look at the word or phrase in **bold** after the verbs when making their choice. Check answers with the class (see answer key). Note that the answers are the same for both the student A and student B worksheets.
- Students work on their own and make sentences they think are true about their partner by filling in the gaps with *'s going to* or *isn't going to*. Students are not allowed to speak to their partner at this stage of the activity.
- ✏️ Focus students on the sentence on the board and elicit the *yes/no* question with *you*: *Are you going to have a party on your next birthday?*. Remind students of the short answers *Yes, I am.* and *No, I'm not.*
- Students work on their own and prepare *yes/no* questions with *Are you … ?* for each sentence on their worksheet.
- Students work with their partner and take turns to ask and answer questions. Students put a tick in the second column of their worksheet if their sentence is correct and a cross if their sentence is incorrect. The student with more ticks is the winner.
- Finally, students can work in new pairs and tell their new partner about the person they have just talked to.

1 have 2 go to 3 watch 4 go
5 move 6 stay 7 get 8 go to

10C▷ After the course p161

Language
saying goodbye and good luck; *be going to*; question words

Activity type, when to use and time
Mingle. Use instead of exercise **8** in lesson 10C, or any time after lesson 10C. 15–20 minutes.

Preparation
Photocopy one worksheet for every twelve students in the class. Cut into separate role cards.

Procedure
- Pre-teach *a club* (a place where you go to listen to music and dance), *invite somebody to something, sail, a journalist* /ˈdʒɜːnəlɪst/, *dive* (go into the sea with scuba equipment to look at fish) and *Nepal* /nəˈpɔːl/. Drill the new vocabulary with the class.
- Give each student a role card. If you have more than twelve students, give out duplicate role cards. (This will not affect the outcome of the activity.) Students are not allowed to look at each other's cards.
- Tell students that the role cards say what they are going to do at the end of their English course. Ask students to read the information and write their own answers for the question words in **bold** on their cards in the gaps.

Be prepared to help any students with ideas during this stage of the activity. Give students time to read their role cards and ask them to remember the information.
- ✏️ Write these prompts on the board: *What are you going to do after the course?*, *I'm going to … , Have a good … , See you … , Good luck with your … .* Drill the question with the class and elicit some phrases for saying goodbye and good luck (*Have a good holiday.*, *See you in December.*, *Good luck with your new job.*, etc.).
- Students move around the room asking each other about their plans after the course. Encourage students to continue each conversation by asking more questions and telling each other the information on their cards. Also encourage students to finish each conversation with a phrase beginning with *Have a good … , See you … *or *Good luck with your … .* If students are not able to leave their seats, they should ask as many students as they can sitting near them.
- Before they begin, tell the class that they must remember other students' plans. Students are not allowed to write anything down at any time during the activity.
- When students have finished, put them into pairs or small groups. Students work in their pairs/groups and see how much they can remember about the plans of the other students in the class.
- Finally, ask each student to tell the class about another student's plans for after the course.

1B ▶ Where's he from? countries; *What's his / her name?*; *Where's he / she from?*

Worksheet A

Shane, Australia
Alberto, Mexico
Layla, Egypt
Tanya, Russia
Isabel, Spain
Helga, Germany
Silvia, Brazil
Ping, China
Scott, the USA
Enzo, Italy
Diana, the UK
Osman, Turkey

Worksheet B

Instructions p114 © Cambridge University Press 2013 **face2face** Second edition Starter Photocopiable

CLASS ACTIVITIES: Photocopiable

Student A

1 *Eminem*	**2** *Natalie Portman*
real name	real name
	Natalie Hershlag
3 *Fatboy Slim*	**4** *Lady Gaga*
real name	real name
	Stefani Germanotta
5 *Katy Perry*	**6** *Bono*
real name	real name
	Paul Hewson
7 *Pink*	**8** *Jay-Z*
real name	real name
	Shawn Carter

Student B

1 *Eminem*	**2** *Natalie Portman*
real name	real name
Marshall Mathers	
3 *Fatboy Slim*	**4** *Lady Gaga*
real name	real name
Norman Cook	
5 *Katy Perry*	**6** *Bono*
real name	real name
Katheryn Hudson	
7 *Pink*	**8** *Jay-Z*
real name	real name
Alicia Moore	

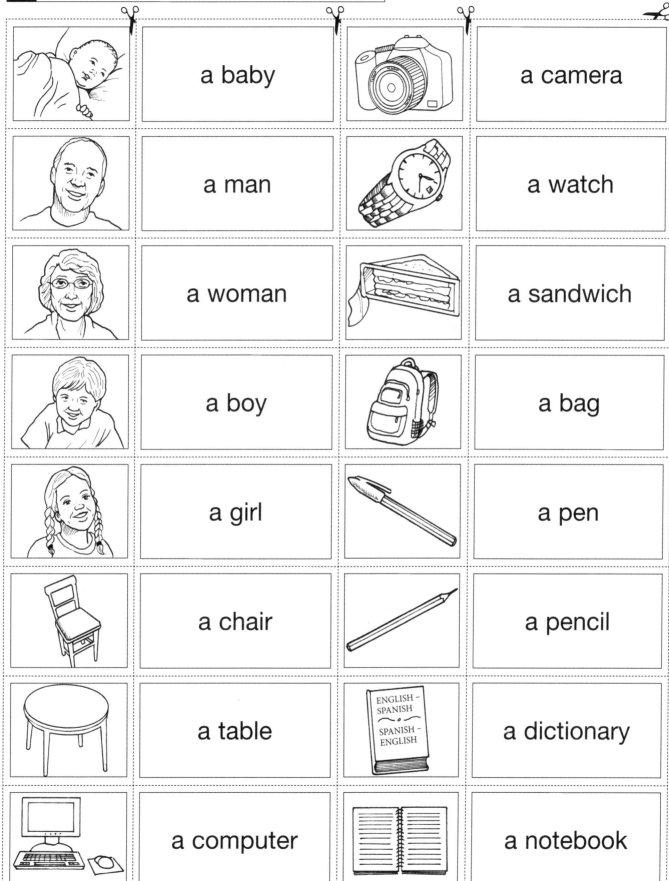

	a baby		a camera
	a man		a watch
	a woman		a sandwich
	a boy		a bag
	a girl		a pen
	a chair		a pencil
	a table		a dictionary
	a computer		a notebook

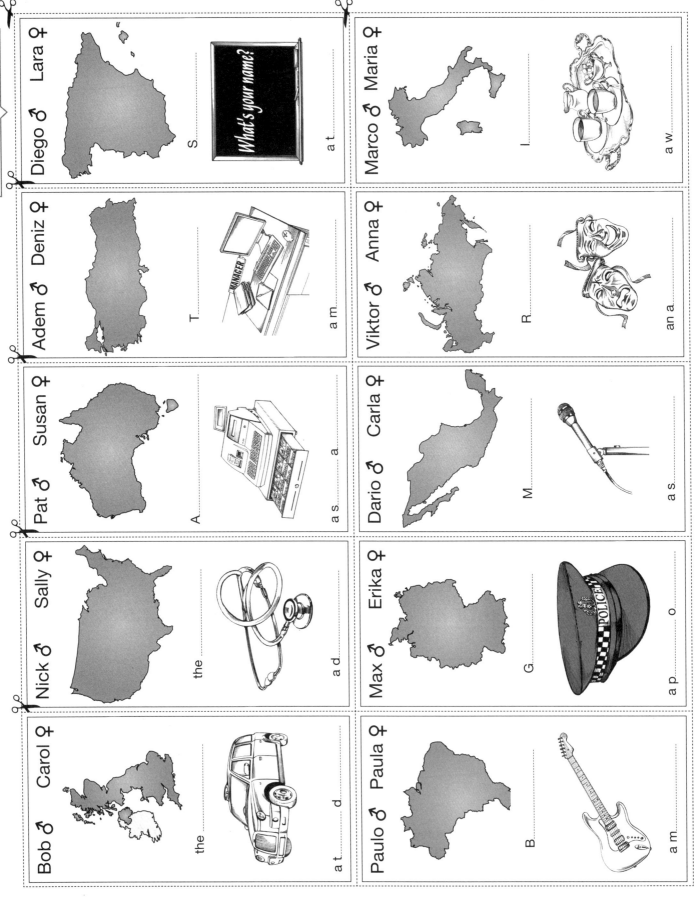

Student A

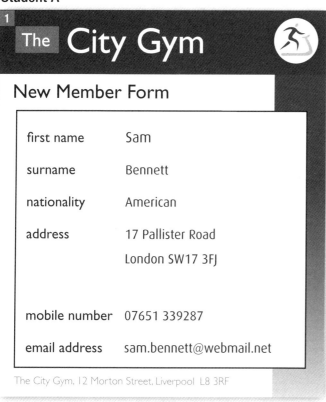

The City Gym

New Member Form

first name	Sam
surname	Bennett
nationality	American
address	17 Pallister Road
	London SW17 3FJ
mobile number	07651 339287
email address	sam.bennett@webmail.net

The City Gym, 12 Morton Street, Liverpool L8 3RF

The City Gym

New Member Form

first name	_____
surname	_____
nationality	_____
address	_____
	_____
mobile number	_____
email address	_____

The City Gym, 12 Morton Street, Liverpool L8 3RF

Student B

The City Gym

New Member Form

first name	Alex
surname	Dickinson
nationality	Australian
address	19 Berringham Road
	London NE5 6GY
mobile number	07128 477201
email address	a.dickinson@netmail.co.uk

The City Gym, 12 Morton Street, Liverpool L8 3RF

The City Gym

New Member Form

first name	_____
surname	_____
nationality	_____
address	_____
	_____
mobile number	_____
email address	_____

The City Gym, 12 Morton Street, Liverpool L8 3RF

CLASS ACTIVITIES: Photocopiable

Student A	
HEAR	SAY
43 ⇨	86
96 ⇨	8
START ⇨	41
35 ⇨	16
29 ⇨	18
0 ⇨	11
17 ⇨	30
71 ⇨	7
50 ⇨	82
12 ⇨	90

Student B	
HEAR	SAY
90 ⇨	19
16 ⇨	100
86 ⇨	12
77 ⇨	60
41 ⇨	15
64 ⇨	17
18 ⇨	80
68 ⇨	0
8 ⇨	23
30 ⇨	70

Student C	
HEAR	SAY
11 ⇨	29
15 ⇨	50
7 ⇨	64
100 ⇨	68
82 ⇨	77
70 ⇨	96
60 ⇨	35
23 ⇨	FINISH
80 ⇨	43
19 ⇨	71

Instructions p116

Student A

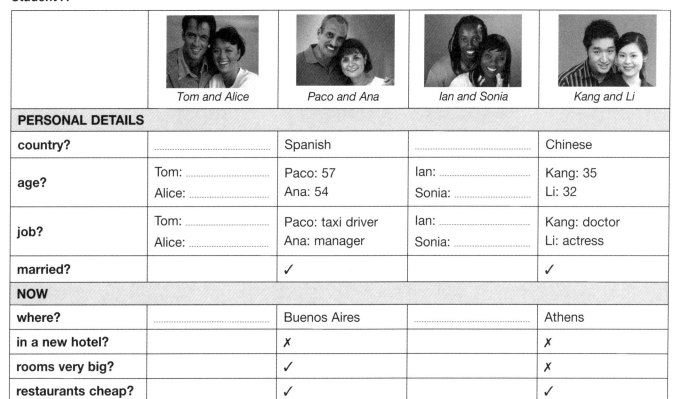

PERSONAL DETAILS	Tom and Alice	Paco and Ana	Ian and Sonia	Kang and Li
country?	....	Spanish	....	Chinese
age?	Tom: .... Alice:	Paco: 57 Ana: 54	Ian: .... Sonia:	Kang: 35 Li: 32
job?	Tom: .... Alice:	Paco: taxi driver Ana: manager	Ian: .... Sonia:	Kang: doctor Li: actress
married?		✓		✓
NOW				
where?	....	Buenos Aires	....	Athens
in a new hotel?		✗		✗
rooms very big?		✓		✗
restaurants cheap?		✓		✓

✂

Student B

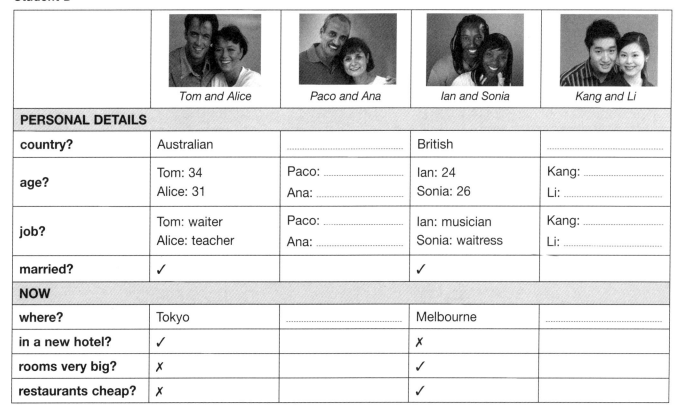

PERSONAL DETAILS	Tom and Alice	Paco and Ana	Ian and Sonia	Kang and Li
country?	Australian	....	British	....
age?	Tom: 34 Alice: 31	Paco: .... Ana:	Ian: 24 Sonia: 26	Kang: .... Li: ....
job?	Tom: waiter Alice: teacher	Paco: .... Ana:	Ian: musician Sonia: waitress	Kang: .... Li: ....
married?	✓		✓	
NOW				
where?	Tokyo	....	Melbourne	....
in a new hotel?	✓		✗	
rooms very big?	✗		✓	
restaurants cheap?	✗		✓	

Student A

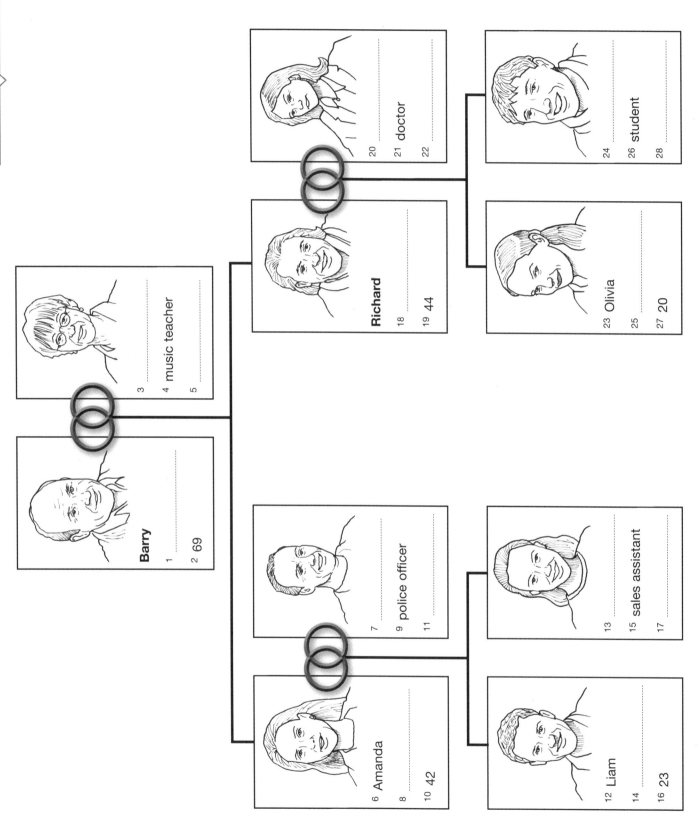

Student B

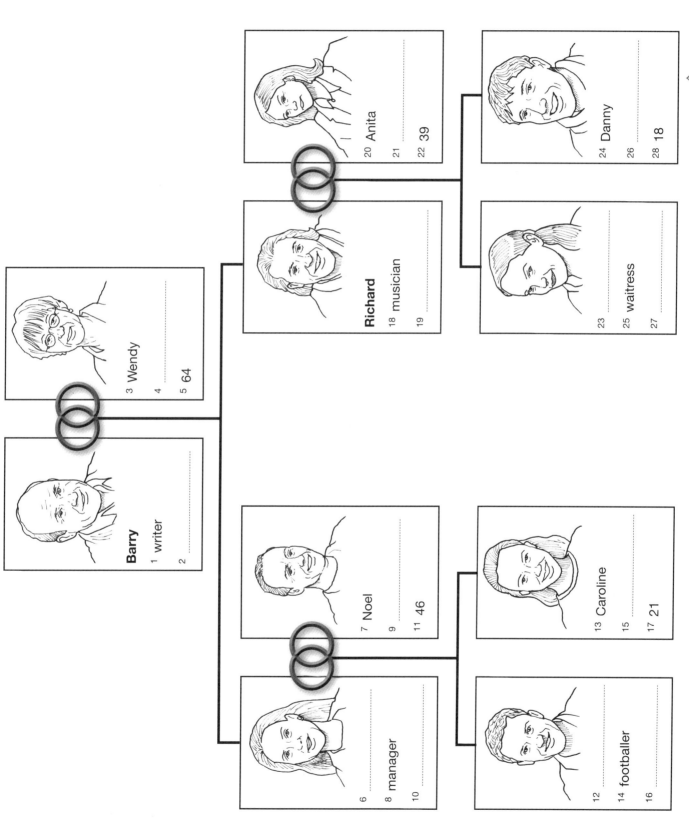

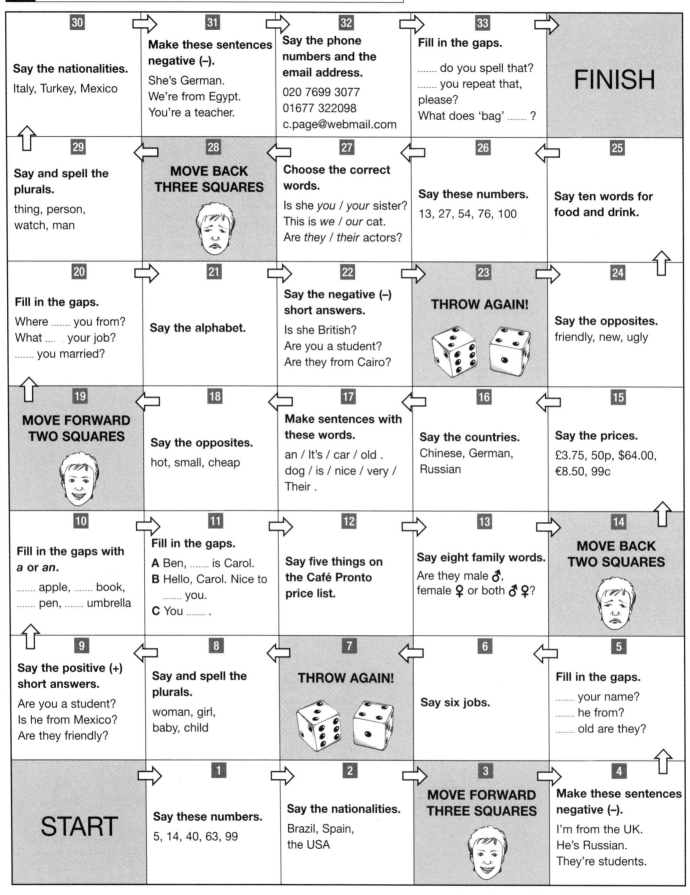

30

Say the nationalities.

Italy, Turkey, Mexico

31

Make these sentences negative (–).

She's German.
We're from Egypt.
You're a teacher.

32

Say the phone numbers and the email address.

020 7699 3077
01677 322098
c.page@webmail.com

33

Fill in the gaps.

.... do you spell that?
.... you repeat that, please?
What does 'bag' .... ?

FINISH

29

Say and spell the plurals.

thing, person, watch, man

28

MOVE BACK THREE SQUARES

27

Choose the correct words.

Is she *you / your* sister?
This is *we / our* cat.
Are *they / their* actors?

26

Say these numbers.

13, 27, 54, 76, 100

25

Say ten words for food and drink.

20

Fill in the gaps.

Where .... you from?
What ..... your job?
.... you married?

21

Say the alphabet.

22

Say the negative (–) short answers.

Is she British?
Are you a student?
Are they from Cairo?

23

THROW AGAIN!

24

Say the opposites.

friendly, new, ugly

19

MOVE FORWARD TWO SQUARES

18

Say the opposites.

hot, small, cheap

17

Make sentences with these words.

an / It's / car / old .
dog / is / nice / very / Their .

16

Say the countries.

Chinese, German, Russian

15

Say the prices.

£3.75, 50p, $64.00,
€8.50, 99c

10

Fill in the gaps with *a* or *an*.

.... apple, ... book,
.... pen, ... umbrella

11

Fill in the gaps.

A Ben, ... is Carol.
B Hello, Carol. Nice to
.... you.
C You ....

12

Say five things on the Café Pronto price list.

13

Say eight family words.

Are they male ♂,
female ♀ or both ♂♀?

14

MOVE BACK TWO SQUARES

9

Say the positive (+) short answers.

Are you a student?
Is he from Mexico?
Are they friendly?

8

Say and spell the plurals.

woman, girl, baby, child

7

THROW AGAIN!

6

Say six jobs.

5

Fill in the gaps.

.... your name?
.... he from?
.... old are they?

START

1

Say these numbers.

5, 14, 40, 63, 99

2

Say the nationalities.

Brazil, Spain, the USA

3

MOVE FORWARD THREE SQUARES

4

Make these sentences negative (–).

I'm from the UK.
He's Russian.
They're students.

 Instructions p117

4B **Find two people** free time activities; Present Simple (*I*, *you*, *we*, *they*): yes / no questions and short answers

Do you …	Name	Name
1 *live* / *play* / *watch* TV a lot?		
2 *go* / *go to* / *work* rock concerts?		
3 *play* / *go* / *live* tennis?		
4 *like* / *go* / *have* out with friends after class?		
5 *watch* / *eat* / *like* out a lot?		
6 *go* / *go to* / *have* shopping with friends?		
7 *work* / *live* / *play* video games?		
8 *go* / *go to* / *watch* the cinema a lot?		
9 *like* / *work* / *have* in an office?		
10 *watch* / *like* / *live* in a flat?		
11 *have* / *go* / *play* a car?		
12 *go* / *work* / *like* football?		

Student A

Student B

Student C

Student D

Instructions p118

twenty past twelve	**2.30**		half past two	**6.50**
ten to seven	**7.40**		twenty to eight	**5.20**
twenty past five	**1.45**		one forty-five	**4.00**
four o'clock	**3.40**		twenty to four	**9.55**
five to ten	**2.25**		twenty-five past two	**1.05**
five past one	**4.15**		four fifteen	**10.00**
ten o'clock	**12.50**		ten to one	**4.45**
quarter to five	**9.35**		twenty-five to ten	**6.30**
six thirty	**3.15**		quarter past three	**2.35**
twenty-five to three	**9.10**		ten past nine	**6.25**
twenty-five past six	**0.00**		midnight	**10.55**
five to eleven	**8.10**		ten past eight	**12.20**

5A My partner's life Present Simple (he, she, it): positive and negative; daily routines; free time activities

Student A

My partner's name		✓ or ✗
1 He / She .... before 7.00 in the week. (**get up**)		
2 He / She .... breakfast after 10.30 at the weekend. (**have**)		
3 He / She .... home before 9.00 in the week. (**leave**)		
4 He / She .... dinner after 9.00 at the weekend. (**have**)		
5 He / She .... to bed before 11.30 in the week. (**go**)		
6 He / She .... video games. (**play**)		
7 He / She .... out in the week. (**eat**)		
8 He / She .... to the cinema a lot. (**go**)		

Student B

My partner's name		✓ or ✗
a He / She .... after 10.30 at the weekend. (**get up**)		
b He / She .... breakfast before 8.00 in the week. (**have**)		
c He / She .... home after 6.30 in the week. (**get**)		
d He / She .... dinner with his / her family in the week. (**have**)		
e He / She .... to bed after 11.00 at the weekend. (**go**)		
f He / She .... tennis. (**play**)		
g He / She .... TV in the morning. (**watch**)		
h He / She .... to concerts. (**go**)		

Student A

CLASS ACTIVITIES: Photocopiable

A week in the life of …
Oliver Richardson, writer

Oliver Richardson writes ^a................................. .... He lives in London with his wife, Ingrid, and their seven-year-old son, Charlie.

Oliver works at home and ¹ *on /* (*in*) */ at* the week he gets up at ^b............................. . He has breakfast at 7.30 with his family. After breakfast Charlie goes to school and then Ingrid goes to work at ^c............................. . She works in a bookshop.

Oliver starts work at ^d........................... . "I like writing ² *on / in / at* the morning because it's very quiet at home," he says. He has lunch at about 1.30 in ^e... and he finishes work ³ *on / in / at* 6.30. ⁴ *On / In / At* the evening Oliver watches TV and he goes to bed ⁵ *on / in / at* midnight.

Oliver doesn't work ⁶ *on / in / at* the weekend. "Saturday and Sunday are family days," he says. ⁷ *On / In / At* Saturday morning he ^f...................................... with Ingrid, and he goes to the cinema with his son ⁸ *on / in / at* the afternoon. "I have a very good life," says Oliver.

---

a What d <u>o e s</u> Oliver w <u>r i t e</u> ?

b What time d _ _ _ he g _ _ up in the w _ _ _ ?

c When d _ _ _ Ingrid g _ to w _ _ _ ?

d What time d _ _ _ Oliver s _ _ _ _ w _ _ _ ?

e Where d _ _ _ he h _ _ _ l _ _ _ _ _ ?

f What d _ _ _ he d _ on Saturday m _ _ _ _ _ _ _ ?

Student B

A week in the life of ...
Oliver Richardson, writer

Oliver Richardson writes children's books. He lives in ª _____ with his wife, Ingrid, and their seven-year-old son, Charlie.

Oliver works at home and ¹ *on / in / at* the week he gets up at 7.00. He has breakfast at ᵇ _____ with his family. After breakfast Charlie goes to school and then Ingrid goes to work at 8.30. She works in ᶜ _____ .

Oliver starts work at 8.45. "I like writing ² *on / in / at* the morning because it's very quiet at home," he says. He has lunch at about ᵈ _____ in a café and he finishes work ³ *on / in / at* 6.30. ⁴ *On / In / At* the evening Oliver ᵉ _____ and he goes to bed ⁵ *on / in / at* midnight.

Oliver doesn't work ⁶ *on / in / at* the weekend. "Saturday and Sunday are family days," he says. ⁷ *On / In / At* Saturday morning he goes shopping with Ingrid, and he ᶠ _____ with his son ⁸ *on / in / at* the afternoon. "I have a very good life," says Oliver.

---

a Where d _o e s_ Oliver l _i v e_ ?

b When d _ _ _ he h _ _ _ b _ _ _ _ _ _ _ _ _ ?

c Where d _ _ _ Ingrid w _ _ _ ?

d What time d _ _ _ Oliver h _ _ _ l _ _ _ _ ?

e What d _ _ _ he d _ in the e _ _ _ _ _ g ?

f What d _ _ _ he d _ on Saturday a _ _ _ _ _ _ _ _ _ ?

---

 face2face Second edition Starter Photocopiable Instructions p119

A

Write **eight** of these people, things, places and times in the boxes. **Don't** write them in this order.

- a person you email **every week**
- something you **don't usually** eat or drink
- a free time activity you **never** do at the weekend
- a place you go to **every month**
- the time you **usually** get up in the week
- something you eat or drink **every day**
- a person you **sometimes** see at the weekend
- a TV programme you **always** watch
- a place you go to **every week**
- the time you **usually** get up at the weekend
- a TV programme you **never** watch
- a free time activity you **sometimes** do at the weekend

Look at your partner's answers in the boxes. Write eight sentences about your partner. Use ideas from box A.

1 You ....

2 You ....

3 You ....

4 You ....

5 You ....

6 You ....

7 You ....

8 You ....

Student A

Student B

Student A

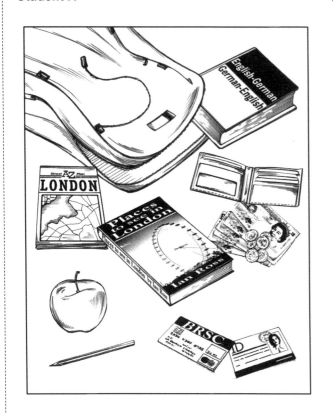

Student B

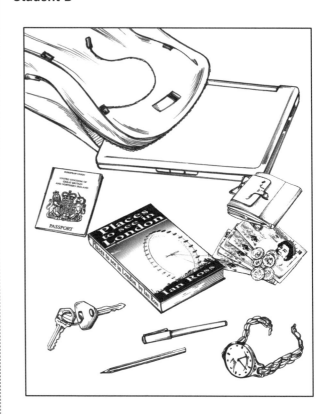

Student C

Student D

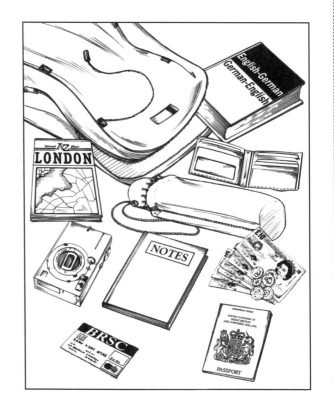

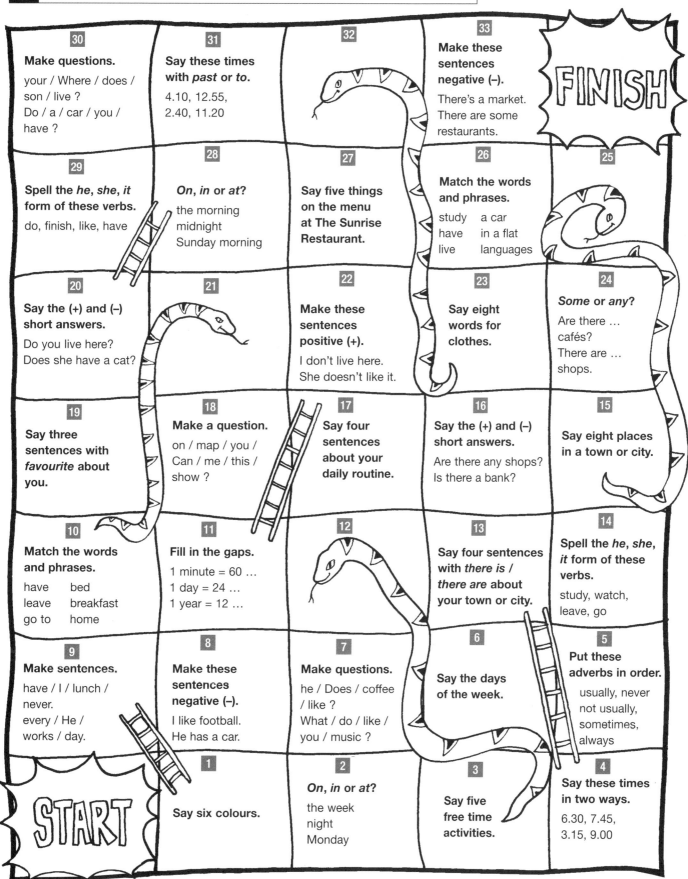

30 Make questions.

your / Where / does / son / live ?
Do / a / car / you / have ?

31 Say these times with *past* or *to*.

4.10, 12.55, 2.40, 11.20

32

33 Make these sentences negative (–).

There's a market. There are some restaurants.

FINISH

29 Spell the *he, she, it* form of these verbs.

do, finish, like, have

28 *On, in* or *at*?

the morning
midnight
Sunday morning

27 Say five things on the menu at The Sunrise Restaurant.

26 Match the words and phrases.

study   a car
have   in a flat
live   languages

25

20 Say the (+) and (–) short answers.

Do you live here?
Does she have a cat?

21

22 Make these sentences positive (+).

I don't live here.
She doesn't like it.

23 Say eight words for clothes.

24 *Some* or *any*?

Are there … cafés?
There are … shops.

19 Say three sentences with *favourite* about you.

18 Make a question.

on / map / you /
Can / me / this /
show ?

17 Say four sentences about your daily routine.

16 Say the (+) and (–) short answers.

Are there any shops?
Is there a bank?

15 Say eight places in a town or city.

10 Match the words and phrases.

have   bed
leave   breakfast
go to   home

11 Fill in the gaps.

1 minute = 60 …
1 day = 24 …
1 year = 12 …

12

13 Say four sentences with *there is / there are* about your town or city.

14 Spell the *he, she, it* form of these verbs.

study, watch, leave, go

9 Make sentences.

have / I / lunch / never.
every / He / works / day.

8 Make these sentences negative (–).

I like football.
He has a car.

7 Make questions.

he / Does / coffee / like ?
What / do / like / you / music ?

6 Say the days of the week.

5 Put these adverbs in order.

usually, never
not usually,
sometimes,
always

START

1 Say six colours.

2 *On, in* or *at*?

the week
night
Monday

3 Say five free time activities.

4 Say these times in two ways.

6.30, 7.45, 3.15, 9.00

© Cambridge University Press 2013

Yes, they love it.	**Do you like flying?**	**No, I hate it.**	**Does your sister like Lady Gaga?**
Yes, she likes her a lot.	**Does your husband like soap operas?**	**No, he hates them.**	**Do your parents like visiting new places?**
Yes, they do.	**Do you like Johnny Depp?**	**Yes, I love him.**	**Does your mother like shopping for clothes?**
No, she doesn't.	**Do your children like vegetables?**	**No, they hate them.**	**Do you like animals?**
Yes, I love them.	**Does your daughter like Beyoncé?**	**Yes, she loves her.**	**Do you like Leonardo DiCaprio?**
Yes, I like him a lot.	**Do your brothers like playing tennis?**	**No, they hate it.**	**Do you like going to the cinema?**
Yes, I do.	**Does your brother like dancing?**	**Yes, he loves it.**	**Do you like Cameron Diaz?**
Yes, I like her a lot.	**Do your grandchildren like Italian food?**	**No, they don't.**	**Do you like horror films?**
No, I hate them.	**Do you like playing video games?**	**No, I don't.**	**Do your daughters like Daniel Craig?**
Yes, they love him.	**Does your wife like Chinese food?**	**Yes, she does.**	**Do your grandparents like classical music?**

7B ▶ What can the class do? *can for ability; abilities*

A

.... students can **play a musical instrument**.

B

.... students can **ride a motorbike**.

C

.... students can **say 'hello' in four languages**.

Hello!

D

.... students can **cook a lasagne**.

E

.... students can **swim a hundred metres**.

F

.... students can **play backgammon**.

G

.... students can **drive**.

H

.... students can **play golf**.

I

.... students can **ride a horse**.

J

.... students can **say 'goodbye' in four languages**.

Goodbye!

K

.... students can **run for twenty minutes**.

L

.... students can **play chess**.

Student A

> You are at ✳ on the map. Ask your partner for directions to these places.
>
> **1** the cinema **2** a post office **3** the market **4** a restaurant **5** a chemist's

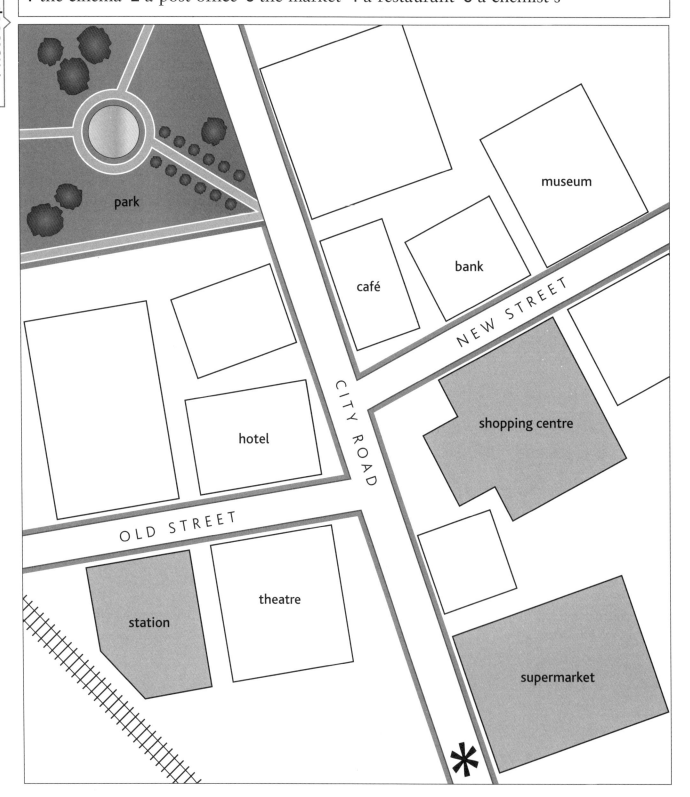

⟨ Instructions p122

It's on the left asking for and giving directions; prepositions of place

Student B

> You are at ✳ on the map. Ask your partner for directions to these places.
> **1** a bank **2** the theatre **3** the museum **4** a hotel **5** a café

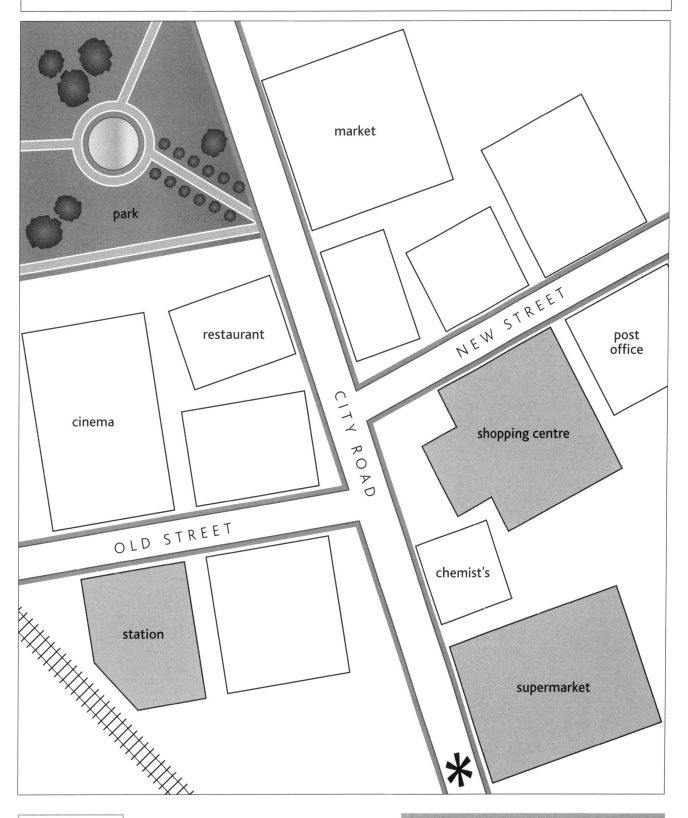

short	long	AWFUL	FANTASTIC
HAPPY	UNHAPPY	bad	good
boring	Interesting	hot	cold
FULL	EMPTY	small	BIG
easy	difficult	NEW	old
WRONG	RIGHT	cheap	expensive
old	young	ugly	beautiful
amazing	TERRIBLE	friendly	unfriendly

8B **Were you or weren't you?** past time phrases; Past Simple of *be*; *was born / were born*

Were you …	Name
1 … at home **yesterday** / **last** / **ago** evening?	
2 … on holiday **yesterday** / **last** / **ago** month?	
3 … born **on** / **in** / **at** December?	
4 … in this town or city five years **yesterday** / **last** / **ago** ?	
5 … with some friends **yesterday** / **last** / **ago** Sunday?	
6 … in a restaurant **yesterday** / **last** / **ago** evening?	
7 … in this class two months **yesterday** / **last** / **ago** ?	
8 … born **on** / **in** / **at** the 1990s?	
9 … at work **yesterday** / **last** / **ago** Friday?	
10 … on a bus or a train two hours **yesterday** / **last** / **ago** ?	
11 … in a café at 10.30 **yesterday** / **last** / **ago** morning?	
12 … in a different town or city two weeks **yesterday** / **last** / **ago** ?	

Student A

HEAR	SAY
May 17th ⇨	2009
December 25th ⇨	6,000,000
2010 ⇨	February 14th
August 19th ⇨	October 8th
750,000 ⇨	1965
45,400 ⇨	60,000
February 4th ⇨	2018
START ⇨	365
July 2nd ⇨	January 30th
60,000,000 ⇨	November 6th

Student B

HEAR	SAY
1965 ⇨	July 2nd
November 6th ⇨	1956
June 20th ⇨	FINISH
January 30th ⇨	54,500
16,000 ⇨	February 4th
April 1st ⇨	1980
60,000 ⇨	May 17th
March 3rd ⇨	45,400
6,000,000 ⇨	January 13th
September 7th ⇨	570,000

Student C

HEAR	SAY
February 14th ⇨	16,000
2018 ⇨	September 7th
1956 ⇨	March 3rd
October 8th ⇨	60,000,000
365 ⇨	April 1st
January 13th ⇨	750,000
1980 ⇨	December 25th
54,500 ⇨	2010
2009 ⇨	June 20th
570,000 ⇨	August 19th

 ⟨ Instructions p123 ⟩

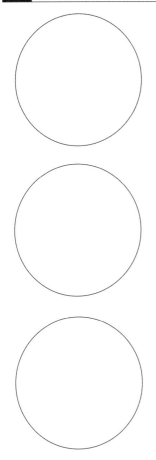

Write **eight** of these people, things, places and times in the circles. **Don't** write them in this order.

- a person you talked to on the phone last night
- something you bought last month
- the town or city you lived in when you were ten
- the time you left home today
- a place you went to last year
- a person you wrote an email to yesterday
- the time you had dinner last night
- something you had when you were a child
- the time you got up last Sunday
- a person you met for the first time this year
- a place you visited last month
- something a friend gave you for your last birthday

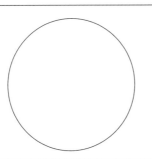 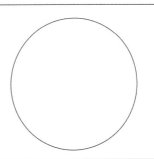

Look at your partner's answers in the circles. Write eight sentences about your partner. Use ideas from the box.

1 I think you ....

2 I think you ....

3 I think you ....

4 I think you ....

5 I think you ....

6 I think you ....

7 I think you ....

8 I think you ....

On holiday last year	Name
1 This person met the American President. **Question:** *Did you* _____ ?	
2 This person bought a tuk-tuk. **Question:** *Did you* _____ ?	
3 This person stayed in a seven-star hotel. **Question:** _____ ?	
4 This person went swimming with dolphins. **Question:** _____ ?	
5 This person cycled 13,000 kilometres. **Question:** _____ ?	
6 This person played football with some famous footballers. **Question:** _____ ?	
7 This person travelled around on an elephant. **Question:** _____ ?	
8 This person took 15,000 photos. **Question:** _____ ?	
9 This person stayed with Daniel Craig. **Question:** _____ ?	
10 This person walked 4,000 miles. **Question:** _____ ?	

 Instructions p124

Role cards

STUDENT A

You went on holiday to the USA last year. You stayed with some friends in Washington. On the last day of your holiday you met the American President at a party. You talked to him for ten minutes and he was very friendly.

STUDENT B

You went on holiday to Thailand last year. On the second day of your holiday you bought a yellow tuk-tuk. You travelled around the country in your tuk-tuk for six months and you had a fantastic time!

STUDENT C

You went on holiday to Dubai last year. You stayed in a seven-star hotel called the Burj Al Arab. It was very expensive and the rooms were very big. There were eight restaurants and cafés in the hotel, and the food was amazing!

STUDENT D

You went on holiday to New Zealand last year. You travelled around the country by bus. The scenery was beautiful and you went for a lot of walks. On the last day you went swimming with dolphins. They were very friendly!

STUDENT E

You went on holiday to Africa last year. You cycled from South Africa to Egypt. You travelled 13,000 kilometres and visited 10 countries. You arrived in Cairo 165 days after you left Cape Town and you raised £10,000 for charity.

STUDENT F

You went on holiday to Brazil last year. You stayed in a hotel near the beach in Rio de Janeiro. You went sightseeing every day and you also went swimming a lot. On the last day of your holiday you played football on the beach with the Brazilian football team!

STUDENT G

You went on holiday to India last year. First you went to a friend's wedding in Mumbai. Then you travelled around the country on an elephant called Raja. You went to some fantastic festivals – at one festival there were 2,000 elephants!

STUDENT H

You went on holiday to Australia last year. You stayed with your brother in Sydney, and then you rented a motorbike and travelled around the country. You stayed in Australia for eight months and you took 15,000 photos!

STUDENT I

You went on holiday to England last year. You stayed in London with the actor, Daniel Craig. You and Daniel are friends because your brother was in a James Bond film with him. You also went sightseeing in London and you had a great time.

STUDENT J

You went on holiday to China last year. You were there for nine months. You walked 4,000 miles along the Great Wall of China. It was an amazing journey and you met a lot of friendly people. You also raised £20,000 for charity.

CLASS ACTIVITIES: Photocopiable

Every person in the game gives you £500!

Grammar card £250

Vocabulary card £750

Give the person on your left £1,000!

Grammar card £500

Double your money!

Vocabulary card £250

Grammar card £600

Miss a turn!

VOCABULARY CARDS

Vocabulary card £400

Grammar card £400

Give the person on your right £1,000!

Vocabulary card £100

Grammar card £200

The person on your right gives you £1,500!

GRAMMAR CARDS

Vocabulary card £750

Grammar card £750

The person on your left gives you £1,500!

Vocabulary card £750

Grammar card £500

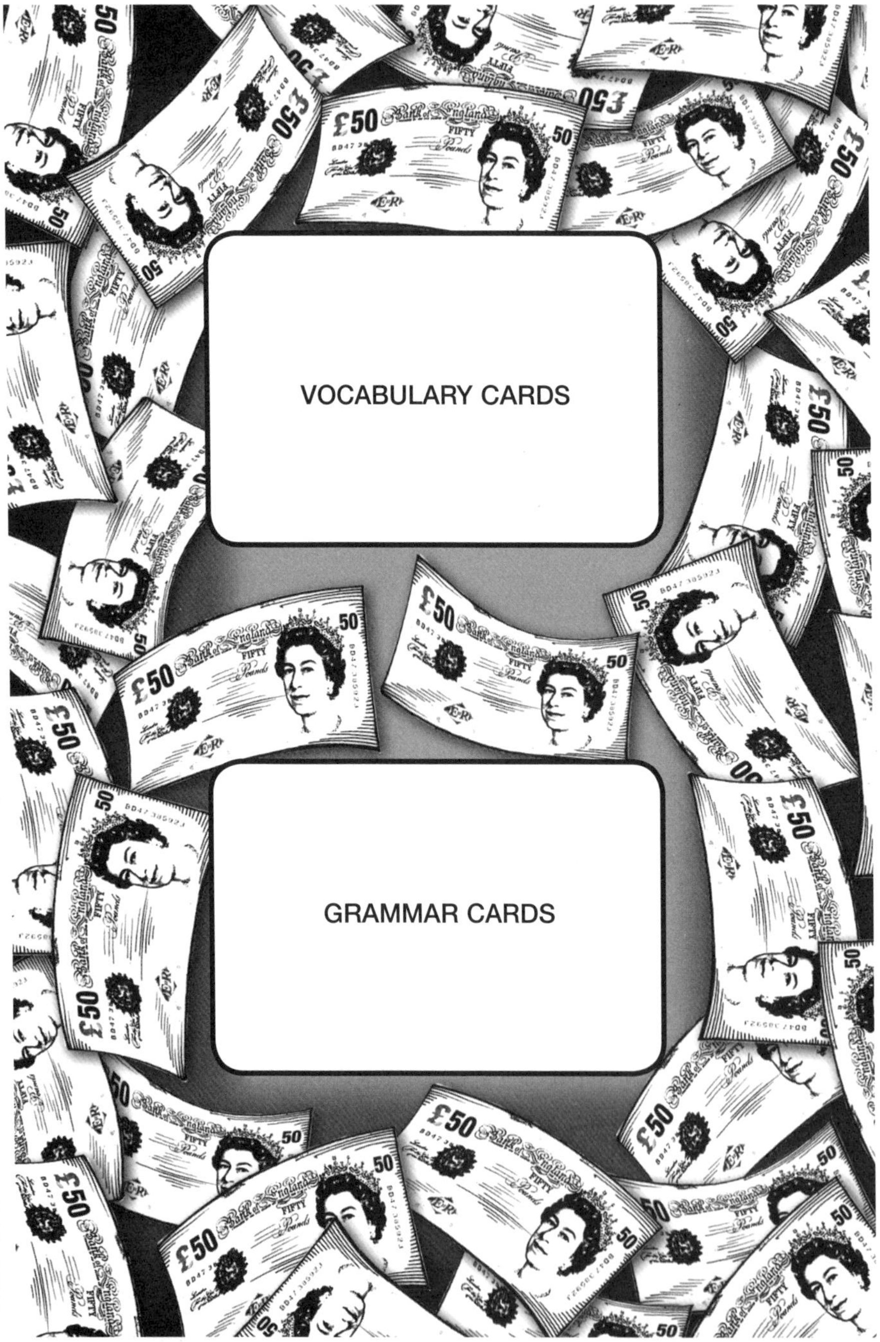

START (you get £1,000 every time you pass this square)

Vocabulary card £600

Grammar card £400

Throw again!

Vocabulary card £250

Give £500 to every person in the game!

Vocabulary cards

V1 Match these verbs and phrases.
visiting — sport on TV
shopping — new places
watching — for clothes

V2 Say these years.
1987, 1998, 2009, 2012

V3 Say the opposites.
long, wrong, difficult, boring

V4 Say the question words.
a thing, a person, a place, a time

V5 *How many* or *How much*?
___ was your car?
___ people were there?

V6 Choose the correct verbs.
take / go photos
travel / rent a car
stay / have in a hotel

V7 Say the months in order.

V8 Match these verbs and nouns.
ride — the guitar
play — German
speak — a bike

V9 Say the opposites.
happy, fantastic, full, young

V10 *Go, go to* or *go for*?
___ the beach
___ sightseeing
___ a walk

V11 Say these big numbers.
850,000
7,000,000
15,450

V12 Say four sentences with *love, like, don't like* or *hate* about you.

V13 Say these dates.
April 1st, May 2nd, June 3rd, July 4th

V14 Match these verbs and nouns.
chat to — music
book — a holiday
download — friends

V15 Say six words for transport (*a car*, etc.).

V16 Choose the correct prepositions.
It's *in / at* New Road.
It's *in / on* the right.
It's *on / near* the café.

Grammar cards

G1 Say the Past Simple of these verbs.
have, travel, go, leave

G2 Say the (+) and (–) short answers.
Can you swim?
Was he at home?

G3 Make a question with these words.
last year / on / did / go / you / holiday / Where ?

G4 Fill in the gaps with *did* or *were*.
Where ___ you?
Where ___ you go?

G5 Make these sentences negative (–).
We were late for class.
I watched TV last night.

G6 Choose the correct words.
They / Them know *we / us* .
She / Her loves *he / him* .

G7 Say the Past Simple of these verbs.
come, get, write, tell

G8 Say the (+) and (–) short answers.
Did he phone you?
Can she cook?

G9 Make a question with these words.
children / afternoon / did / yesterday / What / do / your ?

G10 Fill in the gaps with *was* or *did*.
What ___ he say?
What ___ his name?

G11 Say five sentences with *can* or *can't* about you.

G12 Correct these sentences.
I borned in 1987.
Where did Jo born?

G13 Say the (+) and (–) short answers.
Did you see him?
Were they tired?

G14 Say the Past Simple of these verbs.
buy, meet, give, take

G15 Make these sentences negative (–).
I was at home at 2 p.m.
He went to the beach.

G16 Make a sentence with these words.
ago / bought / four / I / a / months / computer .

CLASS ACTIVITIES: Photocopiable

Student A

	✓ or X
1 My partner .... *go / have / watch* **a party** on his or her next birthday.	
2 My partner .... *go to / go / play* **the gym** next weekend.	
3 My partner .... *go / look / watch* **the news** this evening.	
4 My partner .... *go to / go / get* **shopping** for clothes this month.	
5 My partner .... *move / stay / have* **house** next year.	
6 My partner .... *visit / go / stay* **in a hotel** next month.	
7 My partner .... *get / do / have* **home** before 7 p.m. tomorrow.	
8 My partner .... *stay / go to / get* **bed** before midnight this evening.	

Student B

	✓ or X
a My partner .... *watch / have / go* **dinner** with friends next Friday.	
b My partner .... *go to / go / play* **a party** next weekend.	
c My partner .... *go / look / watch* **a DVD** this evening.	
d My partner .... *go to / go / get* **on holiday** next month.	
e My partner .... *move / stay / have* **to another city or country** next year.	
f My partner .... *visit / go / stay* **at home** next Saturday evening.	
g My partner .... *get / do / have* **married** this year.	
h My partner .... *stay / go to / get* **a wedding** next month.	

© Cambridge University Press 2013 Instructions p125

STUDENT A

It's your birthday on Sunday. You're going to have a party at a famous club in your town or city. _____ (**how many?**) people are going to be there. And _____ (**who?**) is / are going to play at midnight!

STUDENT B

You're going to fly to Nepal tomorrow. Then next week you're going to climb Mount Everest with _____ (**who?**). You're going to come back to this country _____ (**when?**). Then you're going to write a book about the climb.

STUDENT C

You're going to move to Los Angeles next week. You bought Leonardo DiCaprio's house last month for _____ (**how much?**). And in August you're going to be in a Hollywood film with _____ (**who?**).

STUDENT D

You're going to sail around the world next month with _____ (**who?**). You're also going to make a film about your journey. You're going to be away for about _____ (**how long?**).

STUDENT E

You're going to start a new job next Monday. You're going to be a journalist for a famous newspaper called _____ (**what?**). And on Tuesday you're going to interview _____ (**who?**).

STUDENT F

You're going to go on holiday to _____ (**where?**) next week. You're going to stay in a beautiful hotel near the beach. You're also going to learn how to dive. You're going to be on holiday for _____ (**how long?**).

STUDENT G

You're going to fly to _____ (**where?**) for the weekend. You're going to go with _____ (**who?**) and you're going to stay in a five-star hotel. You're going to come back on Monday.

STUDENT H

You're the singer in a rock band called No Future. You're going to play a concert for _____ (**how many?**) people in _____ (**where?**) next week. There were only 200 people at your last concert!

STUDENT I

It's your wedding anniversary next Tuesday. You are going to buy your husband or wife _____ (**what?**). And on Tuesday evening you're going to have a very expensive dinner at _____ (**where?**).

STUDENT J

You're going to start university next September. You're very excited because you're going to study music at _____ (**where?**). You're going to come back to your country in December _____ (**why?**).

STUDENT K

You're going to do an English exam next Monday. Then you're going to fly to _____ (**where?**) on Friday. You're going to study English there, and then you're going to travel around the country with _____ (**who?**).

STUDENT L

You're going to open a restaurant in the city centre next Friday. _____ (**who?**) is / are going to be there! Then you're going to open a second restaurant in _____ (**where?**) next month.

Vocabulary Plus

Instructions

There are ten Vocabulary Plus worksheets (p167–p176). These worksheets introduce additional vocabulary that is <u>not</u> presented in the Student's Book. The topic of each Vocabulary Plus worksheet is linked to the topic of the corresponding unit in the Student's Book. There is an answer key at the bottom of each worksheet, which can be cut off if necessary. You will need to photocopy one Vocabulary Plus worksheet for each student.

- Use these worksheets for extra vocabulary input in class. The instructions give additional communicative stages you can include in each lesson. We suggest you cut off the answer keys and check the answers after each exercise.
- Give the worksheets for homework. You can leave the answer keys on the worksheets so students can check the answers themselves. Alternatively, cut off the answer keys before handing out the worksheets and check the answers at the beginning of the next class.
- Give the worksheets to fast finishers in class. This is often useful when you have a mixed-level class and some students finish speaking activities early. Students can begin the worksheets in class and finish them for homework if necessary. You can then give copies of the worksheet to the other students for homework at the end of the class.

1 ▶ Things in a room p167

Language
a clock, a radio, a phone / a telephone, a TV / a television, a DVD, a DVD player, a CD, a CD player, a door, a window

When to use and time
Use any time after lesson 1D. 10–20 minutes.

Procedure

1 Students do the exercise on their own or in pairs. Check answers with the class (see answer key on worksheet). Drill the words with the class, focusing on word stress. Check that students pronounce the letters in *a TV*, *a CD (player)* and *a DVD (player)* correctly, and point out the capital letters in these words. Also highlight the difference between *a clock* (which goes on the wall) and *a watch* (in lesson 1D). Put students into pairs. Ask students to cover the vocabulary box in **1**. Students take turns to say a number from 1 to 10. Their partner says the thing in the picture that corresponds to the number, for example: **A** *Number 5.* **B** *A radio.*

2 Students do the crossword on their own or in pairs. You can make this a race and the first student or pair to complete the crossword wins. Check answers with the class.

3 Students do the exercise on their own before comparing answers in pairs. Check answers with the class. Point out that all these words have regular plurals with an -*s* added to the singular word. Drill the plural forms with the class.

2 ▶ Countries and nationalities p168

Language
England / English, Switzerland / Swiss, Portugal / Portuguese, Ireland / Irish, Peru / Peruvian, Morocco / Moroccan, Sweden / Swedish, the Czech Republic / Czech, South Africa / South African, Vietnam / Vietnamese

When to use and time
Any time after lesson 2A. 15–25 minutes.

Procedure

1 Students do the exercise on their own or in pairs. Check answers with the class (see answer key on worksheet). Drill the countries with the class, focusing on word stress. Highlight the pronunciation of *England* /ˈɪŋglənd/, *Portugal* /ˈpɔːtʃʊgəl/ and *Czech* /tʃek/. Also point out that we say **the Czech Republic**. Put students into pairs. Ask students to cover the sentences in **1**. Students take turns to point to a person on the worksheet and ask where he/she is from. For example, student A points to person 3 and asks *Where's he from?*. Student B replies *He's from Morocco*. If necessary, demonstrate this by asking the class where two or three people are from before students begin working in pairs.

2 Students do the exercise on their own or in pairs. Check answers with the class. Drill the nationalities with the class, focusing on word stress, and highlight the different stress patterns in *Portugal / Portuguese* and *Vietnam / Vietnamese*. Also highlight the addition of *v* in *Peruvian*.

✍ Write the questions *What's his nationality?* and *What's her nationality?* on the board. Drill the questions with the class. Put students into new pairs. Ask students to cover the sentences in **2**. Students take turns to point to a person on the worksheet and ask what his/her nationality is. For example, student A points to person 3 and asks *What's his nationality?*. Student B replies *He's Moroccan*.

3 **a** Focus students on the table. Point out the endings for nationality words in the first column and the examples in the second column. Students do the exercise on their own before comparing answers in pairs. Check answers with the class.

b Students do the exercise on their own before comparing answers in pairs. Check answers with the class.
Put students into pairs. Ask the class to cover the vocabulary box in **2**. Students test each other on the nationalities by taking turns to say a country from **1**, for example: **A** *Portugal.* **B** *Portuguese.*

3 ▶ Food and drink p169

Language

tomatoes, potatoes, oranges, beer, lemons, red wine, chicken, onions, sausages, bananas, white wine, steak

When to use and time

Use any time after lesson 3D. 15–25 minutes.

Procedure

1 Students do the exercise on their own or in pairs. Check answers with the class (see answer key on worksheet). Drill the words with the class, focusing on word stress. Highlight the pronunciation of *oranges* /ˈɒrɪndʒɪz/, *chicken* /ˈtʃɪkɪn/, *onions* /ˈʌnjənz/, *sausages* /ˈsɒsɪdʒɪz/ and *steak* /steɪk/. Note that *tomatoes* is pronounced /təˈmɑːtəʊz/ in British English and /təˈmeɪtəʊz/ in American English. Also point out that the singular of *tomatoes* is *a tomato*, not *a tomatoe*, and the singular of *potatoes* is *a potato*, not *a potatoe*.

Put students into pairs. Ask the class to cover the vocabulary box in **1**. Students take turns to say a number. Their partner says what the food and drink is, for example: **A** *Number 9*. **B** *Tomatoes*.

2 Students do the exercise on their own before comparing answers in pairs. Check answers with the class.

3 Students do the exercise on their own before comparing answers in pairs. ✐ While they are working, draw the table on the board. Check answers with the class by saying a word from **1** and asking the class which category it goes in, then writing the word in the correct place in the table on the board. Note that although *tomatoes* are botanically classed as a fruit, from a culinary point of view (and in supermarkets, on menus, etc.) they are usually classed as a vegetable.

With a stronger class you can ask students if they know any more words for each category. ✐ Write these words on the board and drill them with the class. Give students time to copy the new words onto their worksheets or in their notebooks.

4 Students do the exercise on their own. Remind students that they can use words from **1** and their own ideas.

Put students into groups of three or four. Students compare sentences in their groups. Finally, ask students to tell the class one or two of their sentences.

> **EXTRA IDEA**
>
> • If you have a monolingual class, teach students the English words for food and drink that is popular in their country. ✐ Write these words on the board and drill the new vocabulary with the class.

4 ▶ Free time activities p170

Language

listen to music, go to the theatre, go clubbing, play golf, go to museums, play cards, read books or magazines, go cycling

When to use and time

Use any time after lesson 4B. 20–30 minutes.

Procedure

1 Students do the exercise on their own or in pairs. Check answers with the class (see answer key on worksheet). Drill the phrases with the class, focusing on word stress. Highlight the pronunciation of *listen* /ˈlɪsən/, *theatre* /ˈθɪətə/ and *cycling* /ˈsaɪklɪŋ/. Point out that we usually say *go to **the** theatre* but *go to museums*. You can compare these phrases with *go to **the** cinema* and *go to concerts* from lesson 4B in the Student's Book. Check students understand that when people *go clubbing*, they go to a club to listen to music and dance. You can also highlight that we often use *go + verb+ing* (*go clubbing, go cycling, go shopping*, etc.).

2 Students do the exercise on their own before comparing answers in pairs. Check answers with the class.

Put students into pairs. Students take turns to say a word or phrase in column B. His/Her partner says the complete phrase, for example: **A** *the theatre*. **B** *go to the theatre*.

3 Students do the exercise on their own. Put students into pairs. Students take turns to tell their partner their sentences. Ask students to tell the class one or two of their sentences.

4 **a** Students do the exercise on their own before comparing answers in pairs. Check answers with the class.

b Students do the exercise on their own. Put students into new pairs. Students take turns to ask each other the questions in **4a**. Students give their own answers. Ask students to tick any of the free time activities they both do.

Finally, ask students to tell the class about things they and their partner both do in their free time, for example, *Martina and I go cycling in our free time*.

> **EXTRA IDEA**
>
> • Give one question in **4a** to each student. If you have more than eight students, give two students the same question. Students move around the room and ask the other students their question. They must try to talk to everyone in the room. Before they begin, tell them to make a note of all the students' answers on their worksheets. Finally, ask students to tell the class the results of their classroom survey, for example, *Six people in the class go cycling in their free time*.

5 ▶ Jobs p171

Language

a nurse, an artist, a journalist, a mechanic, a secretary, a chef, a farmer, a DJ

When to use and time

Use any time after lesson 5B. 15–25 minutes.

Procedure

1 Students do the exercise on their own or in pairs. Check answers with the class (see answer key on worksheet). Drill the words with the class, focusing on word stress. Highlight the pronunciation of *nurse* /nɜːs/, *journalist* /ˈdʒɜːnəlɪst/, *mechanic* /məˈkænɪk/ and *chef* /ʃef/. Also highlight that the stress on a *DJ* is on *D*, not *J*. Note that a *DJ* stands for *a disc jockey*, although this term is rarely used nowadays. Also note that there are two different ways to pronounce *secretary* – /ˈsekrətri/ and /ˈsekrəteri/. You can also teach students that we sometimes say a *PA* /piː ˈeɪ/ (= *a personal assistant*) instead of *a secretary*.

Put students into pairs. Ask the class to cover the vocabulary box in **1**. Students take turns to point to a picture and ask their partner what the person's job is, for example: **A** *What's her job?* **B** *She's a nurse.*

2 Focus students on the example and picture 7. Students do the rest of the exercise in pairs. While students are working, be prepared to help them with any of the new vocabulary in **bold**, or encourage them to check the words in their bilingual dictionaries. Check answers with the class and check any vocabulary in **bold** that students are still unsure about. Drill the sentences with the class.

3 Focus students on the pictures and the example. Point out that students must write their sentences in picture order 1–8. Students do the exercise on their own before comparing answers in pairs. Before they begin, remind students that they must use the *he*, *she*, *it* form of the verbs in **2** and tell the class that all these verbs are regular. Check answers with the class.

Ask students to cover **2** and **3**. Put students into pairs. Students take turns to ask their partner what people do in the jobs in **1**, for example: **A** *What does a mechanic do?* **B** *He repairs cars.*

4 Students do the crossword on their own or in pairs. You can make this a race and the first student or pair to complete the crossword wins. Check answers with the class.

6 ▶ Rooms and furniture p172

Language

the kitchen, the living room, the bedroom, the bathroom, the toilet, the balcony, a sofa, a bed, a cooker, a fridge, a shower, a bath, a carpet, a table, a chair, a desk

When to use and time

Use any time after lesson 6B. 15–25 minutes.

Procedure

1 Focus students on the picture of the flat. Ask the class who lives there (Danny). Students do the exercise on their own or in pairs. Check answers with the class (see answer key on worksheet). Drill the words and highlight the pronunciation of *kitchen* /ˈkɪtʃɪn/, *toilet* /ˈtɔɪlət/ and *balcony* /ˈbælkəni/. Point out that we say **the** *kitchen*, **the** *living room*, etc. because there is only one kitchen, one living room, etc. in Danny's flat. Also tell students that we say **in the** *kitchen*, **in the** *living room*, etc. but **on the** *balcony*.

2 Students do the exercise on their own or in pairs. Check answers with the class. Drill the words and highlight the pronunciation of *sofa* /ˈsəʊfə/ and *fridge* /frɪdʒ/.

Put students into pairs. Ask the class to cover the vocabulary box in **1**. Students take turns to test each other on the rooms and things in the picture, for example: **A** *What's number 8?* **B** *It's a sofa.*

3 Focus students on the examples. Students do the exercise on their own before comparing answers in pairs. Check answers with the class.

4 Students do the exercise on their own before comparing answers in pairs. Check answers with the class.

Students work on their own and write four more questions with *Is there … ?* or *Are there … ?* about Danny's flat. Put students into pairs. Ask students to cover the picture of Danny's flat on their worksheets. Students then take turns to ask their questions and say if their partner's answers are right or wrong.

5 Students do the exercise on their own. You can tell students to look at **3** if they need more guidance about what type of sentences to write.

Put students into pairs or small groups. Students take turns to tell their partner about their flat or house. Finally, ask students to tell the class one or two things about their flat or house.

> ### EXTRA IDEAS
>
> - Instead of doing **5**, ask students to draw a plan of their flat or house, including the things in each room. Put students into pairs. Students take turns to describe their flat or house by referring to their plans. You can demonstrate this before they begin by drawing a plan of your own flat or house on the board and then using this to describe where you live.
> - Alternatively, students can work in pairs and describe where they live from memory.

7 ▶ Parts of the body p173

Language
head, face, arm, leg, hand, foot, back, hair, mouth, eye, nose, ear, teeth

When to use and time
Use any time after 7B. 10–20 minutes.

Procedure

1 Students do the exercise on their own or in pairs. Check answers with the class (see answer key on worksheet). Drill the words with the class. Highlight the pronunciation of *mouth* /maʊθ/, *eye* /aɪ/ and *teeth* /tiːθ/. Point out that the singular of *teeth* is *tooth* and the plural of *foot* is *feet*. Tell the class that all the other words have regular plural forms. You can also tell students that we use *body* to mean your whole body, or the part of your body that isn't your head. Point out that we often use a possessive adjective (*my, your, his*, etc.) with parts of the body: *His eyes are green.*, *It's in her hand.*, etc.

Put students into pairs. Ask the class to cover the vocabulary box in **1**. Students take turns to test each other on the parts of the body of the man in the picture, for example: **A** *What's number 6?* **B** *It's his nose.* Alternatively, students can point to parts of their own body and their partner says the word.

2 Students do the exercise on their own before comparing answers in pairs. Check answers with the class.

3 a ✍ Draw four people on the board, one with long hair, one with short hair, one with a round face and one who is very thin. Use these drawings to teach *long, short, round* and *thin*.

b Focus students on the picture and check they understand what *an alien* /'eɪlɪən/ is. Students do the exercise on their own before comparing answers in pairs. Check answers with the class.

4 Students work on their own and draw a picture of a different alien on the back of their worksheets. Alternatively, they can draw their aliens in their notebooks. Encourage them to use their imagination during this stage of the activity. Students then write a description of their aliens, similar to the description in **3b**. Remind them to use words from **1** and **3a** in their descriptions.

Put students into pairs. Students are not allowed to see their partner's picture. Students take turns to describe their alien to their partner. He/She draws the alien from the description given. When students have finished, they compare pictures and see if they are the same.

If you have a weaker class, ask students to do **4** in pairs, and do the communicative stage of the activity in groups of four.

8 ▶ Places with *at*, *in*, *on* p174

Language
at home, at work, at school, at a party, in bed, in the garden, in the kitchen, in town, in the shower, on holiday, on the train, on the bus

When to use and time
Use any time after lesson 8B. 15–25 minutes.

Procedure

1 Students do the exercise on their own or in pairs. Check answers with the class (see answer key on worksheet). Drill the phrases with the class. Point out that each phrase begins with a preposition (*at, in* or *on*). Note that although it is sometimes possible to use other prepositions with these nouns, the phrases taught on the worksheet are the most common, and the most likely to be used when answering a question with *Where … ?* (*Where are you?*, *Where's John?*, etc.). If you have done Vocabulary Plus worksheet 6 (Rooms and furniture), point out that we also use *in* with other rooms (*in the bedroom, in the bathroom*, etc.) and in the phrase *in the bath*. You can also point out that we use *in* with towns, cities and countries (*He's in New York.*, *They're in Germany.*) and that we can say *at a restaurant/café* or *in a restaurant/café*.

2 Ask students to cover the vocabulary box in **1**. Students do the exercise on their own before comparing answers in pairs. Check answers with the class.

Ask students to cover the sentences in **2**. Put students into pairs. Students take turns to ask and answer questions about the people in the pictures, for example: **A** *Where are the people in picture 1?* **B** *They're at a party. Where's the man in picture 2?* **A** *He's in bed.*

3 Focus students on the nouns in **bold** in **2**. Students do the exercise on their own before comparing answers in pairs. ✍ While students are working, draw the table on the board. Check answers with the class by saying a noun in **bold** from **2** and asking students which box it goes in.

Put students into new pairs, A and B. Ask student B in each pair to turn over his/her worksheet. Student A tests his/her partner on the phrases by saying the places in bold in **2**, for example: **A** *the bus.* **B** *on the bus.* After a minute or two, ask students to change roles.

4 Students do the exercise on their own. Put students into groups. Students take turns to say their sentences to the other people in the group. Students can ask questions about each other's sentences if they wish. Finally, ask students to tell the class one or two of their sentences.

9 ▶ Irregular verbs p175

Language

drive (drove), think (thought), sleep (slept), wake up (woke up), see (saw), break (broke), lose (lost), find (found), send (sent), read (read /red/)

When to use and time

Any time after lesson 9C. 15–25 minutes.

Procedure

1 Students do the exercise on their own or in pairs. Check answers with the class (see answer key on worksheet). Drill the words with the class. Highlight the pronunciation of *break* /breɪk/ and *lose* /luːz/. Check students understand the difference between *wake up* and *get up*.

2 Students do the exercise on their own before comparing answers in pairs. Check answers with the class. Drill the Past Simple forms with the class. Highlight the pronunciation of *thought* /θɔːt/ and *saw* /sɔː/. Also point out that the Past Simple of *read* is pronounced /red/, but the spelling is the same.
Put students into pairs. Ask students to cover the table in **2**. Students take turns to test each other on the verbs in **1** and their Past Simple forms, for example: **A** *think.* **B** *thought.*

3 **a** Focus students on the email. Students read the email quickly and find out if Vicky had a good weekend (she didn't).

b Students do the exercise on their own before comparing answers in pairs. Check answers with the class.

4 **a** Check students remember *an arm*. Students do the exercise on their own. Check answers with the class.

b Students tick the sentences in **4a** that are true for them.
Put students into groups. Students take turns to tell each other which sentences are true for them. Encourage students to continue the conversation if possible. Finally, ask students to tell the class one or two sentences that are true for them.

10 ▶ Weather p176

Language

dry, wet, hot, warm, cold, sunny, cloudy, windy, foggy, (26)° / (26) degrees.

When to use and time

Use any time after lesson 10B. 15–20 minutes.

Procedure

1 Focus students on the pictures. Check students know which countries the cities are in. Tell the class that this is the weather in these cities today. Students do the exercise on their own or in pairs. Check answers with the class (see answer key on worksheet). Drill the sentences with the class. Highlight the pronunciation of *cloudy* /ˈklaʊdi/ and *degrees* /dɪˈɡriːz/. With a strong class you can also teach *It's raining.* and *It's snowing.* However, as students have not studied the Present Continuous yet, we suggest you teach these as fixed phrases at this level.
✎ Write the question *What's the weather like in Sydney?* on the board. Drill the question with the class. Elicit the answer (*It's warm.*) and write it on the board. Point out that we use *like* in the question, but not in the answer (*It's like warm.*).
Put students into pairs. Tell students to cover the sentences in **1**. Students take turns to ask what the weather is like in the places in the pictures, for example: **A** *What's the weather like in Barcelona?* **B** *It's sunny.*

2 Focus students on the table. Check students understand that this is the weather forecast for tomorrow. Then focus students on the example sentence 1 and check students understand that we use *be going to* because we're talking about the future.
Students do the exercise on their own before comparing answers in pairs. Check answers with the class.

3 **a** Students do the exercise on their own. Check answers with the class.

b Students do the exercise on their own before comparing answers in pairs. Check answers with the class.

1 Look at the picture of a room. Match these things to 1–10.

a clock ☐1☐ a radio ☐ a phone / a telephone ☐ a TV / a television ☐ a DVD ☐
a DVD player ☐ a CD ☐ a CD player ☐ a door ☐ a window ☐

2 Write words from **1** in the crossword.

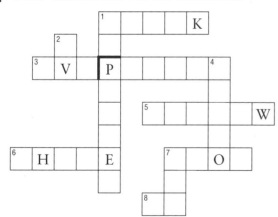

3 Look again at the picture. Write the plurals of words 1–10.

1 c l o c k s

2 d _ _ _ _

3 w _ _ _ _ _ _

4 T _ _ / t _ _ _ _ _ _ _ _ _

5 p _ _ _ _ _ / t _ _ _ _ _ _ _ _

6 r _ _ _ _ _

7 D _ _ p _ _ _ _ _ _

8 D _ _ _

9 C _ p _ _ _ _ _

10 C _ _

VOCABULARY PLUS: Photocopiable

2 ▶ Countries and nationalities

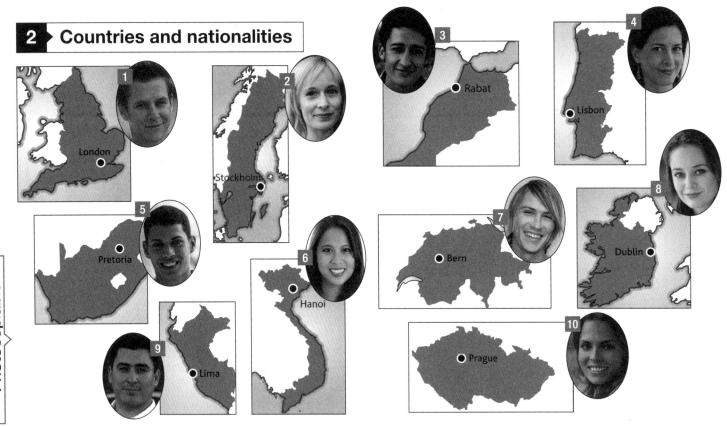

1 Look at the photos and the countries. Fill in the gaps in sentences 1–10 with these countries.

| England Switzerland Portugal Ireland Peru Morocco |
| Sweden   the Czech Republic   South Africa   Vietnam |

1 He's from _England_ .
2 She's from _____ .
3 He's from _____ .
4 She's from _____ .
5 He's from _____ .
6 She's from _____ .
7 He's from _____ .
8 She's from _____ .
9 He's from _____ .
10 She's from _____ .

2 Look again at the photos and the countries. Fill in the gaps with these nationalities.

| English Moroccan Portuguese Swiss Swedish |
| Czech   South African   Vietnamese   Irish   Peruvian |

1 He's _English_ .
2 She's _____ .
3 He's _____ .
4 She's _____ .
5 He's _____ .
6 She's _____ .
7 He's _____ .
8 She's _____ .
9 He's _____ .
10 She's _____ .

3 a Write the nationalities in **2** in the table.

-ish	English
-n, -an, -ian	Moroccan
-ese	Portuguese
other	Swiss

b Write the nationalities for these countries in the table in **3a**.

| Brazil Spain China the USA |
| Turkey France the UK |
| Colombia Japan Italy |

Italian; -ese: Vietnamese, Chinese, Japanese; other: Czech, French.
3 **a and b** -ish: Swedish, Irish, Spanish, Turkish, British; -n, -an, -ian: South African, Peruvian, Brazilian, American, Colombian,
2 2 Swedish 3 Moroccan 4 Portuguese 5 South African 6 Vietnamese 7 Swiss 8 Irish 9 Peruvian 10 Czech
1 2 Sweden 3 Morocco 4 Portugal 5 South Africa 6 Vietnam 7 Switzerland 8 Ireland 9 Peru 10 the Czech Republic

face2face Second edition **Starter** Photocopiable
© Cambridge University Press 2013
⟨ Instructions p162 ⟩

1 Look at the picture. Match these words to 1–12.

tomatoes 9	potatoes ☐	oranges ☐	beer ☐	lemons ☐	red wine ☐
chicken ☐	onions ☐	sausages ☐	bananas ☐	white wine ☐	steak ☐

TIP • The singular of *tomatoes* is *a tomato*. The singular of *potatoes* is *a potato*.

2 Find the words in **1** in the puzzle (→ ↓).

L	E	M	O	N	S	A	W	F	P	C	O
H	W	E	U	F	D	E	H	R	K	H	D
O	R	A	N	G	E	S	I	E	I	I	Y
N	P	S	A	V	C	X	T	Z	E	C	T
I	S	A	U	S	A	G	E	S	A	K	T
O	I	J	E	R	E	D	W	I	N	E	O
N	E	A	X	R	K	O	I	N	E	N	M
S	T	V	S	D	U	I	N	S	B	I	A
D	P	O	T	A	T	O	E	S	E	P	T
W	E	Q	E	J	P	L	E	G	E	Q	O
B	A	N	A	N	A	S	D	O	R	J	E
V	C	E	K	S	R	I	P	B	O	N	S

3 Write the words in **1** in the table.

vegetables	tomatoes
fruit	
meat	
drinks	

4 Complete the sentences for you. Use words from **1** or your own ideas.

1 I like _____ and _____ .

2 I love _____ and _____ .

3 I eat a lot of _____ and _____ .

4 I drink _____ with my food.

5 In my country people eat a lot of _____ .

6 In my country people drink a lot of _____ .

4 ▶ Free time activities

1 Match these phrases to pictures 1–8.

listen to music [8]　go to the theatre ☐　go clubbing ☐　play golf ☐

go to museums ☐　play cards ☐　read books or magazines ☐　go cycling ☐

2 Match the verbs in A to the words / phrases in B.

A	B
listen to	the theatre
go	music
go to	cycling
go	books
read	cards
play	clubbing
go to	golf
play	magazines
read	museums

3 Complete these sentences about your free time. Use phrases from **1** or your own ideas.

1 I _____ .

2 I don't _____ .

3 I _____ a lot.

4 My friends _____ .

5 My friends don't _____ .

6 My friends _____ a lot.

4 **a** Make questions with these words.

1 cycling / you / go / in your free time / Do ?
   Do you go cycling in your free time?

2 the theatre / you / Do / go to / a lot ?
   _____ ?

3 the car / you / in / music / listen to / Do ?
   _____ ?

4 clubbing / Do / with / you / your friends / go ?
   _____ ?

5 in / play / your free time / you / golf / Do ?
   _____ ?

6 you / museums / a lot / go to / Do ?
   _____ ?

7 cards / with your family / you / Do / play ?
   _____ ?

8 you / in English / books or magazines / read / Do ?
   _____ ?

b Answer the questions in **4a** for you.

---

1 go to the theatre 1, go clubbing 6, play golf 4, go to museums 2, play cards 3, read books or magazines 7, go cycling 5
2 go cycling, go to the theatre, go clubbing, read books, read magazines, play golf, go to museums, play cards **4** **2** Do you go to the theatre a lot? **3** Do you listen to music in the car? **4** Do you go clubbing with your friends? **5** Do you play golf in your free time? **6** Do you go to museums a lot? **7** Do you play cards with your family? **8** Do you read books or magazines in English?

1 Match these jobs to pictures 1–8.

a nurse ⑤   an artist ☐   a journalist ☐   a mechanic ☐   a secretary ☐   a chef ☐   a farmer ☐   a DJ ☐

2 Match these sentences to the people in pictures 1–8. Check new words in **bold** with your teacher or in a dictionary.

ᵃ I work for a **news channel**. ᵇ I **cook** food in a restaurant. ᶜ I **paint** pictures.
  ⑦   ☐   ☐

ᵈ I play music in **clubs** or on the radio. ᵉ I write **letters** and answer the phone.
  ☐   ☐

ᶠ I **repair** cars. ᵍ I work in a **hospital**. ʰ I **produce** food.
  ☐   ☐   ☐

3 Look again at pictures 1–8. Write sentences about the people. Use the phrases in **2**.

1 She _paints pictures_ .
2 He _____ .
3 She _____ .
4 He _____ .
5 She _____ .
6 He _____ .
7 She _____ .
8 He _____ .

4 Write the jobs from **1** in the crossword.

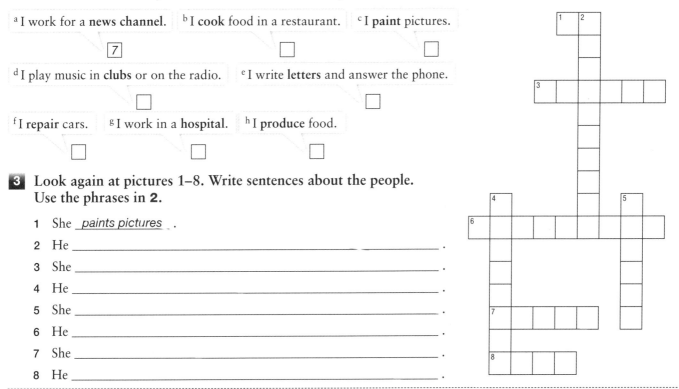

VOCABULARY PLUS:
Photocopiable

1 Look at the picture of Danny's flat. Match these words to A–F.

the kitchen [B]   the living room [ ]   the bedroom [ ]   the bathroom [ ]   the toilet [ ]   the balcony [ ]

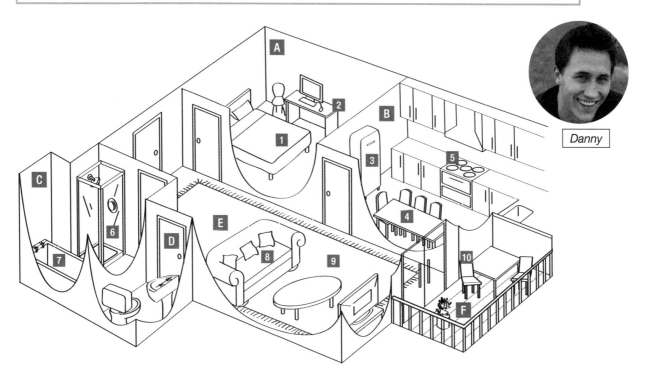

Danny

2 Look at the picture again. Match these things to 1–10.

a sofa [8]   a bed [ ]   a cooker [ ]   a fridge [ ]
a shower [ ]   a bath [ ]   a carpet [ ]   a table [ ]
a chair [ ]   a desk [ ]

3 Tick (✓) the true sentences. Correct the wrong sentences.

five
1 There are ~~four~~ rooms in Danny's flat.

2 There's a bed and a chair in the bedroom. ✓

3 There's a sofa in the living room.

4 There aren't any chairs on the balcony.

5 There's a carpet in the kitchen.

6 There's a bath and a shower in the bathroom.

7 There's a table in the kitchen.

8 There's a cooker in the living room.

4 Answer these questions about Danny's flat.

1 Is there a table on the balcony?
   Yes, there is.

2 Are there any chairs in the kitchen?
   _____

3 Is there a table in the bathroom?
   _____

4 Is there a desk in the bedroom?
   _____

5 Are there any chairs in the bathroom?
   _____

5 Write four sentences about your flat or house. Use words from **1** and **2** and your own ideas.

1 There are _____ rooms in my _____ .

2 There's a _____ in the _____ .

3 There _____ in the _____ .

4 _____ .

---

4 2 Yes, there are. 3 No, there isn't. 4 Yes, there is. 5 No, there aren't.
kitchen. / There's a carpet in the living room. / There's a cooker in the kitchen.
a bath 10, a carpet 1, a table 3, a chair 2, a desk 5   **3** 3 ✓ 4 There **are two** chairs on the balcony. 5 There **isn't** a carpet in the
1 the living room E, the bedroom A, the bathroom C, the toilet D, the balcony F   **2** a bed 4, a cooker 7, a fridge 3, a shower 9,

7 ▸ Parts of the body

1 Match these words to parts of the body 1–13.

> head `1`   face `3`   arm `☐`   leg `☐`   hand `☐`
> foot `☐`   back `☐`   hair `☐`   mouth `☐`
> eye `☐`   nose `☐`   ear `☐`   teeth `☐`

TIPS • The singular of *teeth* is *tooth*.
• The plural of *foot* is *feet*.

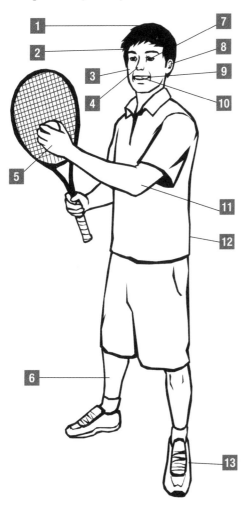

2 Find the words from **1** in the puzzle (→ ↓).

E	Y	E	M	G	H	P	N	S	O	B	J
T	R	I	O	H	A	H	O	Z	Q	A	K
E	L	E	U	I	I	A	S	F	A	C	E
E	A	R	T	L	R	N	E	O	R	K	T
T	U	D	H	E	A	D	K	O	Y	P	Q
H	Y	A	R	M	I	D	F	T	L	E	G

3 a Check these adjectives with your teacher or in a dictionary.

> long   short   round   thin

b Look at the picture of an alien. Fill in the gaps with the singular or plural form of words from **1**.

He has a big ¹ *head* , a round ²_____
and six ³_____ . He has very short
⁴_____ and four small ⁵_____ .
He also has a long ⁶_____ and a very
big ⁷_____ , but he only has five
⁸_____ . He has very thin ⁹_____
and small ¹⁰_____ . He also has short
¹¹_____ and very big ¹²_____ !

4 Draw a picture of a different alien. Then write about your alien. Use words from **1** and **3a**.

VOCABULARY PLUS: Photocopiable

8 ▶ Places with *at, in, on*

1 Match these phrases to pictures 1–12.

at home 6	at work ☐	at school ☐	at a party ☐	in bed ☐	in the garden ☐	in the kitchen ☐
in town ☐	in the shower ☐	on holiday ☐	on the train ☐	on the bus ☐		

TIPS • We use *in* with towns, cities and countries: *He's in New York. They're in Germany.*
• We can say *at a restaurant / café* or *in a restaurant / café.*

2 Look again at pictures 1–12. Fill in the gaps with *at, in* or *on*.

1 They're _at_ a party.
2 He's ___ bed.
3 They're ___ school.
4 She's ___ the bus.
5 They're ___ the garden.
6 She's ___ home.
7 He's ___ the kitchen.
8 She's ___ work.
9 They're ___ holiday.
10 He's ___ the shower.
11 They're ___ the train.
12 She's ___ town.

3 Write the words / phrases in bold in **2** in the table.

at	*a party*	_____
	_____	_____
in	_____	_____
	_____	_____
	_____	_____
on	_____	_____
	_____	_____

4 Complete these sentences about you. Use phrases from **1**.

1 I'm _____ now.
2 I was _____ three hours ago.
3 I was _____ at seven this morning.
4 I was _____ yesterday afternoon.
5 I was _____ last Saturday evening.

---

1 at work 8, at school 3, at a party 1, in bed 2, in the garden 5, in the kitchen 7, in town 12, in the shower 10, on holiday 9, on the train 11, on the bus 4 **2** 2 in 3 at 4 on 5 in 6 at 7 in 8 at 9 on 10 in 11 on 12 in **3** **at** school, home, work; **in** bed, the garden, the kitchen, the shower, town; **on** the bus, holiday, the train

◁ Instructions p165

9 ▶ Irregular verbs

1 Match these verbs to pictures 1–10.

drive 4	think ☐	sleep ☐
wake up ☐	see ☐	break ☐
lose ☐	find ☐	send ☐ read ☐

2 Write the verbs in **1** in the table.

verb	Past Simple
1 *think*	thought /θɔːt/
2 _____	sent
3 _____	broke
4 _____	saw /sɔː/
5 _____	slept
6 _____	woke up
7 _____	read /red/
8 _____	drove
9 _____	lost
10 _____	found

3 **a** Read Vicky's email. Did she have a good weekend?

Hi Harriet
How are you? Jason and I ¹ _went_ (go) away last weekend. We ² _____ (drive) to an old town called Seaford and ³ _____ (stay) in a hotel near the beach. We ⁴ _____ (think) it was a four-star hotel, but it wasn't! The room was very small and the bed was awful. I think Jason ⁵ _____ (sleep) all night, but I didn't. I ⁶ _____ (wake up) at about 4 a.m., then I ⁷ _____ (read) a book and ⁸ _____ (watch) TV.
On Sunday we ⁹ _____ (go) sightseeing. We ¹⁰ _____ (see) some beautiful old buildings, but then I ¹¹ _____ (break) my camera. And then in the afternoon Jason ¹² _____ (lose) his mobile! Of course, he ¹³ _____ (find) it again when we ¹⁴ _____ (get) home – it ¹⁵ _____ (be) in his bag. Next weekend Jason and I don't want to go anywhere!
Love Vicky
PS Did you get the DVDs I ¹⁶ _____ (send) you last week?

b Read the email again. Put the verbs in brackets in the Past Simple.

4 **a** Fill in the gaps with the Past Simple forms in **2**.

1 I _lost_ some money last week.
2 I _____ a good film on TV last night.
3 I _____ at 7 a.m. this morning.
4 I _____ an English magazine last month.
5 I _____ about 300 emails last week.
6 I _____ for about eight hours last night.
7 I _____ to school today.
8 I _____ my arm when I was a child.
9 I _____ my last English lesson was easy.
10 I _____ some old photos last month.

b Tick the sentences in **4a** that are true for you.

1 Look at the pictures. Match sentences 1–10 to the cities.

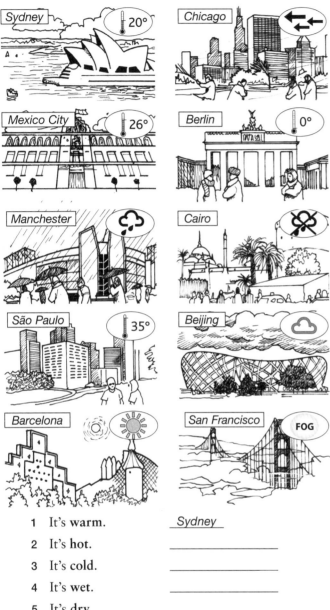

Sydney	Chicago	
Mexico City	Berlin	
Manchester	Cairo	
São Paulo	Beijing	
Barcelona	San Francisco	

1 It's **warm**.   _Sydney_
2 It's **hot**.   _____
3 It's **cold**.   _____
4 It's **wet**.   _____
5 It's **dry**.   _____
6 It's **sunny**.   _____
7 It's **cloudy**.   _____
8 It's **windy**.   _____
9 It's **foggy**.   _____
10 It's **26°**.   _____

TIP • We write 26°. We say *twenty-six degrees*.

2 Look at the weather around the world tomorrow. Make sentences for the places.

Bogotá	
Cape Town	
Dubai	35°
Dublin	
Istanbul	
Lima	24°
Lisbon	FOG
Milan	20°
Moscow	0°
Tokyo	

1 In Bogotá it's going to be ___wet___ .
2 In Cape Town it's going to be _____ .
3 In Dubai it's going to _____ .
4 In Dublin it's going _____ .
5 In Istanbul it's_____ .
6 In Lima _____ .
7 In Lisbon _____ .
8 In Milan _____ .
9 In Moscow _____ .
10 In Tokyo _____ .

3 **a** Look at these questions. Fill in the gaps with *yesterday*, *today* and *tomorrow*.

1 What's the weather like _____ ?
2 What was the weather like _____ ?
3 What's the weather going to be like _____ ?

b Answer the questions in **3a** for the town or city you are in now.

1 It's _____ .
2 It was _____ .
3 It's going to be _____ .

---

going to be cold/3°. **10** In Tokyo it's going to be sunny. **3 a 1** today **2** yesterday **3** tomorrow
6 In Lima it's going to be warm/24°. **7** In Lisbon it's going to be foggy. **8** In Milan it's going to be warm/20°. **9** In Moscow it's
Town it's going to be dry. **3** In Dubai it's going to be hot. **4** In Dublin it's going to be windy. **5** In Istanbul it's going to be cloudy.
1 2 São Paulo 3 Berlin 4 Manchester 5 Cairo 6 Barcelona 7 Beijing 8 Chicago 9 San Francisco 10 Mexico City **2** 2 In Cape

Progress Tests

Instructions

The Progress Tests (p180–p191) are designed to be used after students have completed each unit of the Student's Book. Each Progress Test checks students' knowledge of the key language areas taught in the unit. Some exercises and questions in Progress Tests 5 and 10 also test students' knowledge of language taught in previous units.

It is helpful for students to have done the Extra Practice exercises for each unit in the Student's Book before doing a Progress Test. You can also encourage students to revise for the test by reviewing the relevant Language Summary in the back of the Student's Book and by doing exercises for that unit on the Self-study DVD-ROM and in the Workbook. Note that Progress Tests 5 and 10 also contain a listening section.

- Allow students 20 minutes for Progress Tests 1–4 and 6–9, and 45 minutes for Progress Tests 5 and 10. You may wish to allow more time depending on the level of your class.
- Photocopy one test for each student. Students should do the tests on their own. You can either check the answers with the whole class at the end of the test, or collect in the tests and correct them yourself. Keep a record of the test scores to help you monitor individual students' progress and for report writing at the end of the course.
- Progress Tests can also be given as homework.

Listening tests

There is a listening section in Progress Tests 5 and 10 only. The recording scripts (**CD2** 42 and **CD3** 65) for these tests are in the Answer Key.

Both **CD2** 42 and **CD3** 65 have two separate sections. Focus on one section of the recording at a time. Allow students time to read through the questions for that section in the Progress Test before you start. Play that section of the recording without stopping and allow students time to answer the questions. Then play that section of the recording again without stopping. Repeat this procedure for the other section.

Answer Key and Recording Scripts

1 ▶ Progress Test p180

1 2 your 3 my 4 you 5 You 6 you 7 I 8 you 9 I
2 b eleven c three d eight e twelve f four
3 2 See you soon 3 home number 4 this is
   5 to meet you 6 first name 7 your surname
4 2 His 3 he 4 He 5 Her 6 she 7 She
5 2 Spain 3 Australia 4 China 5 Brazil 6 Russia
6 2 repeat 3 sorry 4 What's 5 spell 6 mean 7 know
7 2 umbrella 3 book 4 apple 5 pen 6 bag 7 pencil
   8 mobile (phone)
8 2 watches 3 people 4 babies 5 men 6 women
   7 tables 8 countries

2 ▶ Progress Test p181

1 2 Spanish 3 American 4 Chinese 5 Turkish
   6 Brazilian 7 British 8 Russian
2 2 'm not, 'm 3 isn't / 's not, 's 4 aren't / 're not, 're
   5 isn't / 's not, 's
3 2 a musician 3 a police officer (a policeman)
   4 a doctor 5 a sales assistant (a shop assistant)
   6 an actor 7 a waitress 8 a taxi driver
4 2 'm 3 Is 4 isn't / 's not 5 's 6 's 7 Is 8 is
   9 Are 10 am 11 Am 12 aren't / 're not
5 (two marks each) 2 What's your surname? 3 How do
   you spell that? 4 What's your nationality? 5 What's
   your address? 6 What's your mobile number?
   7 What's your email address?
6 b forty-six c thirty-three d fifteen e fifty-eight
   f a / one hundred

3 ▶ Progress Test p182

1 2 small (little) 3 unfriendly 4 expensive 5 cold 6 old
2 2 are 3 aren't / 're not 4 're 5 aren't / 're not 6 're
   7 isn't / 's not 8 's / is 9 'm not 10 'm 11 's 12 isn't
3 2 daughter 3 son 4 Pam's 5 sister 6 Steve's 7 father
   8 Jane 9 grandfather 10 children 11 grandparents
4 2 your 3 she 4 Our 5 He 6 their
5 2 please 3 else 4 sandwich 5 away 6 in 7 that's
   8 much 9 welcome
6 2 cheese 3 milk 4 chocolate 5 fruit 6 bread 7 eggs
   8 vegetables 9 tea 10 meat 11 fish 12 water

4 ▶ Progress Test p183

1 2 live 3 work 4 study 5 work 6 have 7 don't have
   8 like 9 don't like
2 2 play 3 go to 4 eat 5 watch 6 go 7 play 8 go to
3 2 What music do you like? 3 Do you like Chinese
   food? 4 Where do your parents live? 5 What do
   you do in your free time? 6 Do your children study
   languages? 7 What food do they like?
4 2 chewing gum 3 batteries 4 tissues 5 a map
   6 a newspaper 7 a magazine 8 a birthday card
5 2 over there 3 How much 4 each 5 These 6 can I
   have that 7 Anything else 8 that's all 9 Here you are
6a 2 Wednesday 3 Thursday 4 Saturday
 b a week b months c hours d seconds
7 b ten past five c (a) quarter past eight d (a) quarter
   to eleven e ten to nine f half past four g twenty to
   three h seven o'clock

5 ▶ Progress Test p184–p185

CD2 42 See p177 for Listening Test instructions.

1
CUSTOMER Excuse me. Do you have any postcards?
ASSISTANT Yes, they're over there.
C Oh, OK. How much are they?
A They're 60p each.
C Thanks. And how much is this map?
A It's £5.95.
C OK. Can I have this map and eight postcards, please?
A Sure. Anything else?
C Er … yes, can I have that box of chocolates, please?
A The big box or the small box?
C The small box, please.
A OK, that's, um, £15.74, please.
C Here you are.
A Thanks very much. Bye.
C Goodbye.

2
TOBY Hi, Eric. How are you?
ERIC I'm fine, thanks, Toby. And you?
T I'm OK, thanks. Eric, this is my sister Vicky.
E Hi, Vicky. Nice to meet you.
VICKY You too. Do you work with Toby?
E No, I don't. We're old friends from school. I work for a computer company. I'm a manager.
V Oh, OK. Do you like your job?
E Yes, I do. But I'm always very busy. I start work at half past eight and I get home at half past seven in the evening.
V Do you work at the weekend?
E I sometimes work on Saturday, but never on Sunday.
V So what do you do on Sunday?
E Well, I always get up late and I usually go to the cinema in the evening. And what about you? Where do you work?

1 (two marks each) 2 60p 3 £5.95 4 eight 5 small
6 £15.74

2 (two marks each) 2T 3T 4F 5F 6T

3 2 has 3 works 4 leave 5 starts 6 has 7 doesn't have
8 finishes 9 gets 10 have 11 watch 12 go 13 work
14 don't work 15 watches 16 doesn't like 17 goes

4 2 do 3 have 4 does 5 work 6 does 7 start 8 Does
9 doesn't 10 do 11 have 12 Do 13 do 14 Do
15 don't 16 Does 17 doesn't

5 2 in 3 on 4 at 5 in 6 at 7 in 8 at 9 on 10 at

6 2 Can I have 3 mushroom pizza 4 would you like
5 for me 6 a bottle of 7 sparkling 8 a dessert 9 Not
for me 10 for me 11 have the bill 12 Of course

7 2 burger 3 chips 4 salad 5 chicken 6 strawberry
7 ice cream 8 apple pie

8 2 We play tennis every week. 3 I'm sometimes late for
class. 4 We never go to concerts. 5 He's usually tired
on Mondays. 6 They eat out every week. 7 We don't
usually get up early.

9 2 Spain 3 Where 4 this 5 for 6 their 7 with 8 past

10 2 I'm sorry, I **don't** understand. 3 My brother's **a**
doctor. 4 What's your mobile number? 5 This is my
new car. 6 I go to **the** cinema a lot. 7 She **studies**
English at school. 8 What music **do** you like?
9 My father's name is Bill.

6 ▶ Progress Test p186

1 2 there's 3 There isn't 4 there's 5 There's 6 there isn't
7 There aren't 8 there's 9 there aren't 10 there are

2 2 there is 3 Is there 4 there isn't 5 Are there 6 there
aren't 7 Are there 8 there are

3 2 a supermarket 3 a market 4 a bank 5 a chemist's
6 a square

4 2 some 3 any 4 a 5 a lot of 6 three

5 2 a wallet 3 money 4 a camera 5 a credit card
6 keys 7 a passport 8 an ID card

6 2 Do you have 3 Where's 4 show 5 Here 6 When
7 from 8 to 9 day 10 on 11 book

7 2 a coat 3 a skirt 4 shoes 5 a jumper 6 a dress
7 a jacket 8 a shirt

7 ▶ Progress Test p187

1 2 operas 3 watching 4 don't 5 visiting
6 likes, clothes 7 films 8 classical, doesn't 9 love

2 2 them 3 him 4 her 5 they, us

3 (two marks each) 2 She can't cook. 3 She can ride a
bike. 4 She can't play the guitar. 5 Brian can swim.
6 He can't sing. 7 He can't ski. 8 He can play
basketball.

4 2 A Can your daughter speak Spanish? B Yes, she
can. 3 A Can Tina's brother play the piano? B No, he
can't. 4 A Can you speak English very well? B Yes, I
can. (Yes, we can.)

5 2 right 3 on 4 opposite 5 is 6 near 7 in 8 left
9 next to

6 2 send 3 chat to 4 read 5 watch 6 book 7 search
8 listen

8 ▶ Progress Test p188

1 2 empty 3 right 4 short 5 terrible / awful 6 easy
7 unhappy (sad) 8 interesting

2 2 was 3 were 4 were 5 wasn't 6 was 7 weren't
8 were 9 wasn't 10 was 11 was 12 weren't

3 2 Were his brothers at the party? 3 they were
4 Was his sister there? 5 she wasn't 6 Where were
Ewan's parents? 7 Was the food very good? 8 it was

4 2 ago 3 in 4 yesterday 5 ago 6 last

5 2 February 3 June 4 August 5 September
6 November

6 2 shall we 3 Let's 4 so 5 Why don't we 6 that's
7 Where 8 at 9 shall

7 d 22nd e 20,000,000 f 1949 g 31st h 200,000
i 2018 j 950

9 ▶ Progress Test p189

1 2 a plane 3 a boat 4 a motorbike 5 a bus
   6 a bike / a bicycle

2 2 had 3 visited 4 met 5 bought 6 didn't stay
   7 wanted 8 left 9 travelled 10 was 11 were 12 got
   13 didn't sleep 14 stayed 15 went 16 wrote

3 2 go on 3 rent 4 go 5 travel 6 go for 7 go
   8 take 9 stay in 10 stay with

4 3 Where **did you** go last night? 4 When did they
   arrive at the hotel? 5 ✓ 6 **Did** Sue go out yesterday
   evening? 7 ✓

5 2 returns 3 When 4 come 5 On 6 That's 7 your
   8 next 9 does 10 in

6 2 How much 3 When 4 Why 5 How many
   6 What 7 How old 8 Who

10 ▶ Progress Test p190–p191

CD3 ▶ **65** See p177 for Listening Test instructions.

1
TOURIST Good morning.
ASSISTANT Hello, can I help you?
T Yes, please. Do you have a map of the city centre?
A Yes, of course. Here you are.
T Thank you.
A You're welcome. Can I help you with anything else?
T Er, yes, please. Where's the Queen's Theatre?
A It's in Market Street, opposite the cinema.
T Can you show me on this map?
A Yes, of course. Um, here it is. It's about ten minutes away.
T Thanks. And where's the City Museum?
A It's in Park Road, near the station.
T Oh yes, I know. When is the museum open?
A It's open from nine thirty a.m. to six p.m.
T Is it open on Sundays?
A Yes, it is. But it's closed on Mondays.
T OK, thank you very much. Oh, one more thing.
A Yes?
T Can I book a walking tour here?
A Yes, of course. They start at 11 o'clock and 2.30 every day.
T How much are they?
A They're £10 per person.
T OK, I'll think about it. Thanks for your help.
A No problem. Goodbye.
T Goodbye.

2
BOB Hi, Louise. Did you have a good weekend?
LOUISE Yes, I did, thanks. It was my husband's birthday on
   Saturday.
B Oh, what did you do?
L We went to Paris for the weekend.
B Really? Did you fly?
L No, we went by train. It's only about two hours from
   London.
B Oh, right. And where did you stay?
L Oh, we stayed in a very nice old hotel in the city centre.
B Hmm. And what did you do in Paris?
L Well, on Saturday we went shopping and had dinner with
   friends. And on Sunday we went sightseeing. Paris is a very
   beautiful city.

B Yes, it is, isn't it? I went there two years ago with some
   friends. We had a great time.
L And guess what – it's *my* birthday next weekend!
B No! What are you going to do?
L We're going to visit my sister – and she lives in Berlin!
B Oh.

1 (two marks each) 2a 3b 4a 5a 6b
2 (two marks each) 2 train 3 in a hotel 4 Sunday
   5 two years ago 6 her sister
3 (two marks each) 2 'm not going to look for
   3 'm going to start 4 's / is going to get 5 aren't / 're
   not going to have 6 are going to move 7 'm going to
   start 8 're going to look for 9 isn't / 's not going to
   look for 10 's going to do
4 2 go 3 go to 4 have 5 go to 6 have 7 go 8 watch
5 (two marks each) 2 Are you going to watch TV
   tonight? 3 Where are your parents going to go on
   holiday? 4 Is your sister going to get engaged next
   year? 5 When are you going to move to the UK?
   6 Are you going to do any exams next month?
6 2 bored 3 sad 4 excited 5 tired 6 angry 7 hungry
   8 scared
7 2 with my brother 3 Have a good time 4 See you
   next 5 Yes, see you 6 visit my parents 7 Have a good
   weekend 8 good luck with 9 very much
8 2 I'm not from the USA. 3 I don't live in London.
   4 They aren't / They're not from France. 5 I didn't
   go out last night. 6 They weren't at work. 7 She
   can't swim. 8 He doesn't like coffee. 9 There isn't a
   market. 10 It wasn't expensive.
9 2 some 3 lives 4 their 5 watching 6 were 7 ago
   8 opposite 9 Why 10 in 11 this 12 by
10 2 Let's go **to** the beach. 3 Where **were** you born?
   4 I went **on** holiday last month. 5 Where did you
   stay in London? 6 My birthday's **on** December 30th.
   7 How **many** people were at the party?
   8 His grandparents **weren't** at the wedding.
   9 This is my **favourite jacket**. 10 I never listen **to** the
   radio. 11 What **shall we** do this weekend?

1 Fill in the gaps with *I*, *my*, *you* or *your*.

BOB Hello, ¹ *I* 'm Bob. What's ² _____ name?
ANN Hello, ³ _____ name's Ann.
BOB Nice to meet ⁴ _____ .
ANN ⁵ _____ too.

KIM Hi, Liz.
LIZ Hi, Kim. How are ⁶ _____ ?
KIM ⁷ _____ 'm fine, thanks. And ⁸ _____ ?
LIZ ⁹ _____ 'm OK, thanks.

⬚ 8

2 Write the numbers.

a 6 *six*
b 11 _____
c 3 _____

d 8 _____
e 12 _____
f 4 _____

⬚ 5

3 Fill in the gaps with these words and phrases.

> ~~Goodbye~~ home number this is first name
> to meet you your surname See you soon

SALLY ¹ *Goodbye* , Colin.
COLIN Bye, Sally. ² _____ .
SALLY Yes, see you.

PAUL What's your ³ _____ ?
DAVE It's 020 7946 0873.

ANDY Tom, ⁴ _____ Lily.
TOM Hello, Lily. Nice ⁵ _____ .
LILY You too.

SALLY What's your ⁶ _____ ,
please?
LUCAS It's Lucas.
SALLY What's ⁷ _____ ?
LUCAS It's Hernández.

⬚ 6

4 Fill in the gaps with *he*, *his*, *she* or *her*.

A What's ¹ *his* name?
B ² _____ name's Peter.
A Where's ³ _____ from?
B ⁴ _____ 's from the USA.

A What's her name?
B ⁵ _____ name's Lisa.
A Where's ⁶ _____ from?
B ⁷ _____ 's from the UK.

⬚ 6

5 Write the countries.

1 T*urkey*   2 S_____

3 A_____   4 C_____

5 B_____   6 R_____ ⬚ 5

6 Fill in the gaps with these words.

> ~~Excuse~~ spell mean know sorry repeat What's

1 ___*Excuse*___ me.
2 Can you _____ that, please?
3 I'm _____ , I don't understand.
4 _____ this in English?
5 How do you _____ computer?
6 What does diary _____ ?
7 I'm sorry, I don't _____ .

⬚ 6

7 Write the words.

1   a *dictionary*   5  a _____

2   an _____   6  a _____

3   a _____   7  a _____

4 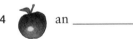 an _____   8 a _____

⬚ 7

8 Write the plurals.

1 chair *chairs*   5 man _____
2 watch _____   6 woman _____
3 person _____   7 table _____
4 baby _____   8 country _____

⬚ 7

1 Write the nationalities.

1 Germany _German_   5 Turkey _____
2 Spain _____   6 Brazil _____
3 the USA _____   7 the UK _____
4 China _____   8 Russia _____

☐ 7

2 Fill in the gaps with the correct positive (+) or negative (–) form of *be*.

1 Serge _isn't_ (–) Italian. He_'s_ (+) from France.
2 I_____ (–) from the UK. I_____ (+) from the USA.
3 Marta _____ (–) from Brazil. She_____ (+) from Colombia.
4 You _____ (–) a teacher. You_____ (+) a student.
5 It _____ (–) a German car. It_____ (+) a Japanese car.

☐ 8

3 Write the jobs. Use *a* or *an*.

a teacher   _____

_____   _____

_____   _____

_____   _____

☐ 7

4 Fill in the gaps in these conversations. Use the correct form of *be*.

A Where [1] _are_ you from?
B I[2]_____ from Egypt.
A [3]_____ your teacher from the UK?
B No, she [4]_____ .
A What[5]_____ his name?
B His name[6]_____ Henry.
A [7]_____ Mrs Jones from London?
B Yes, she [8]_____ .
A [9]_____ you from Mexico?
B Yes, I [10]_____ .
A [11]_____ I in this class?
B No, you [12]_____ .

☐ 11

5 Silvia is at The City Gym. Write the questions.

PETER Right, I need some personal information.
    [1] _What's your first name, please?_
SILVIA It's Silvia.
P   [2] _____ _____ ?

Peter

S It's Thorpe.
P [3] _____ ?
S T-h-o-r-p-e.
P [4] _____ ?
S I'm Australian.
P [5] _____ ?
S It's 39 Park Street, Liverpool, L19 5RF.
P [6] _____ ?
S My mobile number? It's 07900 900478.
P [7] _____ ?
S It's silvia.thorpe@webmail.net.
P Thank you.

☐ 12

6 Write the numbers.

a 20 _twenty_   d 15 _____
b 46 _____   e 58 _____
c 33 _____   f 100 _____

☐ 5

1   Write the opposites of these adjectives.

1   good   _bad_   4   cheap _____

2   big _____   5   hot _____

3   friendly _____   6   new _____

                                             [5]

2   Fill in the gaps with the correct positive (+) or negative (–) form of *be*.

> ○○○   A   ⊘   ➤
>
> Hi Roberto
>
> How ¹ _are_ (+) you? David and I ² _____ (+)
> in the UK! We ³ _____ (–) in London today,
> we⁴ _____ (+) in a hotel in Brighton. The rooms
> ⁵ _____ (–) very big, but they⁶ _____ (+) very
> nice. The hotel ⁷ __ ____ (–) very expensive and
> the manager ⁸ _____ (+) very friendly.
> I⁹ _____ (–) in the hotel now, I¹⁰ _____ (+) in
> a café in Brighton. It¹¹ _____ (+) a beautiful city,
> but it ¹² _____ (–) very hot here!
> See you soon.
> Love Julia
>
>   [11]

3   Look at Roy and Jane's family. Fill in the gaps in these sentences.

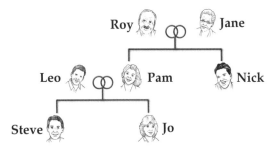

1   Jane is Roy's _wife_ .

2   Pam is Roy and Jane's _____ .

3   Nick is their _____ .

4   Leo is _____ husband.

5   Pam is Nick's _____ .

6   Jo is _____ sister.

7   Leo is Jo's _____ .

8   _____ is Pam's mother.

9   Roy is Steve's _____ .

10   Steve and Jo are Leo and Pam's _____ .

11   Roy and Jane are Steve and Jo's _____ .

                                     [10]

4   Choose the correct words.

1   Where's *I* / *my* bag?

2   Where are *you* / *your* parents from?

3   Is *she* / *her* an actress?

4   *We* / *Our* teacher's name is Caroline.

5   *He* / *His* isn't from Thailand.

6   What's *they* / *their* father's name?   [5]

5   Read this conversation in a café. Fill in the gaps with these words.

> ~~help~~   welcome   that's   else   much
> sandwich   away   please   in

ASSISTANT   Can I ¹ _help_ you?

CUSTOMER   Yes, two coffees, ² _____ .

A   Anything ³ _____ ?

C   Yes, an egg ⁴ _____ , please.

A   Eat in or take ⁵ _____ ?

C   Eat ⁶ _____ , please.

A   OK, ⁷ _____ £6.35, please.

C   Thank you very ⁸ _____ .

A   You're ⁹ _____ .   [8]

6   Write the words.

1   _sugar_   7   _____

2   _____   8   _____

3   _____   9   _____

4   _____   10   _____

5   _____   11   _____

6   _____   12   _____

                                     [11]

         ◁ Answer Key p177

1 Fill in the gaps with the correct positive (+) or negative (–) form of *like*, *have*, *live*, *work* or *study*.

My name's Brigitte and I ^{1} _live_ (+) in Paris with my husband, Bernard, and our two children. We ^{2}_____ (+) in a nice flat in the centre of the city. I ^{3}_____ (+) for a French phone company and I ^{4}_____ (+) English after work two days a week. I ^{5}_____ (+) in an office near our flat. We ^{6}_____ (+) two sons, but we ^{7}_____ (–) a daughter. Our sons ^{8}_____ (+) rock music and tennis, but they ^{9}_____ (–) football or homework!

[8]

2 Choose the correct verbs.

1 (go) / watch out with friends
2 play / go video games
3 go to / go concerts
4 eat / play out
5 play / watch TV
6 go to / go shopping
7 go / play tennis
8 go to / go the cinema

[7]

3 Make questions with these words.

1 do / Where / work / you ?
 Where do you work?

2 music / do / What / like / you ?
 _____

3 Chinese / you / food / like / Do ?
 _____

4 live / do / your / Where / parents ?
 _____

5 do / your / What / free time / in / you / do ?
 _____

6 children / Do / languages / your / study ?
 _____

7 food / they / What / like / do ?
 _____

[6]

4 Write the words.

1 s _weets_
2 c_____
3 b_____
4 t_____
5 a m_____
6 a n_____
7 a m_____
8 a b_____

[7]

5 Read this conversation in a shop. Fill in the gaps with these words and phrases.

Excuse over there each Here you are How much
These that's all Anything else can I have that

CUSTOMER ^{1} _Excuse_ me. Do you have any postcards?
ASSISTANT Yes, they're ^{2}_____ .
C Thanks. ^{3}_____ are they?
A They're 40p ^{4}_____ .
C OK. ^{5}_____ four postcards, please.
 And ^{6}_____ big box of chocolates?
A Of course. ^{7}_____ ?
C No, ^{8}_____ , thanks.
A OK, that's £8.59, please.
C ^{9}_____ .
A Thanks a lot. Goodbye.

[8]

6 a Write the days of the week.

^{1} _Monday_ , Tuesday, ^{2}_____ ,
^{3}_____ , Friday , ^{4}_____ , Sunday

b Write the time words.

a 7 _days_ = 1 _____
b 1 year = 12 _____
c 1 day = 24 _____
d 1 minute = 60 _____

[7]

7 Complete the times.

a _five_ _to_ nine
b _____ _____ five
c _____ _____ eight
d _____ _____ eleven
e _____ _____ nine
f _____ _____ four
g _____ _____ three
h _____ _____

[7]

1 **CD2▶ 42 Listen to a conversation in a shop. Choose the correct answers.**

1 The shop _has some_ / _doesn't have any_ postcards.
2 The postcards are _50p_ / _60p_ each.
3 The map is _£5.95_ / _£5.99_.
4 The customer buys _six_ / _eight_ postcards.
5 The customer buys a _big_ / _small_ box of chocolates.
6 The customer spends _£15.24_ / _£15.74_.

☐ 10

2 **CD2▶ 42 Listen to Toby, Eric and Vicky. Are these sentences true or false?**

Vicky   Eric   Toby

1 Eric is Vicky's brother. _F_
2 Eric doesn't work with Toby. ___
3 Eric's a manager for a computer company. ___
4 He gets home at 8.30 in the week. ___
5 He sometimes works on Sunday. ___
6 He usually goes to the cinema on Sunday evening. ___

☐ 10

3 **Read about Andy's daily routine. Put the verbs in brackets in the correct form of the Present Simple.**

Andy

Andy is a taxi driver in London. He ¹ _gets up_ (get up) at 6.00 and he ² _____ (have) breakfast at 6.30 with his wife, Kathy. She ³ _____ (work) in a café near their flat. Andy and Kathy

⁴ _____ (leave) home at about 7.00. Andy ⁵ _____ (start) work at 7.30. He always ⁶ _____ (have) a coffee and a sandwich at about 11.00, but he ⁷ _____ (not have) lunch. He ⁸ _____ (finish) work at 4.30 and usually ⁹ _____ (get) home at about 5.00 or 5.30. Andy and Kathy ¹⁰ _____ (have) dinner at about 6.30. Then they ¹¹ _____ (watch) TV and ¹² _____ (go) to bed at 10.00. Andy and Kathy ¹³ _____ (work) every Saturday, but they ¹⁴ _____ (not work) on Sundays. Andy usually ¹⁵ _____ (watch) football on TV on Sunday afternoon, but Kathy ¹⁶ _____ (not like) football. She usually ¹⁷ _____ (go) out with friends.

☐ 16

4 **Read about Andy and Kathy again. Then fill in the gaps in these questions and answers.**

A What time ¹ _does_ Andy get up?
B At 6.00.
A When ² _____ Andy and Kathy ³ _____ breakfast?
B At 6.30.
A Where ⁴ _____ Kathy ⁵ _____ ?
B In a café near their flat.
A What time ⁶ _____ Andy ⁷ _____ work?
B At 7.30.
A ⁸ _____ he have lunch?
B No, he ⁹ _____ .
A When ¹⁰ _____ Andy and Kathy ¹¹ _____ dinner?
B At about 6.30.
A ¹² _____ they work on Saturdays?
B Yes, they ¹³ _____ .
A ¹⁴ _____ they work on Sundays?
B No, they ¹⁵ _____ .
A ¹⁶ _____ Kathy like football?
B No, she ¹⁷ _____ .

☐ 16

5 **Fill in the gaps with _on_, _in_ or _at_.**

1 _on_ Sunday
2 ___ the morning
3 ___ Friday morning
4 ___ half past four
5 ___ the week
6 ___ night
7 ___ the afternoon
8 ___ the weekend
9 ___ Friday evening
10 ___ midday

☐ 9

6 Kerry and Dan are in a restaurant. Read the conversation. Then fill in the gaps with these words and phrases.

~~order~~ for me (x2)   have the bill   sparkling   a dessert
a bottle of   mushroom pizza   Of course   Not for me
Can I have   would you like

WAITER Are you ready to ¹ _order_ ?

KERRY Yes. ² _____ the vegetable lasagne?

DAN And can I have the ³ _____ , please?

W Certainly. What ⁴ _____ to drink?

K An orange juice ⁵ _____ , please.

D And can we have ⁶ _____ mineral water?

W Still or ⁷ _____ ?

D Still, please.

W OK. Thanks very much.

W Would you like ⁸ _____ ?

K ⁹ _____ , thanks.

D Fruit salad ¹⁰ _____ , please. And two coffees, please.

W Certainly.

D Excuse me. Can we ¹¹ _____ , please?

W ¹² _____ .

D Thanks a lot.

[11]

7 Write the words.

1 a p _i z z a_   2 a b _ _ _ _ _ _

3 c _ _ _ _ _   4 a s _ _ _ _ _

5 c _ _ _ _ _ _   6 a s _ _ _ _ _ _ _ _ _

7 i _ _ _ c _ _ _ _ _   8 a _ _ _ _ _ p _ _

[7]

8 Make sentences with these words.

1 early / goes / She / to bed / always .
   She always goes to bed early.

2 week / play / We / every / tennis .
   _____

3 I'm / class / sometimes / for / late .
   _____

4 concerts / never / to / go / We .
   _____

5 on / usually / He's / Mondays / tired .
   _____

6 eat out / They / week / every .
   _____

7 early / usually / We / get up / don't .
   _____

[6]

9 Choose the correct words or phrases.

1 What's *you* / *your* first name, please?
2 My wife is from *Spain* / *Spanish*.
3 *What* / *Where* do your brothers live?
4 How much is *this* / *these* watch?
5 I work *in* / *for* a British company.
6 This is a photo of *they* / *their* children.
7 I go out *with* / *for* friends a lot.
8 It's half *past* / *to* eleven.

[7]

10 Correct these sentences.

       's
1 He⌄ from the USA.

2 I'm sorry, I not understand.

3 My brother's doctor.

4 What your mobile number?

5 This is my car new.

6 I go to cinema a lot.

7 She studys English at school.

8 What music you like?

9 My father name is Bill.

[8]

1 Fill in the gaps with *there's, there isn't, there are* or *there aren't*.

> I live in Wolverhampton, a city in England.
> ¹ *There are* (+) a lot of nice buildings and
> ² _____ (+) a beautiful old theatre
> called The Grand. ³_____ (–) a river in
> the centre, but ⁴_____ (+) a nice park
> called West Park. ⁵_____ (+) a station
> in Wolverhampton, but ⁶_____ (–) an
> airport. I live in Albert Road, near West Park.
> ⁷_____ (–) any shops in my road, but
> ⁸_____ (+) a supermarket five minutes
> away. And ⁹_____ (–) any restaurants
> near my house, but ¹⁰_____ (+) a lot
> very good restaurants in the centre.

| 9 |

2 Fill in the gaps with the correct form of *there is / there are*.

A ¹ *Is there* a theatre in Wolverhampton?
B Yes, ²_____ .
A ³_____ an airport?
B No, ⁴_____ .
A ⁵_____ any shops in Albert Road?
B No, ⁶_____ .
A ⁷_____ any good restaurants in the centre?
B Yes, ⁸_____ .

| 7 |

3 Write the words.

1 a b <u>u s s t o p</u>
2 a s _ _ _ _ _ _ _ _ t
3 a m _ _ _ _ _
4 a b _ _ _
5 a c _ _ _ _ _ _ ' _
6 a s _ _ _ _ _ | 5 |

4 Choose the correct words.

1 There's *a* / *any* bus station.
2 There are *some* / *any* hotels.
3 There aren't *an* / *any* museums.
4 There isn't *a* / *some* cashpoint.
5 There are *any* / *a lot of* shops.
6 There are *a* / *three* cinemas.

| 5 |

5 Write the words.

1 a *purse*
2 a _____
3 _____
4 a _____
5 a _____
6 _____
7 a _____
8 an _____

| 7 |

6 Read the conversation. Choose the correct words or phrases.

ASSISTANT Hello. Can I ¹(*help*)/ *helps* you?
TOURIST Yes, please. ²*Do you have / You have* a map of the city centre?
A Yes, of course. Here you are.
T Thanks. ³*Where's / There's* the Royal Theatre?
A It's in Green Street.
T Can you ⁴*help / show* me on this map?
A Yes, of course. ⁵*Here / Where* it is.

T ⁶*When / Where* is the City Museum open?
A It's open ⁷*from / to* 9.30 a.m. ⁸*from / to* 5.30 p.m.
T Is it open every ⁹*day / days*?
A No, it's closed ¹⁰*in / on* Mondays.
T And can I ¹¹*book / books* a walking tour here?
A Yes, you can.

| 10 |

7 Write the words.

 1 j*eans*   5 a j_____
 2 a c_____   6 a d_____
 3 a s_____   7 a j_____
 4 s_____   8 a s_____

| 7 |

1 Fill in the gaps with these words.

| ~~hates~~ love likes don't doesn't films watching visiting classical clothes operas |

1 My sister _hates_ flying.
2 My parents love soap _____ .
3 I like _____ sport on TV.
4 My parents _____ like dancing.
5 Mike and Julie like _____ new places.
6 Gillie _____ shopping for _____ .
7 My sons don't like horror _____ .
8 Zara likes _____ music, but she _____ like rock music.
9 We _____ animals. We have five cats and three dogs! [10]

2 Choose the correct words.

1 (I) / Me love Italian food.
2 Do you know *they / them*?
3 I don't understand *he / him*.
4 Maria's nice. I like *she / her* a lot.
5 Do *they / them* live near *we / us*? [5]

3 Look at the things that Yvonne and Brian can do (✓) and can't do (✗). Write sentences for pictures 1–8.

Yvonne		Brian	
1	✓	5	✓
2	✗	6	✗
3	✓	7	✗
4	✗	8	✓

1 Yvonne _can drive_ .
2 She _____ .
3 She _____ .
4 She _____ .
5 Brian _____ .
6 He _____ .
7 He _____ .
8 He _____ . [14]

4 Make questions with these words. Then complete the short answers.

1 A drive / you / Can ?
  Can you drive?
 B No, _I can't_ .
2 A Spanish / Can / daughter / your / speak ?
  _____
 B Yes, _____ .
3 A piano / play / brother / Tina's / the / Can ?
  _____
 B No, _____ .
4 A well / speak / you / Can / very / English ?
  _____
 B Yes, _____ . [6]

5 Tom is at ✳ on the map. Choose the correct words in this conversation.

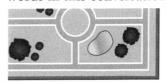 

OLD STREET

museum

bank | post office | theatre

✳

TOM Excuse me. ¹(Where's)/ There's the theatre?
MAN Go along this road and turn ²*left / right*. The theatre is ³*in / on* the right, ⁴*next to / opposite* the museum.
TOM Thanks very much. And ⁵*is / are* there a bank ⁶*next to / near* here?
MAN Yes, there's a bank ⁷*at / in* Old Street. Go along this road and turn ⁸*left / right*. The bank is ⁹*next to / opposite* the post office. [8]

6 Choose the correct words.

1 (download) / book music and apps
2 *send / buy* emails
3 *chat to / book* friends and family
4 *watch / read* a blog
5 *listen / watch* videos and TV programmes
6 *book / send* flights and hotels
7 *search / sell* for information
8 *read / listen* to the radio [7]

1 Write the opposite of these adjectives.

1 young   _old_
2 full   _____
3 wrong   _____
4 long   _____
5 amazing   _____
6 difficult   _____
7 happy   _____
8 boring   _____

[7]

2 Read about Ewan's birthday party. Fill in the gaps with *was, were, wasn't* or *weren't*.

○○○   Ⓐ   📎   ✈

Hi Stephanie
How are you? My weekend ¹ _was_ (+) great! It
² _____ (+) Ewan's 30ᵗʰ birthday party on
Saturday. There ³ _____ (+) about 50 people
at the party. Ewan's three brothers ⁴ _____ (+)
there, but his sister ⁵ _____ (–) there. She
⁶ _____ (+) in France, I think. Also Ewan's
parents ⁷ _____ (–) there, they ⁸ _____ (+) in
Spain. The music ⁹ _____ (–) very good, but the
food ¹⁰ _____ (+) fantastic! It ¹¹ _____ (+) a
good party – sorry you ¹² _____ (–) there!
Love Pia

[11]

3 Make questions with these words. Then fill in the gaps in the short answers.

A party / birthday / When / Ewan's / was ?
   ¹ _When was Ewan's birthday party?_
B On Saturday.
A his / the party / Were / at / brothers ?
   ² _____
B Yes, ³ _____ .
A there / his / Was / sister?
   ⁴ _____
B No, ⁵ _____ .
A were / Where / parents / Ewan's ?
   ⁶ _____
B In Spain.
A the food / good / very / Was ?
   ⁷ _____
B Yes, ⁸ _____ .

[7]

4 Choose the correct words.

1 Peter was at a wedding (yesterday)/ ago.
2 I was in London two years *last* / *ago*.
3 Our son was born *last* / *in* 2012.
4 Where were you *yesterday* / *last* afternoon?
5 Kim was at home an hour *ago* / *yesterday*.
6 I wasn't at work *last* / *yesterday* week. [5]

5 Write the months.

¹ _January_ , ² _____ , March,
April, May, ³ _____ , July,
⁴ _____ , ⁵ _____ ,
October, ⁶ _____ , December [5]

6 Read this conversation. Choose the correct words or phrases.

IAN Hi, Eve. How
   ¹*is* / (*are*) you?
EVE I'm fine, thanks.
   And you?
IAN I'm OK, thanks.
   What ²*we shall* / *shall we* do this afternoon?
EVE ³*Why don't* / *Let's* go to the park.
IAN No, I don't think ⁴*that* / *so*. We always go to
   the park.
EVE OK. ⁵*Why don't we* / *Shall* go to that new
   shopping centre?
IAN Yes, ⁶*that's* / *that* a good idea. ⁷*Where* / *When*
   shall we meet?
EVE Let's meet ⁸*at* / *to* the bus station.
IAN What time ⁹*shall* / *do* we meet?
EVE About three o'clock.
IAN Great. See you there. Bye! [8]

7 Write the years, dates and big numbers.

a nineteen seventy _1970_
b seventh _7ᵗʰ_
c three thousand _3,000_
d twenty-second _____
e twenty million _____
f nineteen forty-nine _____
g thirty-first _____
h two hundred thousand _____
i twenty eighteen _____
j nine hundred and fifty _____ [7]

◁ Answer Key p179

1 Write the words.

1 a _car_

2 a _____

3 a _____

4 a _____

5 a _____

6 a _____   [5]

2 Read about Paul and Sarah's holiday in India. Fill in the gaps with the Past Simple of the verbs in brackets.

○○○   A ✏ ✈

Hi Mum and Dad
How are you? Sarah and I ¹_arrived_ (arrive) in Goa last night. We ²_____ (have) a fantastic time in Mumbai and we ³_____ (visit) some amazing museums. We also ⁴_____ (meet) some nice people and Sarah ⁵_____ (buy) some clothes. We ⁶_____ (not stay) in Mumbai very long because we ⁷_____ (want) to go to Goa. We ⁸_____ (leave) Mumbai at 5 a.m. yesterday and we ⁹_____ (travel) to Goa by train. It ¹⁰_____ (be) a 12-hour journey and we ¹¹_____ (be) very tired when we ¹²_____ (get) to our hotel. Sarah ¹³_____ (not sleep) very well, so this morning she ¹⁴_____ (stay) in bed and I ¹⁵_____ (go) to the beach.
Love Paul
PS I ¹⁶_____ (write) you an email when we were in Mumbai. Did you get it?   [15]

3 Choose the correct words or phrases.

1 *go /go to* the beach
2 *go on / go to* holiday
3 *travel / rent* a car
4 *go / go to* sightseeing
5 *rent / travel* around
6 *go for / go to* a walk
7 *go on / go* swimming
8 *take / rent* photos
9 *stay with / stay in* a hotel
10 *stay with / stay in* friends   [9]

4 Look at these Past Simple questions. Tick (✓) the correct questions. Correct the wrong questions.

             have
1 Did you ~~had~~ a good weekend?
2 What did you do at the weekend? ✓
3 Where you did go last night?
4 When did they arrived at the hotel?
5 Did your parents enjoy the concert?
6 Do Sue go out yesterday evening?
7 Where did you go last weekend?   [5]

5 Read this conversation at a station. Choose the correct words.

TICKET SELLER   Hello. ¹Can/ *Do* I help you?
CUSTOMER   Two ²*singles / returns* to London, please.
TS   ³*When / Where* do you want to ⁴*come / go* back?
C   ⁵*On / In* Sunday evening.
TS   OK. ⁶*That / That's* £54.60, please. Here are ⁷*you / your* tickets.
C   Thanks. What time's the ⁸*next / near* train?
TS   There's one at 10.23.
C   What time ⁹*does / is* it arrive ¹⁰*to / in* London?
TS   At 12.15.
C   Thanks a lot. Bye.   [9]

6 Fill in the gaps with these question words.

~~Where~~ Who What Why When
How much How many How old

1 A   _Where_ are you from?
  B   I'm from Jakarta, in Indonesia.
2 A   _____ is that green bag?
  B   It's £45.
3 A   _____ did you buy your phone?
  B   Six months ago.
4 A   _____ were you late for class?
  B   Because I got up late.
5 A   _____ people were at the party?
  B   About a hundred.
6 A   _____ did you do last night?
  B   I went to the cinema.
7 A   _____ is your daughter?
  B   She's thirteen.
8 A   _____ 's your teacher?
  B   Sally Richards.   [7]

1 **CD3** 65 Listen to a conversation in a tourist information centre. Choose the correct answers.

1 When is the conversation?
(a) In the morning.   b In the afternoon.

2 Where's the Queen's Theatre?
a It's opposite the cinema.   b It's next to the cinema.

3 Where's the City Museum?
a It's in Station Road.   b It's near the station.

4 When is the museum open?
a From 9.30 to 6.00.   b From 9.00 to 6.30.

5 When is the museum closed?
a On Mondays.   b On Sundays.

6 How much is a walking tour?
a £11 per person.   b £10 per person.

☐10

2 **CD3** 65 Listen to Bob and Louise talk about last weekend. Choose the correct words.

1 It was *Louise's* / *Louise's husband's* birthday on Saturday.
2 Louise and her husband went to Paris by *train* / *plane*.
3 They stayed *in a hotel* / *with friends*.
4 They went sightseeing on *Saturday* / *Sunday*.
5 Bob went to Paris *last year* / *two years ago*.
6 Louise is going to visit *her sister* / *a friend* next weekend.

☐10

3 Fill in the gaps with the correct positive (+) or negative (−) form of *be going to* and these verbs.

<del>leave</del> start
get have
look for

Carolina from Spain

I[1] *'m going to leave* (+) school next month. But I[2]_____ (−) a job because I[3]_____ (+) university in September. And my brother [4]_____ (+) married in July. They [5]_____ (−) a big wedding, only about 25 people.

look for (x2)
move do
start

Brad and Amy from the USA

Amy and I [6]_____ (+) to San Francisco in November because I[7]_____ (+) a new job there. We[8]_____ (+) a flat in the centre of the city. But Amy [9]_____ (−) a job because she[10]_____ (+) a computer course.

☐18

4 Choose the correct verbs.

1 *watch* / *have* the news
2 *go* / *go to* shopping
3 *go* / *go to* a party
4 *have* / *go* dinner with friends
5 *go* / *go to* the gym
6 *have* / *watch* a party
7 *go* / *go to* running
8 *watch* / *go* sport on TV

☐7

Answer Key p179

5 Make questions with these words.

1 after class / you / are / What / do / going to ?
   What are you going to do after class?

2 going to / you / Are / tonight / TV / watch ?
   _____

3 your parents / on holiday / Where / go / are / going to ?
   _____

4 get / next year / Is / engaged / going to / your sister ?
   _____

5 move / going to / you / to the UK / are / When ?
   _____

6 any exams / next month / going to / you / Are / do ?
   _____

☐ 10

6 Write the adjectives.

1  h_appy_   2 b_____

3 s_____   4 e_____

5  t_____   6 a_____

7  h_____   8  s_____

☐ 7

7 Read these conversations. Fill in the gaps with these phrases.

> after class   Yes, see you   with my brother   very much
> Have a good weekend   Have a good time   See you next
> visit my parents   good luck with

ULI   What are you going to do ¹ _after class_ ?
JIN   I'm going to have coffee ² _____ .
ULI   ³ _____ .
JIN   Thanks a lot. ⁴ _____ . class.
ULI   ⁵ _____ .

MEG   Are you going to go away at the weekend?
PHIL   Yes, I'm going to ⁶ _____ .
MEG   ⁷ _____ .
PHIL   Thanks a lot. Oh, and ⁸ _____
       your new job.
MEG   Thanks ⁹ _____ .

☐ 8

8 Make these sentences negative (–).

1 She's a doctor.   _She isn't a doctor._
2 I'm from the USA. _____
3 I live in London. _____
4 They're from France. _____
5 I went out last night. _____
6 They were at work. _____
7 She can swim. _____
8 He likes coffee. _____
9 There's a market. _____
10 It was expensive. _____

☐ 9

9 Choose the correct words.

1 I don't know *they* / (*them*.)
2 There are *some* / *any* people in the park.
3 My brother *live* / *lives* in New York.
4 This isn't *they're* / *their* bag.
5 I like *watch* / *watching* TV.
6 Where *was* / *were* you last night?
7 I was in Peru two years *last* / *ago*.
8 The café is *next* / *opposite* the bank.
9 *What* / *Why* are you always late?
10 I play tennis *in* / *on* the evening.
11 Is *this* / *these* your camera?
12 He goes to work *by* / *in* car.

☐ 11

10 Correct these sentences.

  don't
1 I ~~not~~ have a car.

2 Let's go at the beach.

3 Where did you born?

4 I went to holiday last month.

5 Where did you stayed in London?

6 My birthday's in December 30th.

7 How much people were at the party?

8 His grandparents wasn't at the wedding.

9 This is my jacket favourite.

10 I never listen the radio.

11 What we shall do this weekend?

☐ 10

Acknowledgements

Chris Redston would like to thank the following people for their help in the publication of this Teacher's Book: Eoin Higgins for editing the book with such care and attention to detail; Sarah Almy for managing face2face Starter so efficiently under such tight deadlines and for her help with the introduction of this book; Sue Ullstein and Ruth Atkinson for all the work they did during the writing of the first edition of Starter; Gillie Cunningham for her support and friendship since the day we started the face2face journey together, and everyone out there who is doing something positive to help protect our natural world. He would also like to thank Adela Pickles for marrying him on that unforgettable day in May 2013 at the London Wetland Centre – you really are my Lovely Other Dinosaur – and for putting up with book-writing guy for so many years. It's fun-loving guy's turn now, I promise! Heartfelt thanks are also due to Mark Skipper for being the best man at my wedding and for making sure that his speech was considerably less entertaining than mine; Maja Pickles and Lily Pickles for being such wonderful bridesmaids; Will Ord for going round and waking up all the guests at the end of Mark's best man speech; Bill Redston for being just the best dad ever, and Skipper the Bunny for keeping me cheerful with late-night running around and binkies at the end of every working day, and for not moulting during the run-up to the wedding. So, my Lovely Other Dinosaur, now that face2face Second edition is finished, we can finally go on our honeymoon! Love is all.

The authors and publishers are grateful to the following contributors:
Blooberry Design Ltd: text design and page make-up
Hilary Luckcock: picture research

The authors and publishers acknowledge the following sources of copyright material and are grateful for the permissions granted. While every effort has been made, it has not always been possible to identify the sources of all the material used, or to trace all copyright holders. If any omissions are brought to our notice, we will be happy to include the appropriate acknowledgements on reprinting.

The Council of Europe for the table on p14 from the *Common European Framework of Reference for Languages: Learning, teaching, assessment* (2001) Council of Europe Modern Languages Division, Strasbourg, Cambridge University Press. Copyright of the text is held by the Council of Europe exclusively © Council of Europe. Reprinted with permission; *English Pronunciation in Use* Elementary by Jonathan Marks, Cambridge University Press, 2007 and English Pronunciation in Use by Mark Hancock, Cambridge University Press, 2003 for the diagrams on p32, p43, p52, p61, p70, p79, p88, p96, p105. Reprinted with permission.

Photo acknowledgements

The publishers are grateful to the following for permission to reproduce copyright photographs:

Key: l = left, c = centre, r = right, t = top, b = bottom

p128(1): Press Association Images/LANDOV; p128(2): Rex Features; p128(3): Alamy/Chloe Parker; p128(4): Getty Images/ WireImage; p128(5): Getty Images for PCA; p128(6): Rex Features/SIPA Press; p128(7): Corbis/Stephanie Cardinale/ People Avenue; p128(8): Getty Images/WireImage; p133 (Tom & Alice): Photolibrary/PhotoDisc; p133 (Paco & Ana): Alamy /Blend Images; p133(Ian & Sonia): Photolibrary/Digital Vision; p133(Kang & Li): Alamy/Redchopsticks.comLLC; pp141/142: Corbis/Jim Craigmyle; p168(1): Alamy/BlueMoon Stock; p168(2): Shutterstock/Alinute Silzeviciute; p168(3): Alamy/Robert Fried; p168(4): Alamy/Tetra Images; p168(5): Photolibrary/Blend Images; p168(6): Shutterstock/eurobanks; p168(7): Punchstock/Stockbyte; p168(8): Alamy/Radius Images; p168(9): Alamy/UpperCut Images; p168(10): Alamy/ SundayPhoto Europe a.s; p172: Photolibrary/Ken Weingart; p183: Punchstock/moodboard; p184(T): Photolibrary/ Age footstock; p184(B): Alamy/Justin Kase Zsixz; p188(L): Photolibrary/Age footstock; p188(R): Alamy/Uppercut Images; p190(T): Alamy/Joseph Lawrence Name; p190(B): Alamy/OJO Images Ltd.

Front cover photos by Shutterstock/Diego Cervo (TCL); Shutterstock/leungchopan (BR)

Commissioned photography by Neil Matthews: 181.

The publishers would like to thank the following illustrators: Dirty Vectors, Mark Duffin, F&L Productions, Andy Hammond (Illustration), Graham Kennedy, Joanne Kerr (New Division)

Corpus
Development of this publication has made use of the Cambridge English Corpus (CEC). The CEC is a multi-billion word collection of contemporary spoken and written English. It includes British English, American English and other varieties of English. It also includes the Cambridge Learner Corpus, developed in collaboration with the University of Cambridge English Language Assessment. Cambridge University Press has built up the CEC to provide evidence about language use that helps to produce better language teaching materials.

English Profile
This product is informed by the English Vocabulary Profile, built as part of English Profile, a collaborative programme designed to enhance the learning, teaching and assessment of English worldwide. Its main funding partners are Cambridge University Press and Cambridge English Language Assessment and its aim is to create a 'profile' for English linked to the Common European Framework of Reference for Languages (CEFR). English Profile outcomes, such as the English Vocabulary Profile, will provide detailed information about the language that learners can be expected to demonstrate at each CEFR level, offering a clear benchmark for learners' proficiency. For more information, please visit www. englishprofile.org